AIM
HIGH IN
CREATION!

AIM HIGH IN CREATION!

A One-of-a-Kind Journey inside
North Korea's Propaganda Machine

ANNA BROINOWSKI

ARCADE PUBLISHING • NEW YORK

First North American Edition 2016

First published by Penguin in Australia under the title *The Director Is the Commander*

Excerpts from DPRK foreign language publications, films and songs included with gratitude and thanks to the Democratic Peoples' Republic of Korea

Arcade Publishing books may be purchased in bulk at special discounts for sales promotion, corporate gifts, fund-raising, or educational purposes. Special editions can also be created to specifications. For details, contact the Special Sales Department, Arcade Publishing, 307 West 36th Street, 11th Floor, New York, NY 10018 or arcade@skyhorsepublishing.com.

Arcade Publishing® is a registered trademark of Skyhorse Publishing, Inc®, a Delaware corporation.

Visit our website at www.arcadepub.com.
Visit the author's website at www.http://aimhighincreation.com/.

10 9 8 7 6 5 4 3 2 1

Library of Congress Cataloging-in-Publication Data

Names: Broinowski, Anna.
Title: Aim high in creation!: a one-of-a-kind journey inside North Korea's propaganda machine / Anna Broinowski.
Other titles: Director is the commander
Description: First North American edition. | New York: Arcade Publishing, 2016. | Previous edition published under the title: Director is the commander (2015).
Identifiers: LCCN 2016021762 (print) | LCCN 2016035442 (ebook) | ISBN 978-1-62872-676-3 (hardcover: alk. paper) | ISBN 978-1-62872-677-0 (ebook)
Subjects: LCSH: Motion picture industry—Korea (North). | Aim high in creation! (Motion picture) | Broinowski, Anna.
Classification: LCC PN1993.5.K63 B76 2016 (print) | LCC PN1993.5.K63 (ebook) | DDC 791.43095193—dc23
LC record available at https://lccn.loc.gov/2016021762

Cover design by Laura Klynstra
Cover photographs taken by Nicola Daley. Internal and author photographs taken by Nick Bonner, Nicola Daley, and Wendy McDougall, all from *Aim High in Creation!*, courtesy of Unicorn Films

Printed in the United States of America

For Ava

CONTENTS

AIM HIGH IN CREATION!

PYONGYANG

September 6, 2012, 8 a.m.

I'M LYING ON A KHAKI BED at the top of the Yangakkdo Hotel: home to almost every entrepreneur, hack, spy, missionary, NGO and other misfit lucky enough to have snared a visa to the most isolated nation on earth. Unless, of course, you're cross-dressing NBA star Dennis Rodman, in which case you're probably greeting the day in the lavish palace of North Korea's basketball-mad leader, Kim Jong Un.

The Yangakkdo thrusts above Pyongyang from an island in the Taedong River. At a distance it's impressive—an ominous monolith dwarfing the landscape, like Stanley Kubrick's plinth in *2001: A Space Odyssey*. Closer up, the cracked glass and corroded casing reveal that the skyscraper, like so much else in this mysterious place, is a barely functional facade. According to rumours I've collected so far, the forty-six floors below my room are totally empty. Floor Five, which is accessible only via a hidden staircase, reportedly has banks of surveillance monitors—trained on every foreigner on my floor.

A narrow bridge connects us to the city's neat concrete sprawl. You may traverse it daily in a bus or car, chaperoned at all times by a North Korean minder. You may not cross it alone. I discovered this yesterday, when I set out for a stroll and was stopped by the bellboys. There was a choreography to their movements, a firmness behind their smiles, as they manoeuvred me into the revolving door with its plastic flower tubs and spun me back into the cavernous lobby.

I guess I could sneak down to the river and swim across. But the prospect of bellboys in wetsuits, crouching behind the Yangakkdo's clipped bushes, ready to spring with ninja-like efficiency on anyone who tries such a thing, feels too real.

I focus on dozing off my jet lag. And scanning the ceiling for the glint of hidden cameras.

In exactly twelve minutes, I will receive a chirpy call from Ms. K, wondering why I am not at breakfast. That's code for "get in the elevator now": with the Yangakkdo's creaking carcass plagued by power outages, the lift down can take up to eighteen minutes.

Yesterday, my unflappable British cinematographer Nicola Daley and I learnt it's not a good idea to keep Ms. K waiting. We were twenty minutes late, wrangling our cameras, tripods, and battery-powered lights onto rusty trolleys and down to the idling van. Ms. K, in a Hawaiian shirt and hot-pink pants, maintained a frosty silence all the way to our first shoot at the Pyongyang Film Studio.

At the studio gates, the Kalashnikov-toting sentry glared at her watch, shot us a red-lipsticked scowl, and slid open the metal portcullis in insouciant slow-mo. Only once we'd lugged our gear with head-bowed reverence past the Dear Leader Kim Jong Il's statue, and offered chocolates to the chain-smoking filmmakers waiting in the meeting room, did Ms. K relax and flash me her usual half-happy, half-rueful smile.

In a minute I will don the white shirt and slip that are to be my new, respectable front for today's interviews—along with a thick layer of artful makeup. War paint is not my thing, but the North Koreans pride themselves on judging character through the face.

So far, the perky young interpreter Ms. K has chosen for us appears to be editing everything I say. I am not taking any more chances.

I am the only Western filmmaker ever granted total access to the North Korean film industry. I am determined to win the trust of the artists who have built one of the most successful propaganda machines on earth—shaping the thoughts and dreams of an entire nation. I want to discover what motivates them, how they live, who inspires them, and what they know. It has taken me two years to get here. I have two weeks to find out.

I stretch and shuffle to the window. Forty-seven floors below, the iron barge that has punctuated my night with its toe-curling screech continues to scrape rocks, one by one, from the muddy river. It's a quaint soundtrack: the steampunk rattle of a nation stubbornly wedded to growth, despite its nineteenth-century technology. I wonder if the grey-pyjamaed men heaving rocks off the chute go ashore to sleep, or if they are chained to the barge around the clock. With up to two hundred thousand people labouring to their deaths in gulags that Ms. K will never permit me to mention, let alone film, anything's possible.

But the prison camps seem far, far away from the strangely beautiful city spread out before me, with its pastel buildings and lush green parks. The light bouncing up from the river is soft and clean, infusing my drab room with possibility. It silvers the carved arms of the brocade chairs; the peeling veneer of the bar-fridge; the boxy edge of the no-name TV; the wall calendar of Mount Paektu, birthplace of Kim Jong Il, recently deceased.

The Dear Leader's rosy face rises above Paektu's snow-dusted crater, beaming his Technicolor smile. His permed head is haloed by a double rainbow and a star, in a glorious blood-of-the-workers sunset, Juche 100. That's 2012 in my parallel but no longer accessible Western universe: a place which accepts that Kim Jong Il was actually born in a Siberian hut in 1942—where his mother kept him rugged to his eyeballs in Vyatskoye mink for three frozen winters, while his father, Kim Il Sung, waged a bloody guerrilla war to wrest Korea back from the occupying Japanese.

The world I've left knows that the "new star" and "double rainbow" the North Koreans believe miraculously appeared above Paektu the day Kim was born are an elaborate mirage, along with his astonishing ability to drive a car at age three and his genius-level prowess at everything from golf, animal husbandry, fashion design, dam-building, and nuclear weaponry to the magical art of cinema. It's all part of the god-like personality cult woven by Kim Senior, Holy Father of North Korea's Socialist Paradise and Heroic Vanquisher of the Imperialist Japs and Invading Yankee Bastards, and skilfully perfected by his cherubic, platform heel–wearing son.

I officially left that world two days ago, when I handed my phone to a guard at Pyongyang Airport, watching her wrap it up in pink paper and file it away under a hand-written sign: *Mobile phone collection point*. The Yangakkdo's check-in lady stashed my passport away with similar efficiency, informing me with a smile that the Internet is not available anywhere in the country. In an emergency, I may send one email from the hotel's only computer: a nineties dinosaur perched on a doily under an optimistic banner: *Tailor & Business Centre*. The computer is programmed to block all email replies.

I look up at the Dear Leader on my wall, glowing with the lusty certainty of a man who has drunk a lot of A-grade Cognac, and am relieved that at least I know where my passport is. I have spent two years inside this man's strange mind: reading his words, watching his films, hearing stories of people he tortured, surfing websites devoted to deadpan photographs of him giving "on-the-spot guidance" to note-book-carrying minions—in Hungnam textile factories, Pyongyang movie sets, and communal turtle farms in Taedong. Ostensibly, I'm here to make a film. But in reality, like the man who has inspired it, I want to airbrush my life.

Not long ago, my partner sat up in bed and revealed, as partners sometimes do, that he'd met someone else. No, it wasn't just an affair. Yes, he was sorry. But nothing could be done. He was in love, and couldn't wait to introduce her to our daughter—over gelato at Bondi, or testing Ikea futons for their new flat. They were going to spend their lives together in marital bliss—a state which, he correctly pointed out, had mostly eluded us. I was devastated.

But now I am sitting on the forty-seventh floor of the Yangakkdo, the fact that my ten-year marriage is unravelling in Sydney like a mid-life-crisis B movie no longer seems to matter. I am feeling serene, philosophical even. I find it oddly reassuring that Kim, with his finely tuned appetite for young actresses—many of whom he personally trained— would accept it as entirely natural that my ex has replaced me with a student, a girl half my age.

Which proves that I am either emotionally autistic, or being in North Korea has an oddly discombobulating effect on reality. Call me crazy, but I'd rather be here, communing with Kim Jong Il and scanning the lampshades for microphones, than scanning my ex's phone for suspicious numbers back in Sydney. I'm feeling the same calm acceptance you have when you buckle into a long-haul flight with no email access—or fling yourself into space on a bungee cord. The pleasant certainty of knowing there's no option, that you must resign yourself, irrevocably, to fate. For what it's worth: if you're going to go through a divorce, do it in Pyongyang.

I scan Ms. K's itinerary. It promises fourteen blissful days in the company of people who will never know about my crumbling marriage, let alone care. As it turns out, one man will prove me wrong about this. But for now, I focus happily on my film—and the theory I came here to test.

When Kim Jong Il died, on December 17, 2011, the West watched shivering North Koreans hurl themselves at his casket in Pyongyang's snow-locked streets in fascination. Speculation flooded the web: surely these people were crying out of fear that if they didn't cry, they'd be sent to the gulags? Or worse still—they were brainwashed automatons, subhuman groupies who could no longer think for themselves? How could anyone shed a tear for Kim Jong Il, that citizen-slaying monster, the egomaniacal tyrant of *Team America* fame, who wanted to nuke America and everything it stood for, Bad Guy numero uno in George W. Bush's "Axis of Evil"?

Instead of stalking my ex's new girl on Facebook, I watched those grieving North Koreans on YouTube. Then I pasted their wailing faces against video of Western churchgoers whipped up by mic-toting pastors into an evangelical frenzy, and was struck by something: the crowds looked and sounded eerily the same. The fact is, Kim Jong Il knew how to drive people to religious fervor through film, the same way the Bible Belt's best inspire their flocks with the Book.

Kim was a passionate film buff, secretly housing twenty thousand Western movies, which he'd banned his people from seeing, in a vacuum-sealed vault in Pyongyang. He produced more than 1,400 propaganda films over five decades, cunningly adapting Hollywood genres and techniques to transform North Korea's dour socialist cinema into a modern smorgasbord of noir thrillers, rom-coms, sexy melodramas, historical epics, pyrotechnic monster pictures, and big-budget military shoot 'em ups.

Kim Jong Il's regime may have sold his people fear—but his movies sold them hope, beauty, certainty, belief, and love. So, getting back to my theory: is it possible the grief the North Koreans showed the day Kim died was genuine? Could the passion with which they mourned him have something to do with the emotional power of the films he produced? Was Kim Jong Il—that bastard child of Leni Riefenstahl and Steven Spielberg (both of whom he greatly admired), the boy-cineaste who grew up loving Hong Kong chopsocky flicks, James Bond, and everything Elizabeth Taylor ever made, and went on to fix his stagnating film industry with a zealous kind of brilliance—just a frustrated artist who got the wrong job? An artist who, if born in the West, might have become a celebrated auteur, pimped on the Croisette at Cannes for his "revolutionary vision," his "uplifting morality," and the "heart-warming universality" of his David vs Goliath themes?

The North Koreans outside my window would be horrified to know that Kim's only actual appearance at Cannes was in an urn carried by Sacha Baron Cohen to promote his slapstick comedy *The Dictator*. When Baron Cohen, flanked by gun-toting babes and looking like a cross between Saddam Hussein and Prince, announced his dear friend Kim's "deep desire to be here in person," then spilt Kim's ashes all over a gay TV host with the zinger "That's not the first time you've had an Asian man on your chest," he got nearly eleven million hits on YouTube.

But Kim's captive audience of 24.9 million has never heard of Baron Cohen, let alone YouTube. In their Internet-free world, they are totally ignorant of reality TV, the Kardashians, Instagram, twerking, and every other pop-culture fad that has distracted the West since North Korea sealed itself off permanently in 1953. For the people outside my window, the belief that their Dear Leader was a cinematic genius, revered by oppressed workers all over the capitalist world, is blissfully intact. On cue, a burst of music floats over the river: a warbling soprano, ricocheting from speakers across the landscape, like a muezzin's call to prayer. I switch the TV to one of Pyongyang's two channels (the rest of North Korea only has one), and the song continues over portraits of the Dear Leader: straddling a white stallion, waving at cheering crowds, saluting a fat toddler's fist on his proud father's knee. Italics scroll on the screen, karaoke-style: *You pushed away the severe storm. You made us believe, Comrade Kim Jong Il. We cannot live without you!*

I recognise the song from my midnight surfs on North Korea's unofficial web channel, Urminzokkiri. It's "No Motherland without You," the number-one pop sensation Kim penned as a poet at university, where he screened bootlegged copies of *Friday the Thirteenth* in his dorm to seduce the girls. The song celebrates, among other things, Kim's ability to control the weather.

At this distance, the woman's voice is soothing, bathing the city in a cathedral-like calm. Even the dredge has stopped screeching. The pyjamaed men squat on their rock pile, sharing a cigarette. On the other side of the river, a squadron of red-kerchiefed boys do calisthenics on a low stone wall. An SUV glides silently along an empty road. A line of bicycling soldiers threads along a footpath, past the glittering Tower of the Great Juche Idea, and onto the marble colonnades of the Grand People's Study House.

A plume of white vapour drifts from a pipe in the distance, encircling the buildings in cottony fog. Through the mist, Kim grins back at me like a Cheshire Cat from various facades. Red banners hang beneath his portraits, their bold white slogans punctuated with exclamation marks. It's like peering down at a North Korean version of *The Truman Show*. The gentle greens and pinks of the buildings, immaculately mirrored in the uniforms of the people moving around them, the symmetrically planted trees, the ethereal mist, and Kim's ubiquitous, shining face, all create the impression of a perfectly constructed world.

The desk phone buzzes. It's Ms. K. "Miss Anna. We did not see you at breakfast." I explain, like I did yesterday, that I prefer instant coffee. Ms. K giggles. "Let us go to the April 25 Military Film Studio!" Then, something new: "You must bring your passport."

Unsettled, I check the bathroom cupboard. Our black flash drives are stashed where I left them. They are our masters; the orange drives we use on the shoot are dummies. Before we left Beijing, Nicola and I hatched an elaborate plan for saving any footage the North Koreans might want to delete: if either of us says, "I'm terrifically tired," the other must find an excuse to get back to the hotel, run upstairs, and do an emergency data dump from the orange drives to the masters. The dummies can then be shown to our minders, and wiped at will.

Now we're in Pyongyang, the plan feels woefully naive. The kind of thing Maxwell Smart might try, then ruin by blowing up his shoe. I imagine Nicola and me swooning on the red banquettes in the cafe, proclaiming ourselves "terrifically tired" in our best Julie Andrews accents, as Ms. K and her taciturn driver look coolly on. They judge you by your face over here—and, no doubt, your voice. But we're stuck with the plan now. We can no longer discuss it out loud.

I reach for my moisturiser, persuading myself I'll never have to lie to the formidable Ms. K, then stop. There's a note, sitting on top of the washcloth I used yesterday. It is still covered in the foundation I smeared off my face, the tan streaks hardened to a dark, crusty brown. On the note, a single word: NO. I'm horrified. Do the Yangakkdo's cleaners think I'm such a decadent capitalist that I took a dump then wiped my arse on their washcloth? I scrawl a note on the other side of the paper, setting it next to my foundation bottle with a helpful arrow: *Makeup*! I add a little smiley face. I hope it works.

In the lift down, Nicola and I stand beside five crisply pressed Party workers, the Dear Leader's beaming face pinned to their lapels. The workers glance furtively at our Sony camera box, our polyure-thane tripod, the titanium light stands in their Gore-Tex bags. All alien materials, in a country that still uses seventies-era plastics. Eighteen silent minutes later, the lift doors grind open, and we're hovering thirty centimetres above the lobby's polished floor. No one flinches. The bellboys lean in and force the doors open with a practised heave, and Ms. K greets us, all smiles. We're on time.

The van coasts along the bridge to the city, and Nicola and I exchange a grin. It was surprisingly easy to retrieve our passports from the check-in lady. She behaved as if such a thing were perfectly normal, that we could even keep them in our rooms if we like. We hand them over to Ms. K, without comment. Maybe she needs them to show the guards at the film studio. It is not wise to quiz Ms. K too closely about security. She has worked backroom miracles to get us permission to roll as much tape as we like, in a country that regularly sends tourists on the early plane back to China simply for having filmed the Dear Leader's statue at the wrong angle. Silent acquiescence is the best way to preserve the precious access we've been given.

Suddenly, Ms. K barks something at the driver. A thin man in a safari suit is running towards us, leaping over bushes to reach the van. The driver screeches to a stop, and Ms. K pushes our passports through the window. The man grabs them and ducks back into the bushes. The van accelerates before we can process what has happened. We twist around, watching the man's retreating head in disbelief, as it bobs over the bushes and disappears into the foliage under the dimin-ishing Yangakkdo.

"Our passports, where are they going?" I ask Ms. K, lamely. She nods with enthusiasm. "Okay! Let us go to April 25 Military Film Studio! They are waiting!" Nicola and I exchange a look. "But . . .

Ms. K? When do we get our passports back?" I try again. Ms. K sighs and examines her cuticles. She mutters something to the driver. He laughs and toots at an office lady on a bike. She swerves out of the way, shooting me daggers as we pass. I look at Nic. She's wearing her most inscrutable keep-calm-and-carry-on expression. It's a look she perfected while filming a sniper battle in Baghdad from a stalled American tank.

I stare out the window, battling a rising helplessness, as we glide along Yonggwang Street. Past its fluttering North Korean flags, its hand-painted propaganda posters of soldiers and peasant women clenching their fists against the lilac sky. I watch an ancient woman slowly sweeping a leafless pavement with a broom made of sticks, and try to forget that right now, I am in the world's most isolated nation, with a guide who won't answer me, a driver who can't understand me, and an itinerary I have no certainty will happen.

I am making a film about a man who convinced his people to believe he was God, murdered those who didn't, and routinely kidnapped foreigners, to fulfill his dreams of world supremacy.

And now, I have no passport.

Ms. K swivels round cheerfully: "Soon we will arrive at the April 25 Military Film Studio. April 25 is the auspicious day our Supreme Generalissimo Kim Il Sung led the glorious People's Uprising on Jeju Island against the imperialist Japs. You must only film inside. No filming out the window. At all." Ms. K flashes me her half-rueful smile. If I wasn't so intent on smiling back, I might even be scared.

PART 1

GETTING THERE

Comrade Kim Jong Il's love was so great as to enable flowers to bloom even on stones and old trees. It turned into an elixir of life, and finally snatched the actor from the jaws of death.

—GREAT MAN AND CINEMA

THE FREE WORLD

IT ALL STARTED WITH A BIRTHDAY present. In 2009, my partner threw a fondue party for my fortieth, in the film school where he worked. The loveable renegades, jokesters, and other unflushables I'd collected over the years snuck in at midnight and stood around steaming cauldrons, forks in hand, dripping strings of Jarlsberg on the pristine carpet.

Vodka was drunk and lascivious toasts exchanged. The event descended rapidly, as it should, into a retro-punk free-for-all involving pogo dancing to the Sex Pistols and scrums on the marshmallow-smeared floor. By the time the cauldrons were licked clean and filled with brandied chocolate, my mates were paddle-whipping anyone who dropped their strawberry in the sauce, and condemning repeat offenders to sing AC/DC, naked, on the film-school roof.

That's what I heard, anyway. I wasn't there. I was back home under my duvet, nursing the Battlestar Galactica of flus. My immune system was shot by six months' hard labour in an edit suite, making a film about a Chicago impostor called Norma Khouri. Had I known Norma's twisted tale would lead me to Kim Jong Il, I might have thought twice about getting involved with her. She was a dark and doe-eyed beauty, and according to many people I'd interviewed, a truly dangerous dame.

When I started tracking Norma, she was on the lam from the FBI for a reported $1 million worth of fraud. One Chicago gumshoe had spent fifteen years trying to nail her for a string of alleged scams, including an old woman whose signature she claimed Norma had forged to pilfer her life's savings; a businessman who'd given Norma a building, believing she was an "Arab princess" who wanted to house the poor; and a sorry legion of love-struck putzes whom Norma had apparently seduced into proposing marriage, then smoothly milked of their assets.

There were also dubious insurance claims involving Norma's mother-in-law, and her husband John—a sushi-loving playboy with rumoured ties to the Greek mafia and a penchant for white leather shoes. But what had really frightened me was the meeting I'd had with a detective from the Department of Alcohol, Tobacco, Firearms and Explosives, who told me, over key lime pie on an Illinois beltway, that he believed Norma was potentially implicated in the shooting murder of John's tennis partner at a gas station in broad daylight. That bit I left out of the film. Norma's tendency to mention guns in every interview I recorded with her had me spooked.

"Norma's got more brains than John and his mother put together. She's the best con artist operating today," the gumshoe told me bitterly. True to form, Norma had given the FBI the slip—hopping into a taxi to O'Hare Airport with no one but the gumshoe in hot pursuit, and flying to Athens, where—according to one Chicago cop I spoke with—she lived with John and their two kids until the American statute of limitations under which she could be arrested expired. With bills to pay and no Greek, Norma used her Mensa-level IQ to forge a lucrative new career. She sat in an Internet cafe, surrounded by teenagers blasting Arabs to smithereens on Conflict: Desert Storm II, and tapped out a fake first-person memoir.

In potboiler prose, Norma reinvented herself as a Jordanian hairdresser, racked with guilt for her part in the secret affair that led to the brutal murder of her best friend, Dalia. She described the unisex hair salon in Amman where she and Dalia had worked; the secret trysts she'd arranged between Dalia, a Muslim, and her handsome Christian lover, Michael; the Gauloises they'd nervously smoked in Dalia's bedroom the night they realised her brothers were onto them; the agonising sprint Norma had made to Dalia's house on Nablus Street the day she disappeared—only to discover her friend's bloody corpse being dumped in the back of an ambulance.

Dalia had been stabbed twenty-seven times by her father and brothers in bed while she slept, for having dishonoured them by falling in love with an infidel. She was still a virgin when she died. The book ended with Norma's outrage that her chaste and innocent friend could be slaughtered by her own family, yet they could be let off by an archaic section of Jordan's penal code, which allows men to commit "crimes of honour" against female relatives with impunity.

Written in the halting style of someone using English as a second language, Norma's book was utterly convincing, provided you knew nothing about the Middle East. Taking a gamble that Western publishers wouldn't realise unisex hair salons did not exist in Jordan when Dalia was alive, let alone Gauloises, Norma googled literary agents alphabetically. She explained she was a Jordanian virgin on the run from Islamic extremists who'd put a fatwa on her head for speaking out. She feared she'd be killed, but hoped her humble book would help Dalia's legacy survive. By the time Norma got to "F," she had snared superstar New York agent Christy Fletcher.

Forbidden Love: A Harrowing True Story of Love and Revenge in Jordan was the most successful hoax of Norma's career. It secured her a six-figure advance with Simon & Schuster, Random House, and Transworld, and publishing deals in fifteen countries. With George W. Bush beating up the case for bombing Baghdad on the grounds that it would "liberate" the apparently oppressed women of Iraq, Western readers were hungry to know more about the Arab world. Norma's melodramatic page-turner, with its barbaric Muslim men and suffering, burqa-clad women, was an overnight bestseller.

Norma swanned around the world on a five-star publicity jun-
ket—inspiring and reducing readers to tears with her vulnerability and
charm. She told funny stories about what it was like for a thirty-year-
old Arab virgin to wear a miniskirt, see skyscrapers, and drink Bloody
Marys for the first time. She blushed when male journalists asked
whether she'd "ever been kissed," and made female fans swoon with
tender confessions that maybe, if she found the right man, she would
"quite like to have a child." As David Leser, one of many seasoned journalists Norma snowed, put it: "She was like a rock star. If it had been
a concert, they'd have had a mosh pit."

Meanwhile, Hans Blix was scouring Iraq for Saddam's WMDs—
and failing to find them. Dick Cheney's daughter Elizabeth (the
straight one), determined to win hearts and minds to her daddy's
unpopular war, saw Norma Khouri as a useful figure to have in the
public eye. As the head of the State Department's Bureau of Eastern
Women's Affairs, she wrote an emotional letter of support for poor,
hunted Norma, and sent it to the Australian immigration minister.
Norma's passport indicated she was married with two American kids
and therefore telling big fat lies, but the truth should never be allowed
to get in the way of a lucrative literary hoax—or, indeed, the propaganda aims of a pro-war government. Australia, a country renowned
for throwing Arab refugees into flyblown detention centres the minute
they wash ashore, promptly granted Norma permanent residency—in
a waterfront McMansion on Queensland's Bribie Island.

From her tropical oasis, Norma worked her newfound celebrity
on the Australian chat-show circuit, fuelling hatred of Muslims in the
hearts of her adoring fans. Between times, she enjoyed lazy afternoon
barbeques with John and the kids, sipping pineapple daiquiris by the
pool.

Not bad, for an alleged two-bit scammer from Chicago's Southside.

By the time she was exposed by journalist Malcolm Knox in the
Sydney Morning Herald in 2004, I knew I had to make a film about
Norma. She had not only deceived five hundred thousand readers;

she'd convinced the best minds in media and publishing to support her lies. As tens of thousands of innocent Iraqis continued to be slaughtered in the disastrous war, *Forbidden Love* was pulped by publishers all over the world—except for the pragmatic French, that is, who slapped a "Fiction" sticker on the cover and kept on selling.

Norma dumped her children with a kind-hearted neighbor on Bribie Island, extracted enough money for a one-way ticket, and fled to Chicago, where she set about gathering evidence to prove that her story was true, and threatening legal action against anyone who disagreed.

But Norma's "proof" never materialised, and I was hooked. What kind of person, I wondered, could be so amorally brilliant that while on the run from the FBI, she reinvents herself as an uneducated Arab virgin, writes a bestseller, and convinces the whole world she's telling the truth? Was she mad, evil, or just misunderstood? A ruthless femme fatale, as the media portrayed her, or a passionate crusader who had fudged some facts to educate the West about honour crimes? Or was Norma simply a child of the Jerry Springer generation, an opportunistic confabulist from the wrong side of the tracks, who knew that airing your pain in public is the quickest ticket to fame?

I had to make a film to find out. The conviction filled me, as it always does, with exhilaration, and a queasy sense of dread.

Banking on the chance that Norma would be missing the limelight, I wrote to her film noir–ish address (janedoe@lycos.com) and asked if she'd like to work with me. I told her I would interview her detractors—but she would have equal space to rebut them, and could redeem herself to her betrayed fans in the process. Norma didn't just jump at the offer; she promised the jackpot: if I took her to Jordan, she'd prove, on camera, that Dalia had existed, and that her murder was real.

The 1940s master grifter General Strosnider once observed that you can't con an honest man. I was, I'm ashamed to admit, as greedy for Norma's carrot as any other mark. If she were telling the truth,

I had a scoop. If she was lying, I already had a fascinating film. So I let Norma convince me that Jordan's secret police, the Muhabarat, still wanted to kill her, and obeyed her extravagant security demands. I paid thousands for a hunky American Norma claimed was a "military-trained" bodyguard. I hired expensive demountable cameras in London. I bought burqa "disguises" in Sydney. I rented a souped-up escape van with tinted windows in Amman. Norma met me in Jordan on the first day of our shoot, as promised. And then, of course, she conned me too.

The whole crazy journey unspools in my film, *Forbidden Lie$,* which plays like a documentary version of *Catch Me If You Can.* Norma leads me on a high-stakes goose chase through fiction, fact, and faction like DiCaprio's mercurial con man, Frank Abagnale Junior, and I bumble along three steps behind like Tom Hanks's FBI agent, trying to catch her out. *Lie$* had its first screening at the Adelaide International Film Festival to a full house of expectant viewers and a row of nervous investors. Thanks to a technical glitch, it ran at the wrong frame rate. The effect was like Chinese water torture: each careful edit, each CGI sequence we'd spent weeks perfecting, played on that massive screen in excruciatingly subtle slow-mo. A critic published a lukewarm review in Variety. My investors immediately demanded a recut.

Which is how I ended up a bundle of self-pitying misery on the night of my fortieth birthday, buried under the duvet with a pile of wet tissues. My future consisted of cold pizza in the edit suite for two more horrendous months, watching my darlings hit the cutting-room floor. My present was ten minutes away in a cab, in a room full of pogo-dancing friends—whom I was too sick to join. I wished, pathetically, I hadn't told them not to bring gifts. At least I could have been unwrapping them now and reading their cards, feeling I was there with them in spirit.

Thankfully, one friend had ignored me. An old mate from drama school, who had abandoned the Tinseltown dreams we shared to navigate the cutthroat world of factual TV, becoming a top current affairs producer. Just before I'd vomited and left my own party, she'd slipped a paper bag into my hands, with a conspiratorial whisper: "I bought it in Pyongyang." My friend had just made an exposé on North Korea's human-rights abuses. I didn't expect her gift to be uplifting.

Weakly, I tore open the bag. Out slid a discreet brown book, its title embossed in gold:

KIM JONG IL

THE CINEMA AND DIRECTING

Below that, in smaller gold letters:

PYONGYANG, KOREA

1987

No picture, no back-cover blurb. The simplicity made it seem profound, like a Bible. I opened the tissue-thin pages. At the top of each page, in case one might forget the reason the Dear Leader had put pen to paper in the first place, was the clarion call that lost its power in the West back when Thatcher broke the Yorkshire Unions in 1984:

WORKERS OF THE WHOLE WORLD, UNITE!

But stamped on this elegant little book, the words seemed strangely genuine. Romantic, even, to my aging inner punk—who had spent her twenties steeped in Marx and Billy Bragg, raging against the encroaching evils of Thatcherism in a Sex Pistols kind of fury.

I traced the shiny gold letters on the cover, imagining red-star-capped workers applying them on a hand-cranked printing press, somewhere in the nostalgic half-light of the last "pure" socialist nation on earth.

I felt uplifted. I thanked my friend. Then I went to sleep and forgot all about it.

TWO YEARS LATER, I WAS LEANING against a muddy tractor tyre, high on marijuana in a Missouri paddock.

Thanks to the recut, and to everyone's surprise, *Forbidden Lie$* was a success. While it hadn't made the hallowed screens of Cannes, it scored a respectable run in the cinemas, TV sales around the world, and a two-year tour on the festival circuit, where it was showered with prizes. I succumbed happily to the junket, presenting the film to Gaultier-clad Italians in the Renzo Piano cinema in Rome, sipping cardamom coffee with oil sheiks at the Al Jazeera Documentary Festival in Qatar, devouring shashlicks in the beautiful dachas of a Russian province called Tatarstan—which I am still not quite sure exists, despite my passport saying I've been there.

I was lost in a haze of adulation and hotel buffets. *Lie$* had exposed the clichés propagated by the mainstream about the Middle East, and humanised Muslims in my audiences' minds. The Arabs were grateful, and the Americans were intrigued. I had shown people that the streets of Amman, with their happy families and promenading couples, were not that different from downtown New York. That this culture, which Norma had portrayed as a prison, was layered and complex—and that Jordanian women, many of whom didn't wear burqas, had degrees, and could travel at will, were as free as the women of Iraq had been—until Operation Shock and Awe blasted them back to the Stone Age.

My film masqueraded as the portrait of a con artist, but it was really about the nature of truth in the post-9/11 era. People walked out questioning everything: not just Norma's book and the Pentagon spin emanating from the Bruckheimer-designed sets of the Central Command in Doha, but the truth of documentary itself. I jetted around in a business-class bubble, high on hubris and champagne, riding the zeitgeist. I had changed the way people saw things. I had done something good. I couldn't wait for Michael Moore and Errol Morris to call and embrace me as their long-lost bastard child.

But they didn't call—and as I leant against that muddy tractor tyre in Missouri, sharing a joint with the filmmakers of the True/False Film Festival, I had an unpleasant realisation. I had no new project. Filmmaker Alex Gibney, his Oscar for *Taxi to the Dark Side* still warm in his pocket, was enthralling us with the details of a new film he was making on Julian Assange, and I had zip. Two years had passed, the invitations were drying up, and I was doomed to return to the Australian film industry, which tends to operate on the perverse logic that if you've won awards, you're too "up yourself" to employ. If I was going to make another film, I'd have to produce it myself.

The Sydney I returned to was not an inspiring place for an independent in need of finance. The bus stops I trudged past on the way to investor meetings hawked Hollywood's latest 3D blockbusters. Box sets of *Mad Men* and *Breaking Bad* were wowing the home-viewer crowd. In the city's last art-house cinema, punters were avoiding Australian films like the plague. Drama directors were churning out thrillers about serial killers and monster crocs to break into the US genre market. Local documentaries, written off by distributors as "boring," were being straightjacketed into banal confections for the cardigan-wearing faithful of the ABC. Anything about World War I, trout fishing, or fusion food was getting up on prime time. Anything else was a very tough sell.

I retreated to the 7 p.m. news, seeking comfort in the misery of others. This was a mistake. The same free-market greed that had destroyed the audience for Australian films by pitting them against Hollywood's bloated marketing budgets had taken steroids, morphed into Mega-Godzilla, and was plundering the globe. Petrol tankers were breaking apart on pristine reefs. McDonald's was sparking an obesity crisis in India. A mining conglomerate hired guards to shoot Indonesian farmers armed with shovels, so it could plunder their hills for gold. Whales, deafened by sonar testing, were beaching themselves wherever Big Oil put its rigs. A fat cop blasted Occupy Wall Street protesters with capsicum spray and thousands of Facebook sympathisers, too jaded to get off the couch, pasted "Pepper Spray Cop" onto Pink Floyd album covers—circulating it as a harmlessly subversive meme.

My own sunburnt country, with its fragile creatures and ancient caves, was Open for Business. Miners were dredging the seagrass paddocks of the gentle dugong to build the Gorgon gas mine. Drought-stricken farmers were flogging land to Chinese agribusinesses and the GM fanatics of Monsanto. Loggers were pulping Tasmania's old-growth forests, the last habitat of the Tassie devil, for the Asian paper market. The Mandarin-speaking prime minister, Kevin Rudd, who had swept to victory calling climate change "the greatest moral challenge of our time," was busy protecting Big Coal. Along the murderous highways, floral tributes hung from telegraph poles in memory of people killed by road-trains—but the only new railway was a Halliburton-backed freight link that ran straight up to the Ranger uranium mine. You just had to follow the money to see that Cheney and his cohorts would make a killing once the yellowcake was out of the ground.

I looked on in despair. I had capitalism malaise. I had plummeted from photocalls to life in a tracksuit: the universal uniform of the freelancer "between projects." I slid into obscurity, as Sydney, the brassy tart, raked in the dollars. The city's thousand-strong branch of the Occupy movement had shrunk down to a few sodden students in sleeping bags, who bleated slogans at multinationals moving into Martin Place to cash in on the boom. In my little inner-city suburb of Erskineville, developers were about to tear down the possum-filled trees to build 24-storey tower blocks for five thousand new residents. This instant concrete jungle was landing in our backyards with no plans to fix the already inadequate trains, overcrowded schools, and gridlocked traffic.

I developed a bad case of green Tourette's, stomping around my hood like Dr. Seuss's Lorax, muttering about "greed and fucking concrete" as I passed my neighbours' renovated bungalows. I railed at the lawn-bowls club for replacing its eucalypts with view-enhancing hedges. I hectored the childcare centre for uprooting its frangipani trees to attain that curiously Aussie ideal, the shade-free lawn. I sent righteous polemics to city bureaucrats about "lifestyle" vs development, and they swatted back polite form letters in reply. My partner, exhausted by my solo campaign-against-everything, suggested I get a desk job. I agreed, and hung up my boots.

Then one day, as I was reading about a British producer lured south by the high Aussie dollar to snap up some cushy screen job I'd applied for, I saw something strange. A community group had discovered that the NSW premier had quietly given a permit to a company called Dart Energy, to drill for coal seam gas (CSG) near Sydney Park. The park was a five-minute walk from my house, and two kilometres from my daughter's school. She spent her weekends in its playgrounds, chasing dogs around its ponds. Two rare black swans had just built a nest in the prettiest pond and hatched five fluffy cygnets. I was damned if Dart Energy was going to stick its methane-belching needles in our park.

So I put on my Blundstones again and leafleted the streets, yelling at rallies with hundreds of other shocked residents. We were up against an insidious enemy: the CSG industry had saturated the airwaves with ads of happy farmers herding plump cows around pretty gas wells. They'd convinced Australia that gas was clean, green, and cheap. The spin was based on a powerful illusion: gas wells are small and can be concealed by artfully planted trees. The damage they do is invisible— the methane leaking up through the soil, and into the water, cannot be seen by the naked eye.

The fake farmer in the Santos ad shut his gate with a smile: "Santos has been working on my place for a while now. They look after the people, and the land. That's why they're always welcome here." But YouTube posts from Queensland told a different story: in Tara, the CSG cowboys were riding roughshod over farmers and the aquifers they'd relied on for generations, using a law that made everything five centimetres below the topsoil the property of the state. Blue-chip graziers who'd never protested in their lives uploaded shaky videos of police-protected trucks rolling over their Akubra hats and sinking wells deep into their paddocks.

As the protests grew, an unlikely alliance formed: between the farmers and their sworn enemies, the Greens. Sydney lefties trekked north to chain themselves to fences alongside the farmers of the "Lock the Gate" campaign. The CSG industry roped in more security, and a thoroughly un-Australian video surfaced—of a cop in black riot gear throwing Abu Ghraib–style burlap sacks over two middle-aged mums who'd chained their necks to a bulldozer. He sawed their necks free with an angle grinder and threw them, fainting from shock, into a police van. The image was proof that vulture capitalism, whose bullyboy tactics had previously been confined to the Third World, had invaded the genteel West.

The security cameras strung up in the gum trees of the supposedly public Pilliga State Forest affected all of us when we slipped under the wire to inspect a new gas field with activist Tony Pickard, who had been trekking in to collect water samples ever since he'd noticed the forest's normally clear creek running brown. The mining company, Eastern Star, issued a press release blaming the phenomenon on eucalyptus leaves staining the water, but Pickard's samples, lined up in neatly dated Coca-Cola bottles, showed a damning devolution: from sepia, to brown, to an oily black sludge.

We studied Pickard's Coke bottles with the farmers of Lock the Gate, listening to their stories of Santos suits who had driven around snapping up land for exploration wells, pitting neighbour against neighbour with lucrative deals. A dreadlocked lesbian lawyer from Kings Cross, not the sort with whom NSW farmers normally took their tea, held up a Pentagon instruction manual used by soldiers to win hearts and minds in Afghanistan, saying she had proof the CSG companies were using the same tactics in Australia. Instead of heckling her as a Yankee-baiting commie, the leather-skinned graziers listened in polite silence.

Then a seventy-year-old man, who had worked his whole life to ensure his farm would be a rock-solid inheritance for his grandkids, told of the trucks that had driven onto his neighbour's property in Kahlua to set up a pilot production site. The fact he'd locked his own gate made no difference: his neighbour had fled overseas with the pay-out, and the farmer's paddocks were now bordered by thundering bull-dozers as Santos installed its rigs. He spoke of sitting in his kitchen at night, feeling the house shaking as the drills rumbled beneath it: "If I can't stop the bastards, well, I've only got one other option . . . haven't I?" He looked around the room, wild-eyed and desperate. We looked at the floor, struck that his pain could be this great. Then he gently took the lawyer's hand and held her gaze: "It's like a bullet hole, love. One tiny mark, but all the damage is done underneath."

Incensed, I went back to Sydney to march. Luckily, one thing the industry had failed to spin into something more pleasant was "frack-ing," the method by which coal seams are exploded, then pumped full of chemicals to release the gas. This we gleefully parsed on our t-shirts in every possible form: from *Get Fracked* and *Frack Off* to *Stop the Fracking Frackwits*. Fracking was causing mini-earthquakes in Britain—and in the US, children living near gas fields were suffering migraines, nosebleeds, rashes, joint pain, and epilepsy. Louisiana farmers, whose bores had been either polluted with methane or sucked dry by the industry's voracious use of water, now relied on bottled water, deliv-ered by the same companies drilling beneath them.

We shared these stories as we rallied outside parliament. We handed out "frack fluid" in Evian bottles to passers-by and paraded puppets of fat-cat miners and Edvard Munch's *The Scream*. We put our kids in gas masks and lined them up in front of shifty-eyed pol-iticians scurrying out for lunch. Thousands of farmers drove down from Queensland in their trucks and blocked off Macquarie Street for a day. The venerable Country Women's Association, Australia's number-one authority on baking, broke its hundred-year ban on civic protest and dispatched its chairwoman to the microphone, and she declared, with quivering dignity: "This is about a lot more than tea and scones, believe me."

And still, the politicians did not listen. CSG mining was full steam ahead in New South Wales. In the dial-a-dump site next to Sydney Park, Dart Energy was already setting up shop.

I had to do something drastic. But with a seven-year-old child, I couldn't hightail it north, chain myself to a fence, and get arrested. My best option would be to make a film—one that would convert the politicians, and not just preach to the already angry choir. Josh Fox's documentary *Gasland* had inspired us to fight, but it had not stopped the wells rolling out across Queensland, and thousands more threatening New South Wales. I needed to infiltrate the mainstream, which had been colonised by the industry's big-budget spin. Middle Australia was convinced that CSG was safe. I had no idea how to reach it.

Then I remembered my fortieth birthday present, and Kim Jong Il.

At the time, the Dear Leader was no more to me than a YouTube cartoon: the punch-permed star of the epic rap battle *Kim Jong Il vs Hulk Hogan*, where he blasted wrestling superstar Hogan out of the ring with an Uzi, ordering him to "eat my Korean barbeque, you blond arsehole. Your wife says my dick is bigger than yours." Everything else I knew came from the Western newsfeeds: he was a brutal dictator who wore tinted aviators; he ruled over starving citizens who ate the bark off trees; he made incendiary pronouncements against the US; and, once in a while, he'd lob a rocket at Japan—which always missed, and normally fizzled out in the Pacific.

It didn't matter. I wanted to stop CSG, and I needed an idea. So I looked under my bed and found the book exactly where I'd left it. I opened its gold-embossed cover and started to read.

> In capitalist society the director is shackled by the capitalist's money, so that he is a mere worker who obeys the will of the filmmaking industrialists whether he likes it or not. On the other hand, in social- ist society, the director is an independent and creative artist who is

responsible to the Party and the people for the cinema. Therefore, in the socialist system of filmmaking, the director is not a mere worker but the Commander, the Chief who assumes full responsibility for everything, ranging from the film itself to the political and ideological life of those who take part.

Bingo. A light bulb exploded above my head, and a glorious, revolutionary choir started singing "The People's Flag" somewhere in the misty, rose-tinted background. Such things happen, in those rare moments when you have an original idea.

Before I'd finished page one, I knew what I had to do.

I had to use Kim Jong Il's book to make a film so powerful, it would stop the gas mine in Sydney Park.

THE AMAZING KIM JONG IL

Thanks to the prodigious wisdom of Comrade Kim Jong Il and his warm loving care, the cinematic art of Korea is now coming into full flower to contribute to the cause of the independence of the People.
—GREAT MAN AND CINEMA

KIM JONG IL WAS ONE OF the world's kookiest dictators. Anecdotes of his weirdness are legion. He stood at five foot two without his platform heels, drank $650,000 worth of Hennessy a year, and was so terrified of flying he travelled in a bulletproof train—airlifting in lobster, Uzbek caviar, Thai papayas, and Danish pork. He kept a "Joy Division" of nubile starlets to entertain foreign dignitaries, owned seventeen palaces and an army of chefs, and employed two hundred women to ensure each grain of rice he ate was the same colour and length. He forced Pyongyang waitresses to have eyelid tucks to appear more Western, and once flew his sushi chef, Kenji Fujimoto, to Beijing because he craved McDonald's. He only rode white stallions—and after a nasty fall in the 1990s, he put his aides on his painkillers, so he would not be addicted alone. There's a photograph on the web that backs up the playboy rumours: Kim Jong Il, naked and fat, lounges at a table laden with empty Cognac bottles. He looks post-coital, and not at all photo-shopped. Maybe one of his Joy Division babes took the pic.

But Kim Jong Il's eccentricities obscure a more serious fact: he was a brilliant global strategist. With North Korea's $20 billion GDP at his disposal, he used body doubles to foil assassination attempts throughout his career. He built up a missile program credible enough to deter the US from dispatching him in the same way it had dispatched his Axis of Evil colleague, Saddam. Kim's nuclear bargaining chip enabled him to navigate the diplomatic tightrope between trade sanctions and lucrative foreign aid. US Secretary of State Madeleine Albright, the highest-ranking American diplomat ever to meet him, was astonished by his charm and intelligence. The truth is, the man derided on YouTube for his pot-bellied swagger was no buffoon. His rise to the top job, in a supposedly socialist system where inherited power is anathema, was all due to his smarts.

It can't have been easy. Kim, plump and effeminate, had none of the macho charisma of his father, Kim Il Sung—a man who'd earned the love of his people the hard way, by fighting a bloody war against the occupying Japanese, leading guerrilla armies from camps in Siberia and Mount Paektu to drive them out by 1945. Kim Senior loved as passionately as he fought, siring four sons by two wives, along with a squadron of illegitimate children. Lurking in the shadows of his father's personality cult, Kim Jong Il, poet, violinist, and film nerd, worked hard to convince the powerful central party he had the cojones to lead. His half-brother and rival Kim Pyok Il was more similar physically and temperamentally to the boisterous Kim Il Sung. So Kim Jong Il chose a lateral path to power. As the commander of the country's stagnating film industry, he skilfully shifted the focus of North Korean propaganda movies from dry, Soviet-style epics extolling the virtues of communism to full-blown celebrations of the heavenly supremacy of Kim Il Sung.

Elevating his dad from mortal to god in the minds of his audiences shored up Kim's rise through the Party ranks. He took ruthless

measures to stay in Kim Il Sung's good books: when his affair with
married actress Song Hye Rim produced a son in 1971, Kim hid the
baby in secret villas in Pyongyang, stopping the news from spreading
by dispatching Song's friends and relatives to the Yodeok gulag. By the
1980s, he had become the country's chief operating officer, or "Party
Brain." In public, he solidified his reputation as Kim Il Sung's most
devoted son, accompanying the president on "on-the-spot guidance"
visits to factories and power plants. In private, he worked assiduously
to consolidate his influence in government affairs. The strategy paid
off: in 1992, despite having no military experience, Kim was named
Supreme Commander of the Korean People's Army. He became chairman of the National Defence Commission (NDC) the following year.

When Kim Il Sung died of a heart attack in 1994, plunging North
Korea into years of genuine grief, Kim stayed away from the spot-
light, quietly promoting generals loyal to him to strengthen his grip
on power. He resurfaced in 1997, when the Workers' Party of Korea
elected him unopposed to take over Kim Il Sung's position of secretary. In 1998, Kim persuaded the Supreme People's Assembly to adopt
a new constitution, making the role of president unelectable. The dead
Kim Il Sung was now president for all eternity—and Kim Jong Il, as
chairman of the NDC, held the highest mortal office in the land.

New biographies surfaced, remoulding the arty Kim into a manly
warrior, as befitting his new role as Shining Star of Socialism, Ever
Triumphant General, and Highest Incarnation of Comradely Love.
In *Kim Jong Il: A Life*, Kim Il Sung (posthumously) described the
Boy General's unusual start on Paektu, the "sacred mountain of the
revolution":

> He grew up in clothes impregnated with powder smoke, eating army
> rations and hearing shouts of military command. He was upright
> and full of guts from his boyhood . . . He was precocious, proba-
> bly because he grew up under the influence of the guerrillas. Their
> noble feelings and emotions became rich nourishment for his mind

and their mettle as soaring as the peak of Mt. Paektu added flesh and blood to his manly personality.

Kim Jong Il, his biographers enthused, dreamt of being a soldier and sang only military songs at his kindergarten shows. He stayed up late writing patriotic poems for his war-weary father, and always protected children weaker than himself. He was a crack shot with a rifle and a genius at biology, physics, and revolutionary thought. He earned the respect of craggy Soviet generals at age three, when he barred them from entering his humble log cabin, so that Kim Il Sung could finish his supper. Just in case the North Korean people had any doubt about the president's chubby first-born son being the perfect successor, the Dear Leader's extraordinary gifts, forged in the revolutionary fire of the liberation war, were hammered home: "During the years of nation building, Kim Jong Il developed his qualities of curiosity, creative thinking, manliness, magnanimity, audacity, courage, confidence, will-power, frugality, simplicity and modesty."

The revamped Kim was Napoleon, Paganini, and Tiger Woods in one: an expert at everything. He was given credit for the capture of the US spy ship USS *Pueblo* in 1968, and the axe murder of three US soldiers who chopped down a tree in the Demilitarised Zone (DMZ) in 1975. He was the strategic visionary behind North Korea's rise to "world-class power," thanks to his Songun, or military-first policy, which he introduced in 1998. He was a workaholic who slept three hours a day, so devoted was he to advancing the nation. When not designing hydroelectric dams, intergalactic satellites, and fashionable parkas for his people, the Dear Leader wrote six operas, two ballets, one hit song, and four arts manifestos, and became the world's best golfer. In 1994, he shot eleven holes-in-one, achieving a score twenty-five points better than the best player in history. In 2004, concerned that university students needed a quick way to stay nourished, Kim invented the "meat with two breads sandwich"—otherwise known as the hamburger. And to top it all off, the Dear Leader was a Sensitive

New Age Guy: "Comrade Kim Jong Il is more kind-hearted and has more tears than others. When his beloved soldiers die, he mourns more bitterly than anyone else. He even skips his meals and remains wakeful at night."

Kim Jong Il's genius shone brightest of all in the cinema. The North Korean documentary *Kim Jong Il and Film Stars* waxes lyrical about his exquisite sense of craft and his selfless devotion to his crews. Kim's precocious talent revealed itself at age seven, when he spotted a continuity error in the 1949 war drama *My Home Village*, about Kim Il Sung's life on Mount Paektu: the snowflakes on the soldiers' coats were missing in the wide shots. The mortified director immediately reshot the scene. At twenty-six, while providing "on-the-spot creative guidance" to the 1968 military epic *Sea of Blood*, Kim Jong Il surveyed the burning huts, thousands of extras, nervous horses, and rapidly fading light, and proclaimed that the only way to get the battle shot on time would be to film it simultaneously, from three different cameras. He promptly went down in North Korean history as the man who invented the three-camera shoot—which is not a hard sell in a country without sitcom TV. So beloved was Kim by his filmmakers that when a set burnt down in 1983, the crew ran into the fire—not to save the stock or camera, but to rescue the Dear Leader's portrait from the flames.

In March 2010, as I digested these dazzling claims in Sydney, Kim Jong Il was busy antagonising his enemies. North Korea had just sunk the South Korean *Cheonan* warship in a torpedo attack, killing forty-six sailors. Kim Jong Il stood at his gilt-edged podium in Pyongyang, looking out over hundreds of thousands of cheering soldiers, like Hitler in Leni Riefenstahl's *Triumph of the Will*. The display of power was perfectly choreographed, right down to the red banners each soldier waved at exactly the same angle. I was struck by the man's propagandistic brilliance. Rather than respond directly to the angry pronouncements of South Korea and its allies, Kim maintained a god-like silence, using deep-voiced generals to warn the world that any "reckless counter-measures" would be responded to with "an all-out war of justice."

These scenes compounded my eerie sense of certainty that Kim Jong Il was my next subject. The switch from Norma Khouri to Kim made perfect sense: the filmmaker, hoax author, and propagandist are all professional deceivers, after all. Norma had used words to manipulate her readers, and Kim had used images to control his people. I had used thousands of invisible film tricks to create a real-life thriller about a brilliant liar—only to reveal a more complex "truth" about the Arab world. We were all propagandists; the only differences were our goals.

Norma admitted she'd "written the right book, the wrong way, for the right reasons," but justified it on the grounds that if Bush could spin WMDs to invade Iraq, she could "spin Honour Crimes, to stop innocent women being killed." Kim denounced the Hollywood movies he secretly adored, but coopted their techniques to create a manifesto that would smash capitalism, advance the socialist cause, and cement his grip on power. He had succeeded, judging from the mass rallies in Kim Il Sung Square. North Korea's movie-going millions appeared galvanised into a state of permanent, reverential delusion. *The Cinema and Directing* was obviously cinematic kryptonite. Now all I had to do was unleash its power on the unsuspecting West.

I dived deeper into the book. The tension between Kim's love of Western movies and his mission to destroy capitalism on screen was fascinating:

> Today the Cinema has the task of contributing to the development of people to be true communists and to the revolutionization and working-classization of the whole of society. In order to carry out this historic task successfully,it is necessary, above all, to revolutionize direction, which holds the reins of filmmaking. To revolutionize direction means to completely eradicate capitalist elements . . . Just as victory in battle depends on the Commander, the fate of the film depends on the director's art.

The idea of being a commander, unshackled by tycoon producers, was deliciously appealing. But Kim's propaganda techniques, at first glance, were disappointingly mundane: a clumsy mix of Filmmaking 101, as in "makeup should be natural" and "performances must be believable," and bizarre instructions to avoid using "decadent Western film equipment," to "include revolutionary songs" and to make sure the "hand-props" of the capitalist villains were not desirable, so that the people remained loyal to the working-class hero.

I jumped on YouTube to watch the only two North Korean movies that were fully uploaded at the time, the 1968 melodrama *Sea of Blood* and the 1985 Godzilla rip-off, *Pulgasari*. And suddenly, my plan to make a Kim Jong Il–style film to stop a Sydney gas mine felt absurd. Both movies were funny—in a bad way. They looked like early Italian B films: lots of melodramatic acting, jerky camera moves, didactic dialogue, post-dubbed sound, dodgy special effects, and a focus on sentimentality over plot. The unifying elements were people randomly bursting into song, turgid speeches extolling the Dear Leader, and lots of wobbly crash zooms.

But there was also a beauty behind the dogma. The grainy celluloid gave them a nostalgic charm, and the sincerity of the acting was intriguing. *Pulgasari*, in particular, once you got past the eighties hair, was a hoot. Set in feudal Korea, it tells the story of a humble ironworker imprisoned by an evil lord, who is stealing the villagers' tools to make weapons. Starving in his cell, the ironworker makes a little clay monster, imploring it to defend the village. His dying tears bring the monster to life. In kitsch animation sequences involving a rubber Godzilla suit and hand-painted models, Pulgasari becomes a giant fire-breathing dragon, leading the villagers in pyrotechnic battles against the evil lord's army. Woven throughout is a sweetly comic love story between the ironworker's tae kwon do–fighting son and the beautiful seamstress who helped Pulgasari to grow. By the end of the movie, the lord's fort is a pile of ashes, and the lovers sail into the sunset, headed for their glorious, revolutionary future. Socialism has triumphed, and the money-grubbing enemy is defeated: the People, united, have won.

There was enough in *Pulgasari* to convince me that Kim's films, while odd, had a unique kind of appeal. I scoured the web for North Korean operas and movie clips, wishing I could somehow watch them in full. I already knew a film made in Kim's style would be jarring—but as I watched his rosy-cheeked peasant women harvesting corn, his handsome guerrillas lobbing grenades at US tanks, his heroic black-smiths looking up from their anvils as yet another revolutionary song swelled forth, I realised that oddness was the point.

More than 1.8 million people watched Kim Jong Il parodies on YouTube. The Western media was hungry for stories about the hermit kingdom. If I could uncover the secret world of North Korean cinema, I could lure mainstream viewers to my film—and tell them the truth about CSG.

There was just one catch: I'd have to get into North Korea to do it.

THE GREAT NORTH KOREAN VISA CHASE

NEWS FLASH: YOU DON'T GET INSIDE the world's most isolated nation by booking a plane on LastMinute.com. You get in as a tourist, by paying a lot of money to a tour company approved by the regime, agreeing to a strictly controlled itinerary, and taking in nothing more than a stills camera.

But I didn't want to go in as a tourist. I wanted to go as a film-maker, with a professional camera and lights, and sit down with North Korea's top filmmakers. I wanted to ask them whether Kim Jong Il really was a genius, and how to use his techniques to make a film potent enough to stop a mine. If I played my cards right, I might even meet the Dear Leader himself. We'd wander through his movie vault together, discussing Elizabeth Taylor's early work. We'd crack open his Hennessy and chat into the night about why globalisation was destroying the planet. I'd show him my footage of the Pilliga gas wells and he'd be so shocked, he'd bankroll my film himself. I could see us now, storyboarding the script, arguing about the act three crisis. I would be Martin Bashir to Kim's Lady Di: flattered I wanted to pay homage to him in the same way that Brian De Palma had homaged

Hitchcock, and Quentin Tarantino had homaged John Woo, the Dear Leader would tell me everything.

There's a reason no one has tried to do this before. It's impossible.

In his seventy-one years, Kim Jong Il never spoke to a Western journalist. The chance he'd make an exception for me was less than zero, even if I did only want to talk about cinema. North Korean media visas are also rarely granted, no matter what story you're telling. When they are, they can take up to a year to secure. Many journalists avoid the red tape altogether and go in as tourists—concealing HD recorders in their sunglasses and stills cameras to snatch footage of Pyongyang's blighted citizens scouring the ground for food behind the city's showcase tenements. The footage is then packaged into undercover exposés, telling the only story the mainstream media ever tells about North Korea: that it is an evil place, hell-bent on concealing its horrors behind a ruthless propaganda facade.

This story is reinforced by the thousands of people who have escaped over the decades. Think North Korea and terrifying reports of starving, tortured citizens, denouncing relatives to escape execution, spring to mind. The North Korean horror story has spawned books, documentaries, TV series, websites, bestselling novels, and blockbuster spoofs—inspiring outrage, shock, and derision. In the 2004 satire *Team America*, Kim Jong Il sings lonely arias in his Pyongyang palace, wondering why everyone "is so fucking stupid," while feeding UN weapons inspector Hans Blix to his sharks. In the 2014 action comedy *The Interview*, the CIA sends two video journalists on a righteous mission to assassinate the murderous, Taylor Swift-obsessed Kim Jong Un. In Barbara Demick's 2009 book *Nothing to Envy: Ordinary Lives in North Korea*, anonymous defectors remember secret love affairs, conducted in pitch-black parks sans electricity or trust. Adam Johnson's 2012 novel, *The Orphan Master's Son*, charts its hero's horrifying journey from a state-run orphanage to kidnapping Japanese for the regime, and his brutal demise in the gulags; while Blaine Harden's 2012 biography about Shin Dong Hyuk, *Escape from Camp 14: One Man's Remarkable Odyssey from North Korea to Freedom in the West,* makes the gulags horrifically real. In the most notorious prison, Camp 14, where Shin Dong Hyuk was born, even the children of dissenters are punished.

Shin describes eating frogs, rats, and bugs to supplement the camp's watery soup. He looks on with his classmates in silence as a small girl is beaten to death for hiding five kernels of corn in her pocket. At thirteen, he hears his brother and mother planning to escape and tells the guards—hoping for a reward of food. Instead, he is strung up over a fire and tortured. Then he is forced to watch with the rest of the camp as his mother and brother are blindfolded, hung, and shot. When Shin finally escapes, by crawling over a prisoner's electrocuted body on the razor-wire fence, he is shocked. The North Korean villagers outside the camp seem wonderfully "free": they can talk with each other at will; they openly exchange goods for food; they smile, sing, and wear colourful clothes. In an interview uploaded in 2008, Shin sits in a new apartment in Seoul, his dead eyes hooded in his smooth young face:

> *Even today I am still not quite sure of what the concept of freedom actually means . . . I first thought about escaping because I was hungry and tired but I'm not any more. Now I can eat a lot and I can have meat. Physically, I am so comfortable because I don't have to work anymore, but mentally I am still in a lot of pain. Because of what I've been through in the prison camp for twenty-three years, as long as that experience follows me around throughout my life, I don't think I can ever be happy.*

I had to force myself to believe Shin's story. I found it almost impossible to accept that humans were capable of such cruelty. If it hadn't been for the Holocaust, I would have filed Camp 14 away as an exaggeration—the kind of thing defectors might construct to gain favour with their South Korean hosts. Facts about North Korea are notoriously difficult to verify—but the gulags, at least, are real. There are between 150,000 and 200,000 people living in them right now. The biggest is visible from space: it is fifty kilometers long, covering an area larger than Los Angeles. The camps range in severity—from "re-education" centres, in which inmates who have committed comparatively minor ideological crimes are made to study the teachings of Kim Jong Il and Kim Il Sung until they recant, to "complete control districts" like Camp 14, in which an estimated forty thousand political "irredeemables," like Shin and his family, are worked to death.

The gulags have dominated the North Korean story for obvious reasons: their well-resourced, systematic approach to eliminating dissent is horrific. And yet, the more I read about the camps, the more I was struck by the fact that they are only part of the picture. What is life like for the 24.7 million other North Koreans who are *not* in prison? What are *their* stories? Are they all starving? Do they live in a society that is, on every level, unremittingly evil? The famine that killed up to two million North Koreans between 1995 and 1998 happened more than fifteen years ago—but Western newsfeeds continue to run stories about people eating grass to survive. Is this an accurate depiction of what life is like for the *majority* of people living in North Korea today?

Kim Jong Il's books on cinema, despite their ridiculous claims that North Koreans are all "decently dressed and prosperous," do confirm the existence of a thriving film industry, which means there is an audience. North Korea's mortality and nutrition rates place it firmly in the Third World: according to the UN, over one third of its population is malnourished. But the other two-thirds, at least sixteen million people, are a group about whom we never hear. Do they have enough food to lead relatively normal lives? Lives that are poor by First World standards, but normal enough to include voluntary trips to the cinema? These were the people I wanted to find out about: the people Shin Dong Hyuk thought were free, when he saw them in the village after escaping Camp 14. I might never meet Kim Jong Il—but through his filmmakers, I hoped to discover the stories that ordinary North Koreans love, the actors they idolize and the songs they treasure.

There was no way I could do this with a camera hidden in my sunglasses. I would need the full permission of the regime.

When I first tried to get a media visa, in July 2010, my timing was atrocious. North Korea's usual suspicion of Western filmmakers had ramped up to red-hot paranoia, thanks to a documentary called *The Red Chapel*. To make his film, Danish comedian Mads Brügger took in a small theatre troupe, pretending he wanted to forge an artistic exchange with North Korean actors, directors, and playwrights. They gave Brügger their trust, helping him stage a bizarre cross-cultural play. Brügger's ebullient, middle-aged North Korean guide was so grateful for his efforts, she hugged him, declaring that she loved him like a son. With his footage safely in the can, Brügger went back to Denmark and betrayed every one of his subjects by inserting a narration that focused on the brutality of the gulags and the complicity of the North Koreans he'd met. In 2010, not long after *The Red Chapel* premiered at Sundance, Brügger's motherly tour guide disappeared from Pyongyang.

Canadian filmmaker Shane Smith's 2010 web documentary *North Korean Film Madness* was funnier than *The Red Chapel*, but just as contemptuous. The bearded, cool-dude Smith swanned around Pyongyang in a specially tailored Mao suit, poking fun at Kim Jong Il's "crazy-ass, fucked-up world." He winked at the camera as tour guides showed him museums of film equipment the Dear Leader had touched. For all his braggadocio about "uncovering the North Korean film industry," however, Smith failed to locate a single filmmaker. His conclusion was that North Korean cinema was just another lie, and that movies were no longer being made. Smith was wrong. But he got 1.6 million likes on Facebook.

Which made things harder for me.

North Korea and Australia had no formal ties: tensions over Kim Jong Il's rocket tests had seen North Korea shut down its Canberra embassy and leave the country in high dudgeon. So I wrote to the next closest embassy, in Jakarta—enthusiastically requesting permission for a three-month trip around North Korea's cinemas and film studios, to interview directors, actors, and composers about "the Dear Leader's cinematic legacy."

Silence.

I tried again, targeting every North Korean embassy between Phnom Penh and Warsaw, with a more modest ask: a two-day shoot in a film studio, and one interview with a filmmaker, about Kim Jong Il's manifesto. I would speak only to the person they authorised and provide all questions in advance. I signed off with a friendly blurb about how I'd been born in Tokyo, grown up all over Asia, and liked to make films that smashed Western clichés about the East. To save North Korea's cyber-spies the hassle of having to sift through Norma's convoluted deceptions in *Forbidden Lie$,* I added a footnote—I was no apologist for American foreign policy: *Lie$* had exposed an anti-Arab propaganda hoax that went as high as the US State Department.

Out went my request on a humble letterhead, with my Japanese name, Mariko, stamped in a red chop at the bottom. I prayed the little *hanko* would prove my Asian bona fides rather than cast me as the evil spawn of the murderous Japs—Imperialist Enemy Number Two. I posted it snail mail, in case my email didn't get through North Korea's notorious firewall, and waited.

Once again, silence.

In twenty years of filmmaking, I've learnt that rejection usually means you haven't asked the right way. This has gotten me into some strange places: the bed of a teenage geisha for an all-night interview; the 1995 Kobe earthquake zone a day before the rescue teams arrived; the Mount Fuji compound of the Aum Shinrikyo, two weeks before they gassed Tokyo's subways with sarin; an underground fetish party, filming a lesbian having sex with a fish; a face-to-face with the Kyoto Yakuza about drugs, guns and murder; and the movie wing of the Pentagon—where Hollywood scripts are rewritten to be more pro-US in exchange for military hardware. In 2003, I talked my way into a White House press briefing just before the Iraq invasion and asked press secretary Ari Fleischer if Bush would bomb Baghdad if the Pope went there as a human shield. Fleischer stormed out—prompting an amused Texan scribe to drawl: "Jeez, lady, you sure know how to clear a room."

I took it as a compliment, proof that in my game, whether you're trying to embarrass a US president or get inside a highly secretive nation, tenacity works. Perhaps North Korea was like Hollywood, I considered. It's not what you've done, but who knows what you've done. Cold calls are for starry-eyed drama-school grads. If you want to get past the secretary, you'd better know the boss—or know someone who does. After a quick search through the few tour companies operating in North Korea, I had found my go-between.

Nick Bonner is an accomplished British filmmaker, a North Korean art collector, and the head of Koryo Tours in Beijing. He has taken thousands of Chinese and Western tourists into North Korea over the last twenty years, producing three excellent documentaries along the way. *The Game of Their Lives* chronicles the North Korean soccer team's historic defeat of Italy in the 1966 World Cup; *A State of Mind* follows two young gymnasts training for the Pyongyang mass games; and *Crossing the Line* tells the bizarre story of North Korea's most famous movie villain, Joe Dresnok: a US marine who defected over the DMZ into North Korea during the 1960s and has played evil Yankee bastards in Kim Jong Il's propaganda films ever since.

Nick's films reflect his belief that gentle observation, not judgment, is the best way to understand North Korea. This has made him one of the few—perhaps the only—Western filmmaker to have earned the trust of the regime. It has also made him first port of call for access-hungry outsiders like me. When I rang Nick in October 2011, I could hear people working the phones behind him and tourists arguing furiously in Mandarin. Despite the chaos, he listened carefully. I told him I wasn't making another *Red Chapel*. My goal was not derision, but revelation: I wanted to uncover the strange beauty of North Korean cinema. I did not tell him about my crazy plan to use Kim

Jong Il's manifesto to stop a gas mine. There was a slim chance he might steal the idea—and a much stronger chance he'd write me off as a total nutjob. So I stayed vague, promised I'd only shoot where allowed, and be a model client.

Nick agreed North Korean cinema was a curious beast—just yesterday, a Swedish director had rung to pitch him the same idea. I was alarmed: "Yeah, but I really *love* their cinema, Nick. The songs are amazing, and those peasant women are beautiful. *Pulgasari* is hilarious, in a campy kind of way. I know I can do this justice. I can definitely raise the money to go—if you can get us in." There was a long pause. Then Nick chuckled, explained I was part of a very long queue, and, ever so politely, hung up.

I stared at the Koryo Tours logo on my Skype screen: a beaming North Korean worker in a hard hat, air-punching a blood-red sky. I'd made two major gaffes. First, when you're asking someone to use their hard-won contacts to get you inside a place that tends to put people in gulags for backing the wrong project, you'd better tell them everything. And second, *Pulgasari* was made by Shin Sang Ok, a South Korean director Kim Jong Il kidnapped in 1978 to fix his film industry. The strategy worked: Shin's films were light on propaganda and heavy on entertainment, wowing the North Koreans and film festivals all over the Eastern Bloc. But when Shin escaped in 1986, he was wiped from the North Korean history books. Anyone who wants to get inside North Korea knows that you never mention Shin Sang Ok. Officially, he does not exist.

I spent another month working a shrinking range of options. Ms. Kim, the North Korean guide who'd taken in my TV-producer mate two years back, never replied. Nor did the high-ranking cadres in the Pyongyang Culture Bureau, whose addresses I'd been given by the Australian ambassador in Seoul. I began a promising correspondence with a flamboyant character called Alejandro Cao de Bénos—the "Special Delegate of the DPRK's Committee for Cultural Relations with Foreign Countries." For €70,000, Alejandro could get me into

Pyongyang—but he couldn't guarantee I'd meet any filmmakers. He would, however, take me to the Kim Jong Il Cinema Museum, where I could film as many statues, murals, and charts as I liked. My heart sank. This was exactly what Shane Smith had done in *North Korean Film Madness*. North Korea was beginning to look just like the impenetrable bubble the media had portrayed.

Then, on December 17, 2011, when I was about to cut my losses and wire Alejandro the euros, Kim Jong Il died. News screens filled with extraordinary scenes of wailing North Koreans throwing themselves in the snow before the Dear Leader's hearse. Bizarrely, I felt their pain. I'd spent a year discovering the artist behind the dictator, yearning to see the films he'd made, driven by the conviction that if I could get to Pyongyang, I'd meet him. And now he was lying on an embalmer's slab somewhere, being prepared to sleep beside his father for all eternity. North Korea was in lockdown. The regime was bolstering the strongman credentials of Kim's son and heir, Kim Jong Un. The DMZ bristled with guns as South Korean and US troops readied for war. No one knew what Pyongyang would do next. It was not a good time to go in as a tourist.

I sifted through blogs about Kim Jong Il's death, alone in my disappointment. My partner was out every evening, texting me pictures of his office to reassure me he was working. I forced myself not to ask why the film school security alarm was going off with increasing frequency, summoning him from our bed at all hours of the night—and when he wasn't home by breakfast, I'd distract our daughter with YouTube videos of skateboarding cats. In the dark hours before dawn, I buried my fears that our marriage was over in the pain that the Dear Leader's death had unleashed.

North Korean defectors were furious that Kim Jong Il had died before he could be tried for human-rights violations in The Hague. Kim Young Soon, one of the people Kim had thrown in the Yodeok gulag to hide the news of his illegitimate son, said: "I can't ever forgive, ever. North Korea took away the best years of my life. I suffered because of Kim Jong Il." On cable, a British comedian was making a meal of Kim's epitaph: "Here lies Kim Jong (I told you I was) Il." And South Korean and US spies were castigating each other for only finding out about Kim's death two days after it happened—when North Korea's stentorian anchorwoman, tears streaming down her face, shakily announced: "Young and old, men and women, are calling Kim Jong Il, who gave tireless field guidance, totally dedicated day and night to the happiness of the People."

The pundits furiously unpacked the mass grief in Pyongyang. To many, the tears were fake, shed to avoid punishment. Others saw the grief as a display of genuine anxiety, springing from what had happened the last time North Korea lost a leader. Shortly after Kim Il Sung's death in 1994, the country was plunged into a horrendous famine, now euphemistically known by North Koreans as the "Arduous March." An estimated two million people died of starvation, while Kim Jong Il made shiny propaganda movies showing happy peasants eating potatoes around crackling fires and channelled the country's scarce resources into the army. Now, as they gazed at Kim Jong Il's flower-wreathed portrait gliding through the snow-locked streets of Pyongyang, the North Koreans were terrified they'd be sentenced to starve all over again.

As for North Korea's claim that Kim Jong Il had died heroically on his train, travelling to give "on-the-spot guidance" at some rural factory, satellite images from December 17 show the train stationary in Pyongyang. North Korea expert Dr. Leonid Petrov had an interesting theory: Kim had stage-managed the whole thing. The date, the train, the funeral, the grief, all were designed to distract North Koreans from the "Strong and Prosperous Nation" Kim had promised he would deliver them by April 15, 2012, the one hundredth anniversary of his father's birth. Unable to fulfill his promise, and already sickly, Kim discreetly left the building. This gave the regime an excuse to distract people with one hundred days of enforced mourning, shifting the focus of the April celebrations from prosperity (an obvious lie) to the military prowess of Kim's successor, Kim Jong Un. Petrov's theory tallied with the propaganda mastermind I'd met in *The Cinema and Directing*. Now the Dear Leader was dead, I couldn't let him go.

Thankfully, Screen Australia, that capitalist tycoon under whose yoke all Aussie film workers are permanently shackled, was kind enough to accept my proposition that Kim's death was but a hiccup on the way to his canonisation as a cinematic genius. Despite the fact that no one had put Kim Jong Il and coal seam gas in the same sentence before, let alone the same film, they gave me some money. Coupled with a generous grant from the estate of legendary documentary film-maker Solrun Hoaas, I had the funds to pursue my obsession.

If I couldn't get inside North Korea, I would track down the film-makers who had escaped.

AIM HIGH IN CREATION!

*The real objective of cinematic art is not merely to enhance people's aware-
ness of the world, but to develop them as communist revolutionaries.*
—ON THE ART OF THE CINEMA

THE DORMY INN SITS ON A six-lane highway in downtown Seoul. An
all-night chilli-crab diner faces it across the thundering trucks, its dusty
windows permanently empty. Along the grimy pavements, corduroy
couches and plastic chairs spill out from discount furniture stores.
People in shiny headphones walk past fast, hunched against the wind,
headed for somewhere better.

From my window, the city sits under a smog so thick the neon
lights look out of focus: splotches of pink and blue, glimmering
through the haze. LED screens perch on top of buildings like desk
lamps, flashing promos for Samsung, Hyundai, and Daewoo. On the
screen closest to me, the K-pop singers of Girls' Generation wink and
shimmy in perfect unison, their round eyes a dazzling testament to the
eyelid-tuck surgery craze currently sweeping Seoul. Beneath the dancing girls and swinging cranes, nine million people drive, shop, and
chat on their mobiles, living their future-forward lives. In fifteen years,

these industrious people have helped make South Korea the economic powerhouse of Asia.

Inside my room it's warm and clean, the double-glazing reducing the traffic noise to a soothing whirr. The furniture is beige, the walls blank, the fixtures impersonal. It has the flat-packed anonymity of an airport lounge: a space built for transit. I could be sitting in the same room in any city in the free world. The lack of cultural markers makes it the perfect void in which to reflect on the words of Kim Jong Il, dead dictator and unknown cineaste, now lying in a glass box two hours' drive away on the other side of the most heavily militarised border on earth.

My times in South Korea have always been strange. In 1991, I lived for two weeks in a Buddhist monastery run by the country's most enlightened monk. He wore a gold Rolex and giggled like a baby. We meditated together on the cliffs at night, silently asking ourselves the same question that had preoccupied the temple's inhabitants for five hundred years: "Who sees the moon?" I never found out, but in 1994, I was back again, playing one of the evil sisters in a Butoh version of *King Lear*. We performed it to baffled South Korean honeymooners in a hotel that looked like a wedding cake. Somewhere between the meditating and *Lear*, I stood at the DMZ with my father, then the Australian ambassador in Seoul, peering through binoculars at thickly forested hills. I failed to catch a glimpse of a single elusive North Korean. It was like bird-watching, and I didn't have the patience to wait.

Now I am back again, to interview North Korean defectors. I want their advice on how to translate Kim Jong Il's film rules for a Western audience. When *The Cinema and Directing* didn't deliver the ideas I was looking for, I bought Kim Jong Il's bigger manifesto, *On the Art of the Cinema*, from which *The Cinema and Directing* is condensed. *On the Art of the Cinema* is so revered in North Korea there's even a book, *Great Man and Cinema*, about how it was written:

In the early summer of 1971, Comrade Kim Jong Il summoned the officials engaged in cinematic art to his office. They found his desk piled up with manuscripts in thousands of sheets. There was every indication that he sat up all night to write them. They scrutinised the manuscript. The title *On the Art of the Cinema* was written in a vigorous hand on the first page. They could not but be filled with astonishment and admiration, at the thought that he found the time to write the book while shouldering the heavy responsibilities for the revolution and working very hard without a moment's rest . . . Marx worked for four decades to complete *Das Kapital*. By contrast, it took Comrade Kim Jong Il two to three years to write *On the Art of the Cinema*. It was the brilliant product of his unusual intelligence.

Marx has nothing to fear from Kim Jong Il: *On the Art of the Cinema* is turgid, whimsical, and clunky. *Das Kapital*, in comparison, reads like an airport novel. I have no idea if Kim actually wrote his book, or if it was ghosted by one of his minions. But I'm glad I've read it. *The Cinema and Directing*, when fleshed out by the bigger manifesto, contains nuggets of propaganda gold. Kim's first rule is that *The Director is the Commander of the Creative Group*. Before he can shoot a single frame, the director must ideologically train his actors and crew—making them "socialist warriors" in mind and body. People can disagree with the director, but when they are ideologically out of line, he will stage gruelling "self-criticism sessions"—in which the dissenter is shamed by the group until he relents. As creative commander of everything, Kim was a pretty tough critic:

> In one film about life during the Fatherland Liberation War, the barracks of the US Imperialist troops of aggression and the South Korean puppet army were shown as being too luxurious. These may seem to be trifles, but they are distortions of the truth, which undermine the realism of the production, and, furthermore, have an adverse effect on people's education.

I wonder where the director of this film is now. Is there a gulag for directors who've failed? Kim warns that sycophancy towards "capitalist ideas" will be "combated and eliminated once and for all," and I picture the filmmakers who dared to ignore him, scraping rocks in a coal pit with bare hands, their gangrenous feet knotted with rags. I am suddenly grateful for every bad review I've received.

Kim's second rule, *One Must Aim High in Creation!*, involves the *songza*, or "seed," of the movie, which springs "like a tree from a pine cone." The seed unites the creatives behind a single vision—enabling them to make "revolutionary films of high artistic value, to arm people fully with the Party's monolithic ideology." That ideology is Juche, or North Korea's take on socialism.

Developed by Kim Il Sung, Juche is more a religion than a philosophy—seen by North Koreans as a superior version of Marxism, in the same way Muslims see Islam as an advancement of Christianity. Juche Man is master of his own destiny: an "independent and self-reliant warrior." This is puzzling, given the North Koreans are spectacularly good at marching in unison. I guess the idea, from the Juche point of view, is that they have all decided, at exactly the same time, to behave like anonymous cogs inside Kim Jong Il's vast machine.

Filmmakers must "Aim High" when choosing their seed. The goal is not box office, but education. Choosing the right seed is the "most important thing in the process of creation," and no doubt in the process of survival too, if you're making films for Kim Jong Il. From what I can work out, the seeds that will keep you out of the gulags are limited to four:

Seed 1: The People United will Never be Defeated (especially when fighting the Yankee Bastards or Imperialist Japs).

Seed 2: The Person who sacrifices herself for her village, country, or the Dear Leader will be rewarded with glory—but only after extreme suffering.

Seed 3: People who want status and other nasty capitalist stuff will suffer horribly, until a beautiful working-class heroine converts them to the revolution.

Seed 4: Beware of hassling your absent Father or Husband: he might be secretly making nuclear rockets for the advancement of the nation.

Kim's films have limited seeds, but their stylistic range is huge. According to North Korean movie websites, there are noir thrillers (*Unsung Heroes*), melodramas (*Broad Bell Flower*), rom-coms (*Urban Girl Gets Married*), urban satires (*Two Families of Hang Dong*), historical epics (*My Happiness*), buddy movies (*Myself in the Distant Future*), kung-fu action pics (*Pyongyang Nalpharam*), and big-budget war movies (*Wolmi Island*). These titles promise a world of generic wonderment. I wish I could click on them and buy the DVD. But there's no hyperlink. North Korea does not sell its films to the free world. Interviewing Kim's defected filmmakers may be the closest I'm going to get.

In promoting his third rule, *Emotions should be Well Defined in Directing*, Kim Jong Il, like any other dictator with a healthy narcissistic streak, gives Hitler's Aryan ideal a run for its money: "The characteristically photogenic face is a typical Korean face, in which a noble spirit and balanced features form a perfect harmony."

Kim would have taken a dim view of the girls getting eyelid tucks in Seoul. He may have ordered a few Pyongyang waitresses to have plastic surgery to impress the tourists, but his actresses are 100 percent natural. Unlike their decadent Western sisters, their beauty comes from being ideologically pure: "Capitalist cinema, which promotes a few 'popular stars' to curry favour with the audience, reduces the stars to puppets and film to a commodity. There cannot be genuine creative spirit, and the beautiful flower of art cannot bloom, where actors sell their faces, and even their souls."

Kim's actresses are not on screen to sip Red Bull in their hummers, before loading up Glocks for the act three shoot-out. They are there to sell the message that North Korea is the greatest place on earth, the Kims are the greatest leaders on earth, and Juche socialism is the envy of the world. Just like the advertisers he slams, Kim knows that sex (along with humour and desire) is a powerful tool. To sex up his stars so they can inspire total devotion to the nation (and to himself), he sets out a training regime that makes the Juilliard School look like a five-star romp in Fiji:

Work 24/7! The actor must work like a revolutionary. His creative endeavours should fill twenty-four hours of his day. He should live through struggling and struggle even as he lives.

Love the Working Class! An actor who does not love the working class cannot understand its revolutionary spirit. He should always gather experience, so that he can assimilate the ardour of the people of our age, and can feel the very warmth of their breath.

Be ideologically fit! If an actor considers his good looks to be a gift of destiny he will be weeded out before long. As the saying goes, "Even jade has to be polished to make it shine," and the better an actor looks, the harder he should work on his ideological development to improve his screen face.

NEVER show off! When the actor knows ten elements of truth, he should express three or four. If he tries to express ten, he is like someone drawing a puppy when he intended to draw a tiger.

Kim's fourth rule, *Acting Depends on the Director*, is a direct ripoff of method acting. The best way to "draw a tiger," Kim says, is not to research your role, but to live it. The director must make the actor "go and live in a busy iron works or a cooperative farm. At the same time, the actor's home life should be exemplary. He should participate conscientiously in the business of his neighborhood unit, attend parents' meetings at school, and stand duty at his workplace."

This works for actors playing the working-class hero. But for actors playing villains, Kim has a problem. Every socialist propaganda film must have an enemy, as you can't portray the class struggle without one. But in North Korea, there are no bad guys left to research. This is because Kim Il Sung killed them all. The country has apparently been free from oppression since 1953, when the Yankees slunk out of town. Actors playing "Bastard Americans," "Japanese Landlords," or "South Korean Puppets" don't have passports, so they can't research their roles overseas. Instead, Kim helpfully suggests that they "read many excellent literary works, especially revolutionary novels, and conduct their lives like revolutionaries. Visiting historical museums and revolutionary sites can provide actors with invaluable insights into life."

Once an actor has dosed himself up on propaganda museums and novels, he is ready to play the villain. But unlike Western actors, who know that the best way to play a bad guy is to bring out what's good about him, North Korean actors must walk around in a state of perpetual self-loathing:

> To effectively embody the hateful enemy the actor requires a burning hostility. He must have an intense, deeply rooted hatred for the enemy in order to achieve a profound insight into their reactionary nature, [and] the vileness of their actions. If he cannot gaze straight into the enemy's eyes with a feeling of burning hatred, he will not feel the brutality in his bones, and will forget their crimes.

In films set after 1953, there is a different kind of bad guy: the enemy of society. This is a North Korean who is failing in some way—either his village (which he wants to leave), his factory (where he doesn't work hard enough), or the Dear Leader himself, by not sacrificing his all for the nation. I guess these actors don't have to walk around hating themselves: they are among Juche's chosen people, after all. Having not seen a modern North Korean movie, I can only imagine that the North Korean "enemy of society" is a bit like the lone heckler in *Life of Brian:* when the adoring masses stare up at the naked Graham Chapman and chant "We're all individuals," he's the one muttering "I'm not."

The fifth rule, *Exacting Demands Should Be Made in Filming and Art Design*, confirms that Kim would have made a great Madison Avenue PR man, if he weren't a dictator. Kim knows all about the truth driving both advertising and propaganda: Image is Power. Western brands use sex to make their products cool; Kim Jong Il uses objects to sex up his heroes' beliefs: "When they see a film, people try to learn from and imitate not only the words and actions of the positive characters, but even their costumes and hand-props."

In films set in the bad old days before Kim Senior liberated Korea, the heroes' hand-props must be "humble yet noble," while the villains' should be "expensive but crude." But for films set after 1953, in the enemy-free paradise, only one look is acceptable: prosperity. This seems absurd, given North Korea's malnutrition rates. But in 1971, when Kim wrote his book, North Korea was comparatively prosperous. Trade ties with South Korea were growing. The Soviet Union was providing substantial aid. Kim was pouring huge funds into the film industry and producing thirty to forty features a year.

In fact, in North Korean cinema's golden age, from 1970 to the mid 1980s, Kim worried that his filmmakers were so prosperous they would embrace "capitalist culture," which would "cloud the person's mind, leading to degeneration." He urged them to eradicate "undisciplined practices," like "slothfulness." I'm sure being slothful was the last thing on Kim's filmmakers' minds when he diverted their funds to the army during the 1990s famine. They would have been trying to survive. But are they still today?

From the truncated North Korean film clips I've managed to find on the web, it's clear Kim's filmmakers don't have access to the digital equipment used by their cashed-up colleagues in Seoul. They still shoot on celluloid, with no sync sound. *The Art of the Cinema* tells filmmakers to avoid "decadent" Western techniques, like computer effects, elaborate tracks, and complex lighting. Instead, natural light, crash zooms, limited close-ups, and locked-off wides, with the action playing within the frame, are the most "unpretentious" way of communicating a film's noble message.

But North Korean filmmakers do appear to have one asset free of charge: extras. There are thousands running through the battle scenes in *Sea of Blood* and storming the evil lord's ramparts in *Pulgasari*. The special effects for these scenes may be shot in camera, but they are spectacular. One 1950s war movie clip shows that tanks, bombs, and battleships are also freely available. I guess the Pentagon's script wing is not necessary in North Korea. A greenlight from Kim Jong Il gets you access to all the military hardware you need. That's something even Jerry Bruckheimer would envy.

Kim's sixth rule, *The Best Use Should Be Made of Music and Sound*, is about his first love: music. It runs in the family—Kim Il Sung said a "film without songs gives one a feeling of loneliness." Kim Junior, violinist and pop song writer, took this to heart:

> Music is more closely linked to life than any other art because it has emerged directly from the work environment and has been enjoyed there. In our socialist society, where the People are masters of the country, work itself brings the joy of creation and life itself is a beautiful song.

Actors can be dying on a battlefield, pining for a lost lover on a beach, or shovelling manure in a commune—but they are always happy to set down tools and have a good sing. The songs are about collective emotions, not individual feelings—and often involve loving references to the Dear Leader. Music is such an important propaganda tool for Kim there are even songs for each type of scene: "One requires a Labour song for when one is at work, and a Militant song for when one is fighting the enemy . . . Only when film music both conforms with the spirit of the times and suits the situation depicted, can it pluck at the People's heartstrings."

There are also Songs of Motherly Sorrow, Songs of Nature, Songs of the Fatherland, and Songs for Young Women—about the importance of delaying marriage to be a tractor driver. They must be simple enough for people to remember, so they can sing them as they go about their lives. And in keeping with the Italian B-movie aesthetic, it is entirely acceptable for the actors to lip-sync, and be dubbed over by a professional opera singer.

Kim's seventh rule, *The Secret of Directing Lies in Editing*, has a double meaning. Part of directing does lie in editing—but Kim also *directs lies* in the edit. Editing is a dark and manipulative art: if it's done well enough, the audience is unaware of the subtle illusions that shape the way they think and feel. Kim uses these illusions to conceal reality. He tells editors to do the usual things: cut for flow and rhythm and create a dramatic whole. But he also bans the fast-cutting that is fashionable in the West, instructing his editors to use "one cut per scene." This kills two birds with one stone—it saves film stock, and makes the movie play slowly enough to get its message through.

At the height of the famine, when people ate grass and shoe leather and even, it's rumoured, their neighbours' decaying bodies to survive, Kim promoted the message that you can be happy without rice. One film had cheerful labourers roasting potatoes over a fire. Another had laughing farmers pelting each other with chestnuts. *Forever in Our Memory* (1999), the closest Kim got to acknowledging the famine existed, was about "the problem on the farms." Determined to fix it, a group of soldiers save a starving village by replanting its fields with barley. The film ends with Kim Il Sung's Mercedes sweeping into the sunset, the villagers falling into his tyre tracks with gratitude and awe.

Kim's last rule is oddly titled: *The Assistant Director is a Creative Worker Too*. I think it's just an excuse to rant against the West:

The post of assistant director was originally established under the capitalist system. But under this system, the "assistant director" is not a creative worker. Like other artists, he is tied to the purse strings of the tycoons. He is not allowed to express any views of his own; he is

just a kind of "servant" who blindly carries out the instructions of the
director. He is a humble lackey who liaises between the director and
other people, and curries favour with them. In short, he is a servant,
shackled to both the filmmaking industrialists and the director.

I wonder if the North Koreans know that Western assistant directors
are no more oppressed than theirs. A lot less oppressed, if you factor in
the lives they lead off set. I am dying to find out.

I close my notes and make myself a Nescafé in the Dormy's plastic
jug. On the TV, Kim Jong Un stands on a camouflaged platform in
a cashmere coat, watching torpedoes obliterate some tiny island. He
sports the "youth ambition" haircut pundits say has been cultivated
to make him look like his beloved grandfather. Kim Jong Il's "speed
battle" bouffant is obviously not cool any more. But his films may be,
if I can pull this off.

I sip my coffee and gaze at the LED screens flashing messages of
capitalist inspiration in the fading light: *Life's Good. Imagination At
Work. Just Do It*. I imagine myself following Kim's rules in the decadent
West, with an Australian cast and crew. . . .

Me as the Creative Commander, leading the laconic gaffers and
grips in socialist group chants. Ordering my sophisticated actors to
throw away their iPhones and embrace the zealous collectivism of a
Juche boot camp. Putting them through gruelling exercises on Bondi
Beach until their Western egos evaporate. Nurturing in them a fierce
love for the Australian working class by taking them to monster-truck
rallies out west. Introducing them to the courageous anti-CSG farmers
to convert them to our noble cause. Taking the bad-guy actors to the
Pilliga gas wells to ignite in their hearts a burning, murderous hatred
for the enemy.

If anyone dares to question Kim's rules, I will hold marathon
self-criticism sessions until they relent. Together, at Juche speed, we
will create a propaganda masterpiece that starts with a humble gardener discovering that evil miners are drilling under her park and ends

with a thousand villagers rising up to join her in an epic battle against the gas-fracking, capitalist swine. We will use melodramatic acting, post-dubbed sound, minimal cutting, and lots of crash zooms. We will assimilate the People's revolutionary ardour until we can feel the very warmth of their breath. We will passionately devote ourselves to our seed: *The People United Will Never Be Defeated*. And of course, there will be lots of group singing.

Will it work?

Or am I completely insane?

THE DEFECTORS' VERDICT

CHUN CHUL WOO HAS THE CHATTY charisma of someone who sells things on TV. He is a celebrity in South Korea—promoting his grocery franchise through top-rating cooking shows. He thinks my Kim Jong Il–style movie is a terrible idea: "It will be boring. You have to have many speeches about the greatness of the Leaders, and even in the violent fight scenes, the villain must take ten minutes to die, because he has to talk about all the ideological errors he made."

Chun grins at me, teasing: "You will do a better job than a male director, because women are more meticulous. But if you really want it to work, spice it up with a sex scene."

Chun escaped North Korea as a student while studying engineering in Berlin. When the Wall fell in 1989, he crossed over and travelled to Seoul, where he worked his way into broadcasting. Chun's business-savvy approach to life has taken time to learn: when he first moved to East Germany in 1986, he was a proud Juche socialist who believed North Korea was the most affluent country in the world. He lived in denial, stunned that the Germans could buy whatever they wanted in supermarkets and criticise their politicians without punishment. When two African students asked Chun who Kim Jong Il was, he was so outraged he beat them up, locked them in a room, and read them Kim's entire works on Juche until they understood.

It took a year for Chun to decide to defect: "It was hard to come to grips with the huge discrepancy in reality; so much so, I was depressed. However, with time, I realised we had been cheated by the North Korean government and that it was a liar. I thought about why North Korea was so poor, and what on earth my government was on about. Also, I pondered why even in a socialist country like East Germany, it's okay to criticise the president and nobody is charged. But North Koreans cannot say it is wrong to pass power from father to son."

Chun shed his delusions and embraced his new reality in Seoul, with some adjustments. He was used to the emotional way in which North Korean anchors read the news and thought South Korea's low-key TV presenters were dreadful. He avoided the red-light district of Itaewon, where US soldiers drank, because he'd been brought up to believe Americans were subhuman monsters: half-wolf, half-man. He found South Korean movies strange, because there was no clear delineation between good and evil, and you weren't sure who to be happy for when someone died.

Speaking with Chun in his airy office, surrounded by his sparkling awards, it's clear the thing he misses most about North Korea is its cinema: "When watching North Korean movies, I would be taken away by the emotional flow. They are good at capturing emotional moments, unlike South Korean movies, which are subdued. When I was young, I looked forward to the day of the premiere, since new films are not shown on TV for ages. We had no other pastime. People are excited by a premiere; there is chaos as they try to buy tickets. There are rogues who go berserk and use violence. In North Korea, bashing people up is not illegal and no charges are laid."

Chun loved the 1971 melodrama *Flower Girl*—its scenes of the young heroine, being abused by her Japanese landlady, made him cry. He also loved every movie by Shin Sang Ok. He was not alone: Shin's movies were the first to put sex on North Korean screens. Until then, love was expressed through lingering looks or suggestive close-ups of the heroine's silky, ankle-length hem. But *Salt*, which won Shin's wife, Choi Eun Hee, best actress at the 1985 Moscow Film Festival, had a scene in which a Chinese mercenary tries to rape Choi, exposing her milky thigh. Chun and his friends went back to the cinema repeatedly, just to see that brief white flash of flesh.

I ask Chun what happens to North Korean directors when they make a bad film. He slashes his finger across his throat and gurgles: "Execution!" Then he chuckles. "Well, maybe not that extreme, but they will be harshly reprimanded. They'll be sent to a labour camp. And actors who act badly are faced with self-criticism. They don't get promoted. But no director would ever dare to make movies against the regime in the first place." I guess, correctly, that Chun does not think Kim Jong Il was a cinematic genius: "Absolutely not! But even in his political career, cinema was the most interesting field for him. There were many beautiful actresses. His wives were all actresses. They followed his orders without question, and got on TV. He must have enjoyed it."

For a moment, Chun looks uncharacteristically sad: "If Kim Jong Il had given more attention to science and technology and less attention to film, North Korea might be better off today." I ask if he can remember any movie songs, and then he's smiling again. "My favourite is from *Chun-Hyang Story*. It's a remake by Shin Sang Ok. The reason I like it is the lyrics are only about love, and it made young people cry. Any song without politics becomes an instant hit in North Korea."

Chun starts to sway: "*Love, love, my love. Looking this way, you are my love, la-dum-dum my love . . .*" He stops, excited. "There are also heaps of marching songs!" He taps his knees, singing in an exuberant tenor, without irony: "*Comrades, please be ready, with armed hands . . . In a fierce combat, defeat the enemy!*" He moves on to a song from his preschool days, thoroughly enjoying himself now: "*Kids' tank rolling on, our tank rolling on . . !*" Chun has forgotten my camera's there. He bounces and sings, gazing out the window—lost in another world.

Jang Hae Sun is a wiry old man with bright eyes and a ramrod posture. He sits on a brocade couch in his tiny flat, surrounded by bottles of pickled ginseng. The bottles range in size from pipettes to jugs as big as fire extinguishers. The twisted roots suspended inside look like alien foetuses. Behind Jang's head is a magnificent tapestry of a Siberian tiger—which apparently still exists in the unspoilt wilds of the DMZ. Jang watches impatiently as I set up my lights. My interpreter, Monica, a high-flying Seoul commercials producer who has, for some mysterious reason, taken my low-paying gig, distracts Jang with chitchat about the storm clouds amassing outside.

Jang majored in philosophy at Kim Il Sung University and worked as a reporter for Chosun Central Broadcasting for twenty years. Before that, he was a bodyguard for Kim Il Sung. He fled North Korea in 1996, when he could no longer stand the deceptions of popular TV series like *The Star of North Korea*, which portrayed Kim Il Sung as a heroic saviour: "It is a complete lie. People do not know what happened in the '20s and '30s. People who know what's true cannot say anything, so everyone believes Kim Il Sung was a respected hero. If anyone criticised this, they had to escape North Korea—like me."

Jang is writing a book about North Korean defectors. He also has ties with a South Korean activist group which flies hot-air balloons over the border, delivering pamphlets to counter the propaganda North Koreans are fed about South Korean poverty, their own prosperity and the evils of the free world. Jang has a deep love for the people he's left behind, but no respect for their Leaders. He was at university, a few years behind Kim Jong Il and remembers the Dear Leader as a lady-killer: "He was very popular among female students because, owing to his privileged status as the son of Kim Il Sung, he could record new movies and circulate them. He owned many rare films. He utterly neglected his academic work. His brother, Kim Pyong Il, did not mingle with students and was arrogant. We did not want to befriend either of them."

Jang detests North Korean movies. "In North Korea, high-ranking officials commit bad things. But they are portrayed as the good guys.

Kim Il Sung and his son are the worst ones, but they are depicted as the best people. Those who are loyal to Kim Il Sung and Kim Jong Il are shown receiving wealth and privileges. In reality, that doesn't happen." Despite this, Jang still carries a flame for socialism: "In capitalist countries, including South Korea, people only look after themselves. The main characteristic of North Korean movies is the sacrifice of the individual for the benefit of the masses—which seems a good idea to me. I think everyone should learn to sacrifice themselves for the group. Australians are no exception." Jang shoots me a pointed look.

Encouraged, I tell him my film idea. I'm hoping he'll appreciate its socialist undertones. But his eyes flash with disdain: "No one will watch it! The North Koreans won't want to, but will be forced to. If it is shown in free countries like South Korea, who's going to go? No one!" Jang lets out a mirthless laugh and sips his tea. The brutal honesty is something I'm beginning to recognise as a distinctly Korean trait, quite unlike the delicate half-truths I've learnt to use speaking Japanese. I ask Monica to explain the CSG issue to Jang, and why I have to make my film. He thinks carefully, then lights up: "Why don't you make an animation? In South Korea animations are done on computer, but in North Korea they are manually drawn, by over a hundred people. If you can make a children's story about good vs evil, with animal characters like a rabbit or fox, it might work. You can even do a co-production with North Korea!"

I nod politely, imagining my gardener heroine as a rabbit and the villainous miner as a fox, battling it out on a smart-board in my daughter's grade four classroom. Not quite the demographic I want to reach. I hand Jang my copy of Kim's manifesto, asking if he thinks its rules are sophisticated enough to work in the West. Jang slaps the book down on a ginseng bottle, annoyed: "Kim Jong Il believed he was a genius, but he didn't have any talent. He was just an ordinary person who liked film. These are basic rules used by anyone producing a movie: the director is the most important person, music should be included and editing is crucial. They are important principles, but not because Kim Jong Il said so."

Jang tugs at his lapel mic. Conversation over. I ask him feebly if he remembers any North Korean movie songs. Monica shoots me a warning look: I'm pushing it. But Jang leans forward, his autocratic face suddenly wreathed in a beautiful smile: "Yes. It's called 'Fourteenth Winter.' It was very popular with the North Koreans." He starts to sing, in a mournful vibrato: *"Birds are flying away, searching for a warm nest out of the cold wind . . ."*

Jang's resonant voice floats over the rooftops, above the dull rumble of the coming storm.

WALKING INTO MR. C'S CLUTTERED REAL-ESTATE office, I'm feeling deflated. The only uplifting thing about Kim's movies seems to be the songs. Clearly, my film will have to be a musical. For me, hell is a musical, full of tap-dancing and false cheer. It's the most unbearable art form I know.

But Mr. C, a fastidious man with impeccable hair, surprises me. He thinks a Kim Jong Il–style drama about CSG will work: "It will be timely, since the environment is of crucial concern. Your theme is good. I have an inkling it will generate great success." Monica and I look at each other, incredulous. I ask Mr. C if he thinks I'm crazy to want to follow Kim's rules. "No, it makes sense. Kim Jong Il was a genius of art. Even though he is heavily criticised for his evilness, he is well versed in film. The contents of his book are worthy of consideration. I'm not critical of North Korean movies. There are many good ones, made under difficult conditions, with few resources."

Mr. C did not have to leave North Korea. As a Party official, he was one of the privileged few. He moved into politics after ten years' military service, becoming a provincial governor. He met Kim Jong Il at a few official functions and was not a fan: "I saw him twice, giving directions in a rude way. But North Koreans don't know this, because the way he talks is manipulated before being broadcast. They only see him being polite. I have a different opinion about the two Kims. I put

Kim Il Sung in a positive light. He fought to regain the country, and experienced a lot of hardship. But Kim Jung Il, simply on the grounds of being Kim Il Sung's son, inherited power. It is not right that he let the people become poor. The bottom line is, he is a failed politician."

Mr. C defected to Seoul in 2004. It's not clear why. For five years, he ran a newspaper for defectors called *The Settler*, providing employment tips and news from home. He collected the news from secret contacts in North Korea, phoning them from Beijing. Now he sells real estate. If Mr. C hadn't just criticised Kim Jong Il to my face, I'd wonder if he was a spy. Pyongyang regularly sends agents south to keep tabs on defectors. Then again, with the propaganda refocused on Kim Il Sung under his grandson's new regime, maybe it is safe to slam Kim Jong Il now. Maybe Mr. C still is a spy: gathering data for Kim Jong Un and assessing potential threats to North Korea's image—including, perhaps, my film. When I ask why he's here, he is suspiciously vague: "At the early stage of my life in South Korea, I regretted my defection. I enjoyed a good life in the North. But I finally concluded I made the right choice—because of freedom, and the discrepancy of North Korean society."

One thing Mr. C does respect about Kim Jong Il is the way he deified his father on film: "When he joined the Labour Party at twenty-two, Kim Jong Il worked in the Department of Propaganda and Instigation. The first thing he did was use fact and fiction to make war movies about Kim Il Sung's anti-Japanese fight. I liked them very much. My favourites were *Order 027* and *Crude Wings*." Mr. C watched these movies with the soldiers he lived with at the DMZ. He even remembers being shown an American film to study military techniques: "It was called *A Guy Crossing the River*. Despite the fact it was made by an enemy country, we were required to learn the action skills it contained. In my service on the border between the two Koreas, we did a lot of special action training."

I do not know of any American movie called *A Guy Crossing the River*. The real title was evidently lost in translation while being smuggled through China and into the DMZ. I'm guessing the movie is probably David Lean's World War II classic *The Bridge on the River Kwai*, given its anti-Japanese message and detailed scenes of guerrilla warfare. There's something poignant about Mr. C and his mates hunched over a VHS machine in 1992, watching a movie made in 1957 to learn how to fight the Americans—especially when compared with the high-tech 3D computer games the Pentagon uses, simulating terrorist-infested Arab villages and North Korean dungeons crawling with commies, to train its soldiers in the art of modern warfare.

Mr. C has no problem with the fact that North Korean movies use their actors to sell propaganda: "It's same in South Korea. Costumes worn by actors create a fad. South Korean clothing companies put their products in movies to generate a marketing effect. I think humans are inherently the same when it comes to material desire. South Koreans live in an open society and pursue luxurious foreign brands. North Koreans are still cut off from the outside world, with no knowledge of these products. So they crave the clothes of *their* actors, which are modest and tidy."

Mr. C stops speaking and looks up. A group of black-suited men have walked into the main office. They sit on a couch and stare coldly at me and Mr. C through the window of our booth. Mr. C does not acknowledge them, but nor does he look surprised. It's a little creepy. I decide to wrap things up and ask Mr. C to sing. He blushes: "I'm not a good singer. During my military service on the DMZ, we had to sing three times before every meal, especially military songs and songs lauding Kim Jong Il. The one I remember is from my favourite movie, *Order 027: 'Secretly crossing the front, tonight as always . . .'"*

Mr. C stops and laughs. It's true; he's a terrible singer. I laugh too. Through the glass, the men on the couch just stare at me, their expressions unchanged.

That night, Monica takes me out to unwind in a bar so expensive there's no menu. I nibble on a desiccated bubble that tastes of seaweed, and Monica sidles over to an androgynous boy in a caftan. He wears Tibetan beads, jeggings, and thongs. He slouches over a tablet, peering at it through his dreadlocks. Monica flutters around him, giggling. She points at me: "All the way from Australia. A documentary. On North Korea!" Dreadlocks gives me a bored once-over, slides off his stool, and wanders off, followed by a skinny girl with leather boots up to her crotch. Monica gulps her margarita, flushed with excitement. Dreadlocks is the highest paid commercials director in Seoul: one of the bright young things driving the Korean Wave—the avalanche of cutting-edge art, technology, media, and pop culture that has revolutionised Asia.

In the city's neon-bright streets, innovation is everywhere—in the gadgets, fashion, and architecture, and on the ubiquitous HD screens. Gazing at the uber-cool, glittering crowds, I have the same feeling I had twenty years ago in Tokyo: that I've slid exactly five years into the future. On the circular screen of a crenulated yellow skyscraper, Japanese teenagers mob a pudgy South Korean pop star, begging for his autograph. His grin is as shiny as his silver suit. Monica tells me he's a minor celebrity, known for his anti-Americanism. In 2002, he smashed a US tank on stage after a US military convoy ran over two schoolgirls in Yangju. In 2004, he sang rock band N.EX.T's anti-US anthem to protest against the Iraq war. In 2010, when South Korea replaced its permissive North Korean "sunshine policy" with a hard-line stance, he called it a "tragedy" and begged for peace. "Who is he?" I ask Monica, curious. We're still four months away from the song that will make this man a YouTube mega-star, feted by everyone from Ban Ki Moon to Obama. Monica shrugs and parks her car on the kerb: "Oh, some guy called Psy."

We slip behind the plastic flaps of a barbeque joint and wedge ourselves around a smoking brazier. Monica covers the grill with succulent strips of marinated beef, showing me how to parcel it up in lettuce leaves with tangy pickles and kimchi. We wash it down with icy OB beer. It's cheap and delicious: the soul food of Seoul. Around us, people swap jokes and laugh, relieved to be out of the freezing wind. "What do South Koreans think of North Korea?" I ask Monica.

She laughs: "They don't. North Koreans are crazy! They're backwards and savage. When they come here, they can't handle it. They have an old-fashioned way of speaking, which is hilarious. Lots of our movies make fun of them."

"So you don't welcome North Korean defectors with open arms?" I ask.

Monica frowns. "We don't trust them. They spy on us and have weird ideas. We are scared that one day, when they run out of food, they will all want to come here. Then what will we do? Where will they go? What will they eat?"

Monica scoops up a glistening hunk of japchae noodles and lowers her voice. "Our government never tells us anything about North Korea. That's why I took your gig. I want to know more."

NORTH KOREAN JESUS

MAYBE IT'S MY HANGOVER—BUT I'M SURE the man facing my camera is Kim Jong Il. He has the same fleshy features and teddy-bear build. He even has fluffy hair. But that's where the likeness ends. Choi Myoung Min is polite, considerate, and shy. He hates Kim Jong Il. Before he escaped North Korea seven years ago, Choi taught computing in a Pyongyang high school. His former students are now the cyber-spies who routinely attack South Korean banks from Beijing—and, more recently, if Western reports are to be believed, the mainframe of Sony Pictures, before its release of the Kim Jong Un assassination spoof, *The Interview*. Choi runs a small film studio, Hana Culture, in Seoul. He has been tracking North Korean hackers since 2009 for a thriller he's making on cyber-warfare.

The attacks are a big problem for South Korea: 95 percent of the population uses high-speed Internet to bank, shop, and store data online. North Korea, with no Internet, is immune from counterattack. It has staged more than six thousand cyber-strikes since 2010, using an estimated army of three thousand hackers working from "command and control" servers in China. In 2013, they shut down the South Korean president's website, hit six banks and thirty thousand computers, and disrupted financial services worldwide—causing economic damage totalling $769 million. The second-most-damaging strike, in 2009, cost $47.5 million to clean up. The third strike is the one Choi is researching. It targeted banks in 2011, costing them $9.6 million in lost transactions. At the Nonghyup Bank alone, more than thirty million customers couldn't use ATMs or online services for days. The bank had to spend $476 million on security upgrades.

Choi's office is a comfortable cave—soft brown couches, low ceilings, and wood-panelled walls. Hanging above the gently steaming kettle are two North Korean soldiers' jackets with red stars and gold epaulettes. They look like something out of a James Bond film, but they're real. Choi shows me a trailer for his last film. Two men in the soldiers' jackets beat up a girl in a cell. The scene is stiffly acted and badly mixed—but the violence is horrific. It pulls out of focus and dissolves to the same girl, in a sundress, skipping in slow motion through a fairground. The kitsch sentimentality reminds me of *Sea of Blood*. Choi's movie is about North Korean refugees in China. If they are lucky, they survive as sex workers and labourers until they can get to South Korea. But if the Chinese authorities catch them, they are handed back to the North Koreans—who torture and, sometimes, execute them. Choi made his film with unpaid defectors in Seoul. It's low budget, raw, and full of anger.

As a fellow director, Choi is courteous enough to treat my interest in Kim Jong Il seriously, despite loathing the man: "Of course he may possess a flair for art, but it's too much to say he is gifted. If you show his book to South Koreans, they won't be impressed, as his rules are not new. What's interesting is why he wrote them. *The Director is the Commander* comes from the fact that Party officials used to control filmmaking. But Kim Jong Il said: "The director should not be touched." *The Assistant Director is a Creative Worker* was written because when Kim Jong Il took over the industry, the AD was a lazy guy who sat in the corner taking notes. This pissed Kim Jong Il off. He thought it was slothful. He ordered ADs to set up scenes, get them shot on time, and keep the director happy. Now, being an AD in North Korea is how you become a director."

Choi moves on to Kim's micromanaging style as the nation's only film producer: "His word is everywhere: actors should be good-looking, costumes should be modern, acting should be natural, hooligans should look like real hooligans . . . he controls the whole thing. In *The Nation and Destiny*, the exiled hero returns home to seek his mother's forgiveness. She is drinking. Kim Jong Il cut the scene, because 'North Korean mothers do not drink.' In *Till the End of the World*, the filmmakers challenged the idea of traditional love by showing an affair between a man and two women. The writer was expelled, even though Kim Jong Il, who had many mistresses, liked the film. It's a double standard: 'It's a romance if I do it, but a criminal act if you do it.' He rejected hundreds of high-quality scenarios. The hand-held camera of Western movies is prohibited, because Kim Jong Il felt dizzy watching it. And no matter how excellent the director is, there's always the danger of being sent to the camps."

Kim also controlled film classification through the Song Mu Bureau, which translates all imported films, including porn. Instead of using the West's G, PG, and R ratings, Kim Jong Il rated films as "Suitable for the People" (mostly Chinese and Russian movies), "Suitable for Officials" (mostly James Bond, James Cameron, and Jackie Chan), and "Suitable only for himself" (everything else). Choi sips his tea, full of disgust for the country he's left behind.

I wonder if he finds North Korean propaganda movies as awful as the regime they promote, but he quickly defends his colleagues: "The standard of North Korean filmmakers is not low at all. They are well qualified. They have simply been cut off from the outside world." So does Choi think a film made using Kim's rules will fail? "Not at all. The key point is how you touch people's emotion. If you just mimic the North Korean style, you will make a parody, and it won't move people. But if you can make a film in Australia that shows North Koreans' daily lives . . . a North Korean–style Australian movie, if you like, that would be good."

I smile. I have no idea what Choi means. He smiles too. We just sit there, smiling, overwhelmed by the strangeness of my idea. Then I ask Choi if he'd mind singing, and he sighs: "Most North Korean songs are propaganda songs, so we don't sing them. There is one popular one, from *Lim Guk Jung*. It's about fighting the ancient Korean lords." He starts to sing in a whispery monotone: *"The noise of people's resentment and deplorability, echoing in the air . . ."* He stops, amused by the irony: "This song implies that high-ranking officials are exploiting ordinary North Koreans. So it was banned."

Choi beckons over a lean man in a leather jacket who has been listening from the doorway: "Look, you want a real expert on Kim Jong Il, talk to this guy." Jimmi has the sharp cheekbones, sinewy grace, and rough skin of a Hong Kong action star. He slides into Choi's seat, locking eyes with my lens: "Please take a good shot—I might have a fan club in America one day." He is magnetic, an edge of danger behind the charm. Jimmi's a black belt in tae kwon do. Before he fled North Korea in 2003, he was going to be a movie star. Now he works on Choi's films for nothing, cleaning hospitals to pay the bills: "I graduated from the Pyongyang University of Film and Theatre. But I was implicated in a serious incident so I had to leave. I don't want to talk about it."

Jimmi's the first defector I've met who knows Kim Jong Il's manifesto better than I do. He studied it for four years. North Korean drama school sounds more like a military boot camp: as a student in the action-movie stream, Jimmi had to do hand-to-hand combat, wrestling, shooting, judo, jeep driving, and marathon running, and train with the North Korean Special Forces. He also had to learn Kim's teachings by heart.

Jimmi is offended when I confess that North Korean acting seems pretty hammy, from what I've seen in *Pulgasari* and *Sea of Blood*. He politely points out that a Godzilla rip-off and a sixties melodrama are hardly an accurate indicator of contemporary North Korean drama practice. Overacting is definitely frowned upon.

To explain, Jimmi describes a scene in a naturalistic drama, *Star of Chosun*, in which a dying soldier speaks his last words to the men who have shot him. "The scene is the climax of the movie. They filmed it for three days in the woods, in minus forty degrees. The actor had to say: 'Comrades, please choose the right path,' with a warm-hearted face. This was acting of maximum difficulty. He had to do two things simultaneously—suppress physical pain, and through his bloody, disfigured face, inspire audiences with passionate loyalty to Kim Il Sung."

Jimmi acts out the death speech on the couch, and Monica and I are transported to the freezing North Korean woods. He's extraordinary.

Jimmi knew he wanted to perform from age eight, when his mother took him to the Big Top in Pyongyang. He found the clowns and trapeze artists dazzling. At nine, he saw the people of his village mobbing a group of travelling film stars and was struck by the happiness they inspired. He became a performer while in the army, which sounds odd—until you realise that many North Koreans spend their first adult decade in military service before moving onto civilian careers. Jimmi's beautiful voice gave him his break. As a young cadet, he did daily broadcasts in the barracks: "Dear Party members and labourers. The Great Leader Kim Jong Il has pointed out the following . . ."

Later, he was put on loudspeakers in factories, theatres, and farms, wherever his unit was stationed. He eventually became a state radio announcer, broadcasting North Korean propaganda to China and Japan. He spoke in heavily accented English about the "imperialist US warmongers" and used a friendlier voice for the Chinese, as North Korea's brotherly comrades. Kim Jong Il allowed theatre and film students to watch foreign films at the university, which Jimmi entered after eleven years in the army. He saw movies from America, England, Russia, France, Italy, Japan, Romania, and Hong Kong. He liked Hong Kong movies best, followed by the Japanese ones, because they had sex scenes. The American films were mostly war movies, and usually old. They were not properly subtitled and were often truncated.

"If we understood the content, there was the danger we would get to know the American mind-set and lifestyle, which are undesirable elements," explains Jimmi. "We just watched the scenes to learn character behaviours."

Jimmi loves acting, but says North Korean performers never use the word "love" to describe what they do. Instead, they say: "Fulfil your acting faithfully." He thinks my Kim Jong Il–style film could have a major impact: "North Koreans know about the US, China, and Japan, but they think of Australia as an island far away. There is less hatred towards Australia than to the US. If you make your film from an Australian perspective, you will help change North Korea. But it is very important you do it a certain way."

Jimmi speaks slowly, making sure Monica translates exactly what he says: "Your actors must not act skin-deep. Develop a bond with the North Koreans. Immerse yourselves in their lives. You know the problems they face. You are on a mission, to create a better understanding of them. Above all, do not use images of North Koreans produced in South Korea. That will make your film a mockery, and breed hatred. Mockery is not art. Art is something that generates shared feeling. It is enough that you faithfully make a film in the North Korean style. It will generate worldwide interest."

Jimmi beams at me, full of hope. I have no idea what he's said, because Monica has stopped translating. She is wiping back tears: "I feel so stupid," she sniffs. "He has been through so much. Your film must open a window. For all of us." Jimmi says something softly to Monica, and her eyes widen in horror. "He left North Korea because three of his acting friends were executed," she says. "He knew he was next."

Without my prompting, Monica asks Jimmi to sing. He thinks for a beat, then shuts his eyes. His voice is low and beautiful, and unutterably sad. *The long and winding road, a cruel smoke like the blowing wind . . . when I walk alone.*

On the outskirts of Seoul, where the skyscrapers give way to battered industrial blocks, is a dirty building with a broken elevator. Its four floors are derelict, their blown-out windows facing a shabby gas station. At the top of the stairwell, there's an iron door. It leads onto the roof and a breathtaking view of Seoul—all glass and telephone poles, stretching to the distant hills.

A small chipboard hut sits on the roof, wedged between a satellite dish and a boiler. This is the studio of Sunmo, the only defector who won't let me film his face. He waded across the Yalu River into China ten years ago, looking for something to eat. He then trekked south, all the way to the jungles of Laos, where he got lost. He would have died if some villagers hadn't found him and taken him to the nearest town. He wanted to keep walking to Thailand, then stow away on a boat to South Korea, but he was too sick. So he handed himself over to the Laotian police, pretending to be a South Korean tourist. It worked. He was arrested and sent to Seoul.

Sunmo is an artist. In North Korea, that means a propaganda artist—there is no other kind. As a young boy, Sunmo saw Kim Il Sung, whom he revered like a god, praising some children for their artwork on TV. He desperately wanted Kim Il Sung to praise him too, so he started to draw. He got into art school, but when he graduated, he was not deemed skilful enough to be given the supreme honour of painting the Leaders' portraits. So he drew them in secret, then burnt them. In North Korea, the Leader's image is sacrosanct. Even folding a newspaper so the crease falls on the leader's face can send you to the gulags. If Sunmo's portraits had been discovered, he would have been charged with treason and sent to Camp 14. He might even have been shot.

Given all this, I am stunned by the lightness and beauty of Sunmo's canvases. They are masterpieces of technique and expression, rendered in delicate pastels. They celebrate the North Korea Sunmo left behind with his parents and one sibling, a life he says was "filled with happiness and pride." Sunmo lights a Marlboro and tugs down his baseball cap, deadpan cool: "Of course I want to show my face. I am very good looking. But if I do, my family will be caught and put under enormous hardship." He is definitely attractive—not just physically, but because of his sly humour. His beautiful paintings are undercut by a cynicism that is both funny and disturbing. This is North Korea seen by a North Korean artist, from the other side of the mirage. It still looks like propaganda, but it feels like anarchy. Sunmo is the North Korean Banksy.

On one canvas, a grinning schoolgirl throws her arms wide, haloed by a pink carnation. Underneath is a bold red slogan: *Let Us Grow Up on Freedom Mountain and Sing the Song of Joyful Paradise!* On another, eleven identical pink-cheeked schoolgirls link arms over a bright yellow slash: *We Are All a Bunch of Happy Kids!* A smaller painting shows a toddler on tiptoes, reaching up to pull down a curtain. Through the fabric, a single word: *Open.* There is an evocative image of a tiny old woman bicycling up a steep hill, dwarfed by a sack on her back. A word appears through the snowdrifts: *Escape.* Two canvases capture the reunification dream that all Koreans share: in one, a North Korean girl spins inside a hula hoop with a South Korean girl in a pink onesie: *Where shall we play?* In another, a sexy woman in hot pants walks arm in arm with a North Korean policewoman, made up like a fifties movie star: *Let's Dance!*

I ask Sunmo if he still paints the Leaders, and he pulls out a circular canvas of Kim Jong Il smiling his Prozac smile through a bushy hippie beard. It's the North Korean Jesus. "He wasn't a very good Jesus, was he?" Sunmo muses, showing me more: Kim in Sony headphones and a red jumpsuit, pirouetting on one foot. Kim in a hospital bed, gazing at a schoolgirl—who pours Coca-Cola into his drip feed. There are bigger canvases of North Korean soldiers in Ray-Bans, pointing guns: *Let's Destroy the American Imperialists! Let's Liberate the South!* They are impeccably painted, but in Banksy's stencil style: graphic reds and blues over bold pink slogans.

Sunmo loved North Korean movies. He misses them deeply. As he speaks about them, I remember the Camp 14 escapee Shin Dong Hyuk in a documentary I saw—standing in a supermarket in Seoul, staring at rows of food with glazed disinterest. Shin confessed he missed the simple routine of the gulag—where each day was a blunt challenge to survive. Shin managed to find real happiness in North Korea, just like Sunmo: "We were forced to watch movies continuously, whether we wanted to or not. I adored them. Especially ones that evoked patriotism and loyalty to the state. My favourites were *Nation and Destiny*, *A Star of Chosun,* and *A Sun of the People.*"

Sunmo sings a song, low and soothing. I don't know which movie it's from, because our camera has broken down in the heat of the studio. There is no footage to translate. All I have is my memory of Sunmo swaying as he sings, lost in a gentle reverie. I'm struck by the resilience of the human spirit: its capacity, even in hell, to find joy.

MONICA AND I DRIVE AT BREAKNECK speed around Seoul, using her satnav to find ATMs that will covert dollars to won. Monica has shown a tender side during our three days together, but she's merciless with money. Tonight is our last interview. I'd hoped it would be with Choi Eun Hee, the actress Kim Jong Il kidnapped in 1978. But after repeated attempts to come up with an appearance fee Choi will accept, she has announced that she is "incapacitated" in a private hospital without a phone. Monica has got me the next best thing—an interview with Choi's South Korean agent. He also wants a fee, and Monica is making damn sure I pay it, in cash, before I fly out.

She hustles me from bank to bank, peering over my shoulder to count the notes, demanding each time that I hand them to her. She's upbeat in the face of my obvious discomfort, as if there's nothing rude about her behaviour. This is apparently how South Koreans do business. I wonder if the bullishness is something they've had to learn during their ascent to global powerhouse. Or if it's a national trait, shared by their communist cousins in the north. "Give me ten thousand more, for the calls I made yesterday," says Monica, staring me down in the biting wind. She's not going to unlock the car door until I do. I suddenly understand why the Koreans are said to be the only people the Japanese really fear. And then Monica's all smiles again as she pockets the cash and delivers me to the studio of Chung Sun Min, secretary-general of the Shin Sang Ok Memorial Project.

Chung is imperious, expensively dressed, and wearing socks. As is customary, we've left our shoes at the door. The space is magnificent, filled floor to ceiling with Shin Sang Ok's film canisters, cameras, instruments, and props. I want to film it in a wide, but Chung won't talk until I cut off the frame at his knees. His socks may be argyle, but they do not convey the gravitas he's going for as Shin Sang Ok's executor. Chung has never heard of Kim Jong Il's manifesto. But he knows all about his ambition. Thanks to the Dear Leader's desire for cinematic glory, Chung's best friend, Shin Sang Ok, and his wife, Choi Eun Hee, spent five years in the North Korean gulags.

Chung tells their story: "Choi was a top South Korean movie star in the '70s, but her career was on the wane. While relocating her new film school in 1978, she got an invitation from Wang Dong Il in Hong Kong—who promised to invest in the school and get her movie work. This was a trap set by North Korea. At the time, Choi was divorcing her husband, Shin Sang Ok. But they were still in contact, and he opposed her going to Hong Kong. She went anyway, and that's how she was abducted. In January 1978, Kim Jong Il came to Nampo port in North Korea to greet Choi in person. Then he sent her to prison. She didn't see him for another five years.

"Kim Jong Il knew Shin would try to find Choi. He did, and was interrogated by the South Korean secret police, who suspected he was involved in her kidnapping. This meant he could no longer make movies in South Korea. When Shin received an offer to export fifteen of his films to Hong Kong, he took it, because he was broke. He went to Hong Kong to set up the deal, but it took too long and his visa was in danger of expiring. His friend Lee Young Saeng, who was really a North Korean spy, suggested a way to extend the visa. Shin was desperate, so he followed Lee to meet a broker. On their way, they met robbers, who kidnapped Shin and handed him to the North Koreans. The whole thing had been an elaborate plan set up by Kim Jong Il.

"Shin and Choi were kept in separate labour camps and brainwashed with ideology. After five years, they finally saw each other at a party thrown by Kim Jong Il. He told them it was time to contribute to North Korean cinema. They wanted to get out of prison, so they agreed. Kim Jong Il forced them to remarry in public, as 'revolutionary filmmakers' who had voluntarily defected from the South. Then he appointed Shin as chief adviser and Choi as a deputy-chief adviser on all movies. Choi made a secret recording of Kim Jong Il explaining why he had chosen them. She remembers he spoke with great anger: 'We send our people to East Germany to study editing, to Czechoslovakia to study technology, to the Soviet Union to learn directing. We cannot send our people anywhere else, since they are all enemy states. I acknowledge we lag behind in filmmaking techniques. We have to know we are lagging behind, and make efforts to raise a new generation of filmmakers.'"

What happened next to Shin is well known. Kim showed him through his air-conditioned movie vault, where he kept over twenty thousand foreign movies, including everything Shin had made. Kim's favourite Shin movie was *Evergreen Tree*, a passionate plea for Korean reunification, that had moved South Korean president Park Chung Hee to tears. Kim told Shin it had also deeply touched the North Koreans. Shin went on to make seven movies for the dictator, providing advice on another thirteen. He was given all the money and equipment he needed—including, on one film, a real train to blow up. Shin had access to a private jet, shopped in the foreigners-only store, and was allowed to run his movies through his own studio in Pyongyang. While making *Pulgasari*, Shin complained to Kim Jong Il about the standard of North Korean animators, and Kim promptly flew in the entire Japanese special-effects team Toho Studios, the makers of Godzilla—including Kenpachiro Satsuma, the actor who wore the monster suit. Kim's largesse was rewarded: Shin's films were hits in North Korea and won awards all over the Eastern Bloc. But Choi's story is less well known. I can't help identifying with her as a woman in her forties, trying to reconfigure her public life while going through a nasty private breakup. What must it have felt like, as a newly single woman, to travel to Hong Kong to set up the school that was supposed to support her in old age, only to find herself thrown into a North Korean gulag? Was Choi stunned when, after five years of hard labour, she stood sipping champagne at Kim Jong Il's cocktail party and saw her ex-husband across the room? Did she fall in love with him again? Was it torturous, or pleasant, to marry him a second time, live with him in a Pyongyang condo, and star in his films? What guts must it have taken to buy a recorder in the foreigners' store, pretending she needed it for "voice training," then secretly record the dictator who could send her to the firing squad?

Choi is credited as director on Shin's first North Korean film, *A Secret Envoy of No Return*. Chung says this is because Shin was embarrassed by it and wanted his name removed. But Choi was a talented filmmaker in her own right. When *Secret Envoy* won best director at the Karlovy Vary Festival, she must have felt proud. Even prouder, perhaps, when she won best actress for *Salt* in Moscow in 1985—despite the fact that the suffering she'd depicted on screen was real.

Chung confirms Choi enjoyed working on North Korean movies, even though she was as keen to escape as Shin. But there's another view, promoted by Japanese film critic Tetsuo Nishida: the couple weren't kidnapped, but went to North Korea willingly—Shin because South Korea's conservative government was no longer backing his movies, and Choi because she was too old to play leading roles at home. Nishida's book *Fictional Image* portrays the couple as ambitious survivors: like Leni Riefenstahl, who was dubious about Hitler's politics but happy to accept his patronage, Shin and Choi did whatever it took to keep making films. Even if that meant defecting to North Korea.

I put Nishida's theory to Chung and he rejects it crossly, pointing out that Kim regularly kidnapped foreigners to teach North Koreans various skills. Japanese newspapers from the 1980s and 1990s are full of stories of people disappearing from Kamakura beaches while walking their dogs or being thrown into boats moored off Jeju Island at night, only to resurface years later as tutors in Pyongyang. Listening to Chung's account of how Shin and Choi finally escaped, I suspect his version is true.

The couple were clever: when their movies began winning awards, Kim gave them his trust. They persuaded him that the best way to show the world they had willingly defected to North Korea would be to set up a studio in Hungary, from which they could shoot films needing European locations and come and go at will. Kim appointed them an army of minders and left them to it. In Vienna in 1986, after several unsuccessful attempts, Shin and Choi finally got away.

The way Chung tells it, their escape unfolded like a Hollywood thriller: "On March 13, with the help of a Japanese reporter, they ran from their minders and jumped in a taxi. On their way to the American embassy, they were pursued by North Korean agents, who radioed taxis all over the city to find out if an Asian man and woman were on board. The Japanese reporter paid the cabby to lie and say he was going in the opposite direction. Shin and Choi slightly passed the front gate of the embassy to distract their pursuers. Then they ran in. They said it was like a slow-motion movie, the gate seemed so far away. Shin ran in first and Choi followed."

Once free, Shin and Choi went their separate ways—Shin to make the popular *3 Ninjas* movies in LA under his new alias, Simon Sheen, and Choi back to Seoul, where she wrote a book about her time with Kim Jong Il. Many times on the streets of Seoul, Chung has seen North Korean defectors approach Choi, in tears, thanking her for her work in *Salt*.

I wish I could meet this indomitable woman in person. But she is hidden away from me, along with the movies she made with Shin. The

South Korean government considers them too sympathetic to North Korea to be screened. If Chung released them, he would be jailed. As a result, *Salt, A Secret Envoy of No Return, Love, Love, My Love, A Chronicle of Escape,* and fifteen other brilliant films are rotting in metal canisters on both sides of the DMZ.

The propaganda cuts both ways: South Koreans are banned from seeing Shin and Choi's movies, and the North Koreans have been told to forget they exist.

CHASING GODZILLA

COASTING TOWARDS KYUSHU IN CATTLE CLASS, I study the satellite map on TV. The lights of South Korea glitter brightly against a jet-black sea. To the north and west, China and Japan are lit up like funfairs. Looking closer, I realise the black void between them is not the sea: it's North Korea. I feel a rush of anger at the goose chase I've been led on by this stubborn country: a place so paranoid, it doesn't even turn its lights on at night. Then I remember the crippling poverty. At least North Korea, by default, is doing something to reduce global warming.

I have three precious days in Japan, my last chance to meet someone who actually worked with Kim Jong Il. Kenji Fujimoto, who was the Dear Leader's sushi chef before he flew to Okinawa to get abalone and never came back, watched many movies with Kim in his Pyongyang palace. Charles Robert Jenkins, one of the four American GIs who defected to North Korea in the 1960s and played Yankee bad guys for Kim Jong Il, now lives on Sado Island with a Japanese wife. And Kenpachiro Satsuma, the actor who wore the monster suit in Kim's Godzilla rip-off, *Pulgasari*, tends a community garden in Tokyo. I have contact numbers for all of them. South Korea and the US have just started their annual military training exercises, and North Korea is threatening a full-scale nuclear attack. Things are tense in Japan, but I am still optimistic they'll talk.

First, however, I need to meet an ex–grave digger from Leipzig. Johannes Schönherr belongs to a small but devoted club of North Korean cinema fans on the Internet. They exchange information via anonymous posts, downloading North Korean DVDs smuggled in from China and streaming them to each other from all corners of the globe. Johannes defected to Bonn in 1983 and forged a colourful career distributing underground films. At first, he tracked the violent offerings of Eurotrash filmmakers like Ruggero Deodato, the maker of *Cannibal Holocaust*. Then he toured Japanese cyberpunk movies around Europe and screened the works of Cinema of Transgression pioneers Nick Zedd and Richard Kern at underground clubs in Nuremberg. These events were often shut down by outraged German feminists—which made Johannes proud. His hunger to uncover films the world wanted to censor eventually led him to North Korea. As he says between drags on his ever-present cigarette: "You can't get more underground than that."

Fittingly, Johannes lives in Beppu—a hot-spring town the Japanese like to say sprang from the gaseous bowels of hell. Roughly 950 kilometres to the north, Fukushima's shattered nuclear reactors are belching their toxic waste into the Pacific—but the denizens of Beppu, in their *yukata* and wooden clogs, clip-clop from bathhouse to dumpling shop as if they're living two hundred years ago. They might as well be: Beppu is the real-world version of the spirit world in Hayao Miyazaki's animated fantasy *Spirited Away*—a steampunk wonderland of eighteenth-century brass pipes and bubbling, acid-green canals. I stand on the stone steps of my *ryokan*, waiting for Johannes. Along the cobblestones, fluffy cats snooze on air ducts, warmed by sulphurous blasts from deep underground. An old lady with a wart on her chin totters past under a paper parasol, clutching a bag of mandarins. The steam thickens and swirls over the jigsaw of tiled roofs, and emerging from it, like a ghoul from hell, is Johannes.

He's a hulking black figure with waist-length hair, a carefully wrapped sack dangling from his bony fingers. His glasses have fogged up in the steam. He blinks at me shyly, clearly more comfortable in front of the blue glare of a video screen: "Would you like some noodles?" I follow Johannes into a little wooden bar and we wolf down piping-hot bowls of silky ramen, spiked with shiitake mushrooms and ginger. Then Johannes gently spreads his North Korean treasures on the tatami-mat floor of my room.

Kim Jong Il's DVDs, books, and movie posters gleam on the mat like precious artefacts, painstakingly collected during Johannes's 1999 trip to Pyongyang. He was invited there by a North Korean embassy contact in Bonn for whom he used to dub Western films so they could be sent in the diplomatic bag to Kim Jong Il. Johannes spent his time as a guest of the Pyongyang International Film Festival (there really is such a thing), chatting up Korfilm, the state-owned distributor. He left with a handful of North Korean movies, which he toured around Europe. Then he slammed their mind-numbing propaganda in a 2002 book, *Trashfilm Roadshows*, and North Korea labelled him an "imperialist spy." He has never been invited back.

Johannes has written an impressive book, *North Korean Cinema: A History*. But his intimate knowledge of North Korean filmmaking stops around the time of *A Schoolgirl's Diary*, which was script-edited by Kim Jong Il in 2006. Another six years' worth of films have since been made, about which hardly anything is known. Johannes's collection of bootlegged North Korean movies confirms what I suspected—Kim not only borrowed from Hollywood blockbusters, he reproduced them: *Souls Protest* is the North Korean *Titanic*, *Hong Kil Dong* is its *Karate Kid*, and *Unsung Heroes* is a Juche-style James Bond. And while North Korean movies may be an acquired taste, a few are truly exquisite.

On Johannes's small TV, I watch the 1971 melodrama *The Flower Girl*, which has been transferred from celluloid to DigiBeta to DVD. The dubbing process has made it jittery, its pixels as big as sugar cubes. But the power of the story shines through.

Kotpun is a young Korean girl living under Japanese rule in the early twentieth century. Her mother, beaten mercilessly by their evil Japanese landlord, is dying. To pay for her medicine, Kotpun sells flowers in the marketplace to drunk Japanese and their scornful Korean prostitutes. They spit at her, but Kotpun is proud: when her little sister attempts to sing for money, she stops her. They're not beggars but noble daughters of Korea. When the Japanese landlady flings boiling oil at Kotpun's sister and blinds her, Kotpun's life becomes hell. Her mother dies of exhaustion, and Kotpun's sister goes mad with grief and runs away. The landlady, tormented by guilt, falls sick—and the landlord decides to murder Kotpun to get rid of the "evil demons" possessing his wife.

Beautifully shot scenes of melancholy songs and extreme suffering follow. After two hours of relentless torment, things finally look up for Kotpun. She flees to the hills and finds her brother, a handsome guerrilla fighter who looks uncannily like Harrison Ford's Han Solo in *Star Wars*. He rouses the villagers with a passionate speech about how they must build "a new society, free from oppression," and they join him in a violent battle against the evil Japanese occupiers. The villagers triumph, the three siblings are reunited, and Kotpun walks through the marketplace once more, her beautiful young face framed by red flowers, singing with joy.

Flower Girl shows that Kim Jong Il knew what he was doing. It is as elegant as an Akira Kurosawa movie, engaging despite the melodrama, and exquisitely acted. The world thought so too: in 1972, the film won a prize at the World Film Festival in Czechoslovakia, and is still known in film circles today as a North Korean classic.

Johannes unwraps a pamphlet bound in green leather, *Great Man and Cinema*—a collection of anecdotes about Kim Jong Il's movie career, which the prologue insists will "be enshrined in the hearts of those who lived, live and will live, benefiting from the birth of the Juche-oriented cinematic art and its eternal prosperity, and will go down in history as imperishable legends." The pamphlet celebrates Kim Jong Il's work on several films, including his editing and casting of *Flower Girl*. Kim didn't let the superior morality of Juche stop him from resorting to an age-old Hollywood technique when choosing Kotpun—he passed over the experienced actresses and went for a barely legal beauty:

> A group was organized to select a fit woman. They looked closely for her not only at the film studio but also at all the art organizations of the country, but could not find the right actress. In these circumstances, Comrade Kim Jong Il said that it was advisable to cast the part of the heroine to a young actress who had never appeared on the screen.
>
> This was a bolt from the blue. The officials were swayed by misgivings, wondering if a novice could play the role of the heroine in such an important film. But Comrade Kim Jong Il said that her simplicity and unsophistication struck his fancy, and advised them to cast her.
>
> The nominated heroine appeared on stage. She wore her straw shoes in the reverse way. She had never put them on in her life. Comrade Kim Jong Il said she did not know how to wear straw shoes because she had grown up happily without the hardship of the old days, and he taught her how to put them on.
>
> Afterwards, he gave her meticulous guidance in her acting, costume and props. Under his warm leadership the heroine developed into a famous actress who commands the love and respect of the People.

I wonder if Kim Jong Il's warm leadership extended to teaching his young star other activities, off-set. His impressive strike rate with young actresses doesn't fill me with hope. But at least *Flower Girl* shows that Kim's propaganda techniques can produce powerful cinema.

Inspired, I walk off the *tonkatsu* cutlets I've eaten with Johannes. It's snowing heavily, and we hug the edge of the canal, warming ourselves in its heat. I tell Johannes the plot of my movie. He groans with disappointment. "It cannot work," he says. "There is no leader. To make it truly North Korean, the villagers can only win if they are led by a leader like Kim Il Sung."

"But we don't have leaders like that in Australia," I protest. "They're tossers. The audience will laugh."

"Then the villagers must lose, and the miners must win," Johannes replies with Teutonic finality. "At the end, you can have a big song about how, one day, a revolutionary fighter will save the village. Then show Kim Jong Il, on a white horse or something, rising above Sydney Park."

I sit neck-deep in the *ryokan's* hot spring, thinking about Johannes's idea. Maybe he is right. Maybe I should make a pro-CSG movie so heavily laced with propaganda, sophisticated Western audiences immediately get the message. North Korean spin or capitalist spin—it's one and the same. Or perhaps I should make a film cobbled from the advice the defectors have given me—which would mean an animation about a rabbit and a fox, shot as a musical, with plenty of sex, ten-minute death speeches, and authentic scenes of North Korean life, shot in the middle of Sydney. All without—and here's the kicker—a trace of irony. Impossible. I might as well use Kim's rules to make an ad for Hummer. At least then I could upload it as a YouTube parody and reach the forty-two million fans of *Hulk Hogan and Macho Man VS Kim Jong-il - Epic Rap Battles of History 5*.

Defeated, I slide under the scalding water, letting it sting me awake. I remember the joyful conviction with which the defectors, no matter how scarred, sang songs from North Korean movies. There has to be a way of capturing that power, of using it to instil the same joy in jaded Western hearts.

I throw on a *yukata* and head down to the manager's office to use the only phone line out of this antiquated place and receive more discouraging news. Tepco has just admitted the radiation leaks at Fukushima are on par with Chernobyl. The ABC journalist who was going to give me the real name of Kim's sushi chef, Kenji Fujimoto, has to fly north to investigate. Fujimoto is still being tailed by North Korean agents. His contact cannot be handed out on the phone.

Struggling to stay positive, I call the souvenir shop on Sado Island where Charles Robert Jenkins, retired North Korean movie villain, now spends his Saturdays. The lady who answers is polite but evasive. Yes, Mr. Jenkins received my letter requesting an interview. Yes, he works on Saturdays, but for some reason not today. No, I cannot have his home number.

I cancel my ferry ticket to Sado Island and book a flight to Tokyo. Somewhere in that seething metropolis of thirteen million people is the one man left who can tell me what it was like to work with Kim Jong Il.

SHIMOISHIWARA IS A RUN-DOWN SUBURB on the outskirts of Tokyo. It nestles, forgotten, under a thundering overpass. I stand beneath the girders, looking at a dusty vegetable patch. To my left is a row of ramshackle two-storey flats. To my right, the path I have been walking up and down for three hours, trying to find Satsuma: community gardener, Godzilla actor and—according to the postman who has ridden past twice now—unknown at this address. I had hoped the letters I posted to Satsuma from Sydney went unanswered because he couldn't reply in English or was too reticent to respond. I'd banked on him being an *erai shito*: the kind of Japanese VIP who will only grant an interview if you approach him the old-fashioned way, in person. But I was wrong.

I tear open the *omiyage* of candied chestnuts I bought for Satsuma in Beppu. They're crushed from the walk, oozing from delicate paper packets. I fling them at the overpass, consumed by apocalyptic despair. Images of Godzilla—smashing Tokyo Tower with a scaly paw, obliterating Yokohama with a sweep of its tail, shooting fireballs at Mothra through massive fangs—flash through my mind. And I see the brilliant Satsuma, moving inside his monster suit, breathing life into the nuclear nightmare that has plagued the Japanese ever since Little Boy destroyed Hiroshima. Satsuma was the Andy Serkis of his day—an artist so accomplished Kim Jong Il hired him to smash feudalism clean off the collective North Korean retina. But Godzilla is elsewhere now, and a new nuclear monster is destroying Fukushima.

And I am alone in the city of my birth, only two hours away from the country in which I most want to be. This is where my great North Korean visa chase has left me: standing in a veggie patch with an empty candy box and smelling faintly of cabbage. I head for the station, beaten.

North Korea to Aim Missile Test at Australia

A long-range missile which North Korea plans to test next month will for the first time be aimed towards South-East Asia and Australia. "If the test proceeds as North Korea has indicated, it will impact in an area roughly between Australia, Indonesia and the Philippines," Mr. Campbell said.

ABC News, March 24, 2012

I returned to Sydney filled with a sense of impending doom. The rushes in my camera did not match the film in my head: North Korea was missing. When Kim Jong Un and his girlfriend were seen at a concert in Pyongyang, laughing at a Mickey Mouse on ice skates, the West saw it as a hopeful sign the new leader would be more open. But now Kim Jong Un was pointing rockets at Australia, it was clear he intended to carry on the family tradition. My chances of getting in had evaporated.

As North Korea's nuclear posturing took Asia to the brink of war, the tensions at home exploded. My partner was spending repeated nights away and not even calling at breakfast. On our daughter's eighth birthday, as she and her friends slept off a midnight feast in a jumble of blankets in her room, he told me about his new love. He wouldn't tell me how young she was at first, but after an emergency counselling session, the truth came out. My immediate reaction was to laugh, but I was hiding my shock.

I sat on our rotting deck for three days, howling. But strangely resigned. We'd been battling for years, I realised; as far back as *Forbidden Lie$*. I'd criticise his driving when he collected me from the airport; he'd throw the awards I'd won out the car window in disgust. Over time, these petty assaults had built up a world of shared pain. I blamed his inability to realise his dreams. He blamed my inability to be kind. Our bodies had imprinted parallel trenches in the mattress, from which we lobbed psychological grenades at each other, but rarely moved. We were eviscerated husks. I felt no jealousy for my younger rival. A woman my own age might have been a threat. As it was, part of me was happy for him. He'd found someone to adore him, the way I no longer could.

Then reality hit. I didn't have time to work through the five stages of grief: I had to get to Pyongyang. Without North Korean access, I wouldn't get a production budget. Without a budget, I couldn't take over the mortgage. My sunny daughter was not going to lose her home just because her dad's priorities were elsewhere. So I fast-forwarded through denial, anger, and depression, cut to acceptance, pulled myself together, and hit the phone.

Going in as a tourist was still off the cards: Pyongyang was calling for South Korea's president, Lee Myung Bak, to be "struck with a retaliatory bolt of lightning" and threatening to turn Seoul "to ashes." I would not be welcome as an ally of the puppet state. My only option was to beg Alejandro Cao de Bénos to wrangle a media visa, whatever his price. Then my producer, Lizzette Atkins, who had been following my progress from the sanity of her Melbourne office, wisely intervened. I should call Nick Bonner one last time, she urged. What did I have to lose? He could only say no.

Koryo Tours' grinning North Korean worker popped up on my screen, and Nick greeted me like we'd spoken yesterday. I was impressed—it had been over a year. I took a deep breath and told him the truth. My film wasn't just about North Korean cinema, I said; I also wanted to use Kim Jong Il's manifesto to make a short drama, in their style—and I wanted the advice of their filmmakers to do it. I wasn't just taking; I was giving back.

Nick sighed. "Darling, why didn't you tell me that in the first place?"

With rising hope, I confessed I'd already interviewed defected North Korean filmmakers. They'd been pretty negative about Kim Jong Il: was that a deal-breaker?

Nick gave a dismissive chuckle: "Why go to them, when you can go straight to the horse's mouth?" And just like that, we were in.

PART 2

THE FIRST TRIP

The communist society to which we aspire is a truly popular society in which people of a new type enjoy rich and cultured lives as masters of nature. Writers and artists have a significant role to play in building this great society, a unique role, in which they are quite irreplaceable.

—ON THE ART OF THE CINEMA

FLYING AIR KORYO

WALKING TO PICK UP MY DAUGHTER from school, it's hard to believe that in forty-eight hours, I'll be on a plane to Pyongyang. When I tell the harried mums, they smile, then do a double take. "Wait. *North* Korea? Not South?" I can see skeletons and death squads flashing in their eyes. "That's right," I say, trying to stay upbeat. "Not good Korea, bad Korea. The one with the gulags."

My daughter, on the other hand, is blasé. She's used to my short trips to unusual places; she knows I always come back. To her, North Korea is a land where the hotels serve stale bread and the children don't get toys for Christmas. Last night, she helped me pack according to the detailed instructions of Koryo Tours: a torch for the blackouts, gifts for the minders, and family photos to break the ice. She was fastidious about making sure I did not pack any "offensive foreign literature," "devices with GPS capability," or "weapons of any kind." *Who* magazine and George Orwell's *1984* have stayed out of my bag, along with my satnav and pocketknife. We have already bought Imodium tablets, in case I forget to boil the water and get Pyongyang belly.

Lizzette and I are meeting Nick in Beijing. He's set up a three-day recce with North Korea's elite filmmakers through his trusted Korfilm contact in Pyongyang, Ms. K. I'm only allowed to take happy snaps this time—but if I earn Ms. K's trust, I'll be let back in to shoot the film for real. It's the Asian way of doing business: contracts mean nothing if you can't look a collaborator in the eye. I'm used to it after dealing with the Kyoto Yakuza. They once granted me an interview because my production manager was sleeping with their boss. He was in jail, so he sent his tattooed henchmen. They told us everything we wanted to know about drugs, guns, and murder on two conditions: we hide their faces, and never show the interview in Japan. I agreed to all this over a cup of green tea in a hotel they were extorting. When the Australian Film Commission demanded the Yakuza sign a legal release form, they faxed back a haiku about cherry blossoms.

I've told our investors not to expect anything in writing from the North Koreans. An oral promise is what counts. If Ms. K decides to invite us back, the offer will be made during our trip, and probably over a meal. There will be no follow-up correspondence: Ms. K and her Korfilm colleagues, between them, share one heavily monitored email address. An access-all-areas film shoot inside the North Korean propaganda machine is too risky a proposition to negotiate in writing.

Nick has already warned us our mobile phones will be confiscated at the airport. I assume the "no GPS" rule is to stop foreigners taking in other devices that could trigger a bomb via satellite, or provide location stats for North Korea's secret military facilities. The little pro-am camera I've chosen for the trip is too low-tech to speak to a satellite. But it'll be my only chance to capture North Korea, if Ms. K pulls the plug on trip two. I swaddle it in a scarf and place it in my handbag on top of a pair of $10,000 German lenses. At least whatever I am allowed to shoot will look pretty on screen.

Tucking in my daughter that night, I'm relieved she only has a vague idea that her parents separated three months ago. My ex will stay with her the week I'm away, then return to dividing his time between our home and his "new office"—which she believes is the place he now goes to write. She's happy with the arrangement, because Mummy and Daddy aren't fighting any more. She doesn't know that Daddy's office also contains a girlfriend. She breathes calmly, flushed from another busy day, and I know we've done the right thing. We've protected her sense of stability. It will cushion her when it's time for her to face the most difficult news of her young life.

The phone rings.

I check my watch. It's past midnight. I pick up. The line clicks a few times. Then a disembodied voice comes through. The accent is precise and slow: part high-Raj colonial, part LA. "Madam Broinowski," it says. "You want to come to my country?" "Yes," I laugh nervously. "Yes, please. Where are you calling from?"

The voice ignores my question: "How long do you intend to stay?"

I start to feel uneasy. Is this an officer from one of the embassies I approached, or someone more malevolent? "Umm, only three days," I answer, keeping my tone light. "I believe there is a visa waiting for me, at your embassy in Beijing?" The voice says nothing. I can hear it breathing, through the clicks. I panic and blurt: "I love the films of your country. I really do. That's why I want to come. To understand your movies."

"Ha, ha," the voice says coldly. "I know." And hangs up. I immediately want to cancel everything and stay with my little girl. What if I don't come back? She needs me now, more than ever. I have become what the system identifies as "the primary carer"—and what my daughter knows as the parent-who-is-most-around. Then I remember Nick—brilliant, efficient Nick—who has been in and out of North Korea, unscathed, for the last twenty years. He will be beside us, every second of our stay. I kiss my daughter one last time and turn out the light.

BEIJING IS HOT AS A SAUNA, locked under a blanket of pollution. People in face masks hustle past, too cowed by the smog to notice the blue-sky tropical resorts on the billboards above. Nick works in an old part of town, a place still clinging to the city's pre-revolution grandeur. Tucked behind a fruit market and an ornate iron gate, Koryo Tours fills the ground floor of an elegant thirties apartment block. It faces a small alley crammed with bicycles. Lizzette and I dodge a glistening wad of phlegm, freshly hoicked by a man playing Go, and pass a woman dangling her baby over a gutter to poo. We arrive at a pair of carved mahogany doors, and there's the North Korean worker in the hard hat again—not a logo this time, but a real picture, on a real wall. We push the doors open and step inside.

Nick Bonner in 3D is even more energetic than he appears on Skype. Roguishly charming with electric blue eyes, he's working three calls at once, briefing a guide, and flicking through stills from *Comrade Kim Goes Flying*, a European–North Korean feature film he's just shot in Pyongyang. He gives us each a bear hug, then becomes distracted by a Danish backpacker and leaves us to peer around the lobby. It's a portal between reality and North Korea's parallel world. The walls are hung with propaganda posters: smiling women holding sheaves of golden corn, men waving flags, and North Korean soldiers doing ghastly things to pointy-nosed Americans. In one, a boot smashes a GI's skull. In another, a fist slams nuclear missiles to splinters. In a third, a compass skewers a screaming Yankee to the paper. They are beautifully done, in the same graphic style I saw at Sunmo's. But these slogans are painted by people who mean every word: *Let us celebrate our bumper cotton crop! Let us advance the textile industry with Juche speed! Let us kill a hundred enemies with a hundred blows! Let us make the Yankee wolves kneel and drown in a river of blood!*

Lizzette and I share a look. What are we getting ourselves into? Then Nick bursts in like a cyclone, demanding passports, photos, and euros. He crams the lot into a vinyl Air Koryo satchel, jumps on his bicycle, and zooms off. Apparently, we don't need to front up to the North Korean embassy in person: Nick and the customs officer are old mates. Before we've finished our tea, he's back again—with the precious media visa it has taken me two years, and a one thousand-kilometre detour through Tokyo and Seoul, to get.

Nick ushers us out to the chipped tables of Café Egypt and unleashes a torrent of Mandarin abuse at a beggar hustling Lizzette for money. Then he politely orders three coffees and gets down to business. The first thing we must understand about North Korea, he explains, is that the Leaders are gods: "Never just say 'Kim' when referring to them. Say 'Your Dear Leader Comrade Kim Jong Il' or 'Your Great General Kim Jong Il.' They know they're not your leaders, but as a visitor, you must show respect. The second thing is, be careful what you film. Portraits of the Kims can only be shot wide: if you zoom in to any part, even the face, you can be sent home." To help us understand how grave an offence this is, Nick reminds us how Muslims all over the world rioted when a Dutch cartoonist drew Mohammed: "The Kims are not politicians; they are a religion. Shoot only what the minders say, and don't push it: no filming soldiers, or people in the street, or out of the van." Nick looks at me, dead serious: "Ms. K will be watching. You need her trust." I nod, daunted. I've met the formidable Ms. K once, on Skype. She has a strong jaw, no-nonsense hair, and a tight smile. Ms. K has worked with Nick for twenty years; she's one of the few North Koreans trusted enough to travel. She Skyped me from Beijing, where she and Nick were setting up a tour of North Korean artists to Brisbane. Pyongyang had just tested a missile, and Australia refused to grant the North Korean visas. I was outraged at the censorship and keen for Ms. K's approval. So I told her that my father was once the Australian ambassador in Seoul, known in Canberra as "Red Dick" thanks to his left-wing proclivities—I'd ask him to help. Ms. K giggled at Nick as if I wasn't there: "She's saying she's important. She's showing off." Her voice was light, but I got the message. Ms. K has a bullshit meter a mile wide. I'm not going to push it.

Nick continues his survival tips. Once we are in Pyongyang, we will no longer be able to talk openly: in our hotel, the restaurants, or anywhere else. Whatever Ms. K has arranged is what we'll do—without complaint. This may include doing things that seem completely nonsensical. But North Korea has its own kind of logic: as first-time visitors, we could cause serious problems without even realising it. I ask Nick to use the code word "rabbits" if we do anything wrong. The whole thing's beginning to feel like *Mission Impossible*. Nick grins, gulps down his coffee, and jumps up. He's got a gorgeous Italian girlfriend to say goodbye to. He tells us to make sure we've got enough batteries, cash, and snacks to take in: there are no ATMs or shops. "Oh," he says, straddling his bike, "never call it North Korea. That's a big no-no. It's the Democratic People's Republic of Korea. And get some duty-free. But don't give it to them on the first day, or they feel compromised. Do it discreetly. Cheerio!"

Nick trundles off into the traffic, and Lizzette goes searching for euros and yuan: the only currency we can use, once inside. I wander through the mall to soak up my last taste of capitalism. The Apple logo and Nike swoosh glow back at me like old friends. At the top of a glassy skyscraper, Cate Blanchett cradles a jar of SK-II Essential Power Cream. I gaze at her ethereal face, struck by the absurdity of fate. I once acted in a play with Cate, before she shot to stardom. We earned $200 a week and swapped fart jokes in the pre-show warm-ups. Standing beside her luminous presence on that tiny Sydney stage, I knew she was destined for greatness—and my own less-salubrious future belonged firmly behind the lens. And now there she is, my earthy former colleague: a million-dollar brand at the top of the consumer juggernaut, endorsing moisturiser to support her kids. And here I am, about to step off the same juggernaut to support mine—by travelling back to 1953. That's the year the Democratic People's Republic of Korea sealed itself off, permanently, from materialism. The North Koreans have never heard of Essential Power Cream. I wonder what else they don't know.

Lined up in front of Air Koryo's check-in counter the next morning, I feel a shiver of excitement. Our trip back in time has already begun. Lizzette, Nick, and I are the only people in jeans. Everyone else wears mid-century suits and twinsets, with shiny buttons of Kim Jong Il on their lapels. They are fit, thin, and impeccably groomed. The men have pomaded crew cuts, the women neatly permed updos. It's like encountering rare wildlife, or alien beings. Holy shit, I tell myself. I am standing in a line with living, breathing North Koreans. They're not extras from a James Bond film. They're real. Then I look down. We do have one thing in common: we're all holding duty-free bags.

I CLIMB UP THE STAIRS OF an old Soviet Ilyushin and step inside a squeaky-clean cabin. A beautiful young woman greets me with a dazzling smile. It's not the fake smirk of a free-world trolley-dolly; it's genuinely friendly. She wears a red-and-white suit and a girl-guide scarf. She shows me to the seat that has been chosen for me—a window, above the wing. Lizzette and Nick are also seated alone, at opposite ends of the plane. On my way down the aisle, I notice a pudgy man in gold aviators and a khaki Mao suit, with a fake tan and fluffy perm. He's a dead ringer for the Dear Leader, and he's sitting at the pointy end. Is he one of Kim Jong Il's famous body doubles? And if so, how does he earn a living now? Or did Kim actually never leave the building? Was the funeral just his way of retiring, so he could lie on a beach somewhere in Bermuda? I try to get a closer look at the man, but the hostess nudges me forward with her sunny smile.

The Ilyushin bumps along the runway, and I feel the wheels leave terra firma. For the next three days, I will have no idea what is happening in the outside world. North Korea could nuke Seoul, and I won't know until I get back. The plane starts climbing the cloud line, and the hostess plumps down beside me and buckles her seatbelt. She asks what I'm writing.

"It's a letter for my daughter," I lie. She is giggly and persistent: "You are a journalist, right?" "No," I say, firmer now. "Just a tourist." I hunch over my notebook, trying to show her, in the politest possible way, that I am busy. But she leans against my arm, reading my words out loud. I look at her, astounded. She claps her hands in delight, as if we're playing a little game: "You *are* a journalist!" Now I'm spooked. I've heard that one in five North Koreans is a spy, more ruthless than the Stasi. This hostess is keeping tabs on me. She knows about my film.

As soon as we land, they're going to take my notebook and throw me in a gulag. I tear out the page, fold it in a tiny square, and, as surreptitiously as I can, tuck it into my sock.

I gaze pointedly out the window. I can feel the hostess's hundred-watt smile, warming the back of my head. Then, as if nothing weird has just happened, she stands, wishes me a lovely time in Pyongyang, and walks off.

As we hurtle towards North Korean airspace, the cabin—which appears to be held together by fresh paint and Blu-Tack—rattles. Loudly. It still carries 1960s-era emergency equipment and a safety brochure that does not inspire confidence. A safety video shows my hostess friend doing the usual things with an oxygen mask, but her orange vest looks disturbingly retro, and there don't seem to be any inflatable slides. The video segues to a crane, the symbol of Air Koryo, soaring through a glorious sunset. A voice kicks in over a military choir. It's the same bizarre accent I heard on the phone back in Sydney, all soft American Rs and crisp colonial Ts. The North Koreans must all learn English from the same two people, I decide: a Mumbai call-centre worker and one of Kim Jong Il's captured American movie villains.

"Welcome to the Socialist Paradise of the Democratic People's Republic of Korea!" the voice-over intones, as the camera pans over a shaky shot of Pyongyang. "What kind of place is Pyongyang, and what kind of country is Korea? Many countries have environmental damage by growth of industry. But what is most attractive about Pyongyang is its fresh air. People who visit it call it 'The City in a Park!'" A shot of Western tourists in seventies leisure gear appears. They stroll by a tree-lined river full of happy people paddling yellow, duck-shaped boats.

The shot dissolves to a black-and-white still of Pyongyang, circa 1953, smashed to smithereens. During the war, the city endured one of the most concentrated bombing campaigns in US military history. General MacArthur had planned to end the war in ten days, by dropping twenty-six atom bombs on North Korea and thirty to fifty more, "strung across the neck of Manchuria." But his proposal was turned down—so he opted for conventional ballistics. In 1950, the US dumped 700 bombs, 175 tonnes of delayed-fuse demolition bombs and 10,000 litres of napalm on Pyongyang—reducing its population from half a million to 50,000 within a year. In 1952, 6,000 people were killed in a single air strike, having been given fifteen minutes' warning—just enough time for anyone trying to flee to be caught in the open. By the end of the war, an average of three bombs had fallen for every man, woman, and child in Pyongyang. The city was flatter than Hiroshima.

On the screen, skeletal people pulling dead babies from the rubble appear, and the voice-over grows stern: "The US imperialists had not planned that the city would rise again, in a hundred years. But Pyongyang has created a civilised urban culture, like today. It is really surprising!" Then the image snaps back to happy Technicolor, and laughing children run towards us in slow-mo on a bright green hill. Thanks to a technical glitch, the sound plays back warped and slow, along with the picture. The kids sound like they're screaming.

There is no other audiovisual entertainment on board. But there is a newspaper. The *Pyongyang Times* is available in English and Korean, across a range of dates. Written in florid, sweeping phrases, the newspaper celebrates North Korea's supremacy in everything and makes Rupert Murdoch's publications look like fair and balanced news.

The three Kims—Senior, Junior, and Junior 2.0—beam from every page under inspiring headlines. Their names are always set in a slightly larger font. The articles are all about winning: from the Third World flower festival, where "Kimjongilia" has just won first prize, to the bumper cotton crop of Wonsan, which will be used to make world-class jackets designed by **Comrade Kim Jong Il** for grateful workers everywhere. The domestic news section features a story, "Inscriptions on Rocks Mirror Koreans' Faith and Will," about some Junsan farmers who carved the words **Peerless Patriot General Kim Jong Il** into the cliffs of Mount Sokta to commemorate his birthday. The foreign news section states that **Beloved Comrade Kim Jong Un** has just stopped the heinous military provocations of the US aggressors and their South Korean lackeys by "successfully" detonating a rocket in the Sea of Japan. Meanwhile, in Pyongyang, international tributes to **Generalissimo Kim Jong Il**, the deeply mourned son of **Supreme General Kim Il Sung**, "are continuing with vigour" eight months after his death.

"Baskets of Messages, Gifts, Tributes Flow!" declaims a headline, above rows of red flowers lined up at the Palace of the Sun, where Kim Junior now lies in a glass box next to Kim Senior. "Pyongyang People and Service Personnel Part with Leader in Bitter Grief" reminds another, set over a picture of Kim Junior 2.0 handing out hot buns to the freezing masses as his father's hearse trundles past. I have to hand it to Kim Jong Il: if he did design his own funeral, then the hot buns were a masterstroke. No one knew who Kim Jong Un was until a year ago. Kim Jong Il needed an effective way to position his youngest son as a benevolent saviour, like the heroic Kim Il Sung.

Unlike his father, Junior 2.0 had no competition for the top job: Kim Jong Il thought his other sons were idiots. Junior 2.0's oldest brother, Kim Jong Nam, whose existence Kim Jong Il had hidden in the 1970s by sending his mother's relatives to the gulags, cosseting him in private villas with miniature movie sets and child-sized sports cars, had grown up to become an over-indulged playboy. In 2001, Kim Jong Nam was caught attempting to get into Tokyo Disneyland on a fake passport and Kim Jong Il promptly dumped him as successor. Junior 2.0's second oldest brother, Kim Jong Chul, was last seen at an Eric Clapton concert in Singapore and was always considered by Kim Jong Il to be "too feminine" for leadership. Which left the 28-year-old Kim Jong Un—international man of mystery, and now the world's youngest head of state.

According to Kenji Fujimoto, the defected sushi chef I failed to track down in Tokyo, Kim Jong Un likes shark's fin soup three times a week, just like his dad. He also "knows how to be angry and how to praise. He has the ability to lead people . . . he loves basketball, roller-blading, snowboarding, and skiing . . . I watched him play golf once and he reminded me of a top Japanese professional." I look at the chubby, Swiss-educated Kim Jong Un being mobbed by female athletes on the sports page of the *Pyongyang Times*. He seems cheeky and upbeat—more Prince Harry than Prince William. The sort of prankster who'd have a healthy Twitter profile and an active network of drinking buddies; a guy who'd go to a costume party dressed as Hitler for kicks. Then again, it's July 2012. Kim Jong Un hasn't executed anyone—yet.

I unbuckle my seatbelt and sneak a look at the passengers. They are a perfect hybrid of the *Mad Men* cast and a 1950s Soviet documentary. The women wear lacy twinsets and pink lipstick. The men sport starched white shirts, tortoiseshell glasses, and dark, boxy jackets. Many are reading the *Pyongyang Times*. The story about the Junsan farmers is open on laps, with a picture of a ten-metre sign on a cliff over the breathless assertion that "the People carved letters on the rocks in reflection of their boundless respect for the revolutionary exploits of **Dear Leader Comrade General Kim Jong Il** who devoted his life to the sacred cause of the prosperity and the wellbeing of the People, generation after generation."

I think even Rupert Murdoch would baulk at the excesses of the *Pyongyang Times*.

Just when things can't get much stranger, the hostess serves me a hamburger. It sits in a yellow-and-white wrapper on a small plastic tray. It is icy cold. And heavy. Closer inspection under the bright yellow bun reveals a patty made from three types of unrecognizable meat, and what appears to be a pickle. This must be Kim Jong Il's famous "meat with two breads sandwich." I haul the thing up to my mouth and take a bite. It tastes like no burger I've ever eaten—intensely salty and sweet, and strangely delicious. Apparently, not all foreigners think so: under the tray is a white paper bag, stamped with the Air Koryo crane and a helpful suggestion: *For Your Refuses*.

As we descend over the misty hills encircling Pyongyang, I see something I'll never forget. Below us, in a rice paddy next to the airstrip, is a group of waving farmers. They are all women, and look like they've stepped straight from one of the North Korean music videos on YouTube: rosy-cheeked and stout, with floral head scarves and thick cotton skirts bunched around their waists. We draw closer, and I can see they are carrying straw baskets, from which they hurl fresh-cut flowers at our plane. They are singing and dancing, waving frantically at us as they run. They seem to be filled with joyous ecstasy, simply because we've arrived. It's completely surreal.

Pyongyang airport is a large metal shed with a baggage carousel down one side and two souvenir counters on the other. Kims Senior and Junior look down from the wall. Junior 2.0 is notably absent. There are no other pictures, and only two queues—one for foreigners to hand in their mobiles, and one in which soldiers herd passengers towards a stern guard in a customs booth. The whole place seems to have been passed through a monochromatic filter—everything, from the uniforms of the guards to the suitcases on the baggage rack, is a shade of grey. Perhaps it's the low-wattage bulbs. Or the lack of neon. Popping through the gloom like golden ingots are our bright yellow duty-free bags. They look like alien life forms in this faded world: new and loud and made of plastic—stubborn stowaways from Planet Capitalism.

I catch up with Nick and Lizzette, still a little spooked by my encounter with the Air Koryo hostess. The form she gave me demands that I declare "all weapons, ammunition, explosives and killing devices; all drugs, exciters, narcotics and poison . . . publishing of all kinds, including type, unit and quantity." I have no idea how to explain the note hidden in my sock, let alone the *Vanity Fair* I bought in Beijing. Kristen Stewart from *Twilight* is slouching in a strapless gown on the cover, and a poll inside says 66 percent of readers answered the question "Would you go to North Korea if it was free?" with "You've got to be joking." I tug Nick's sleeve, whispering behind my hand: "Is *Vanity Fair* 'offensive literature?' Should I declare it?" Nick chuckles, takes my travel documents, and calls out to the customs guard: "Oi! Tongji!" Astonishingly, the guard breaks into a wide grin. Nick is clearly famous around here. Relieved, I leave him to negotiate, and study the souvenirs. There are stamps of the Leaders, hand-carved toothpicks and two slim, pale-blue phrasebooks.

If I didn't already know I was in North Korea, I do now. *Welcome. Speak in Korean!* lists the five words foreigners are most likely to use in Pyongyang: "Comrade! Waiter! Driver! Interpreter! Guide!" The other one's a dictionary—of sorts. Under the word "Respect," the English–Korean Workbook offers the phrase "We respectfully wish President Kim Il Sung, the respected Leader, a long life." "War" brings up "The Fatherland Liberation War." "Square" mentions "Kim Il Sung Square." And the words "Propaganda," "Murder," "Oppression," "Dictatorship," and "Poverty" are not in the book at all. At least, not directly—when you look up "March," "The Arduous March" appears.

Nick jokes his way through the queue, and we're soon out under the pale sun in a small car park. Ms. K hurries through the crowd and kisses Nick on the cheek. She's shorter than I imagined, and wearing a bright pink shirt. The square jaw and mannish features are still there, along with the no-nonsense hair—part bob, part eighties mullet. But she's soft-voiced and sweet, almost cuddly. Nick kisses her back, and she blushes. I am so grateful for what she's done to get us here, I want to give her a hug. Instead, I smile brightly and hold out my hand: "Thank you for having us, *tongji*." Ms. K flinches. *Tongji* is how you address comrades older than yourself. I've pegged Ms. K at fifty. Clearly, I am wrong. She narrows her eyes: "You can already speak Korean." It doesn't sound like a compliment.

Nick chuckles and promises Ms. K he'll get the crazy Aussie to get her eyesight tested. Lizzette makes a gracious remark about the balmy weather and soon Ms. K is smiling again, climbing into the front seat of an unmarked van beside Nick. They giggle together like teenagers as Lizzette and I pile into the back. The driver flicks his cigarette away without acknowledging us and slides the door shut. We pull out, then stop at a gate beside the highway. A soldier, no more than twenty, peers in at me. He wears the same jacket I saw in Choi's movie in Seoul and a huge hat decorated with a cheap-looking red plastic star. The thin fabric and fake brass buttons make his uniform look like it's been sourced from a discount costume store: "North Korean Bad Guy" dress-ups. Then I see the Kalashnikov on his back and the bayonet in his belt. His eyes dart from my North Korean dictionary to my face, more curious than suspicious. He nods, steps back, and waves us on.

The road to Pyongyang is spacious, quiet and clean. People in different shades of khaki and grey ride bicycles, wait at bus stops, walk with their children, and read books in the sun. Others squat on pavements, clipping grass from the kerb or weeding small vegetable plots beside the road. I peer eagerly between the buildings, scouring the landscape for signs of starvation. No one is fat. But no one is dropping dead in the street either, or shuffling around in chain gangs, or staring at the ground in brainwashed stupors.

They look purposeful, fit, preoccupied, thoughtful, and, strangest of all, content. Take away the colour-coordinated outfits, and they could be normal people in any city in the world, just getting on with their day.

We turn into a wide boulevard fluttering with red-and-blue North Korean flags. An ancient trolley bus trundles along, its joints freshly covered in crimson paint. Schoolboys in sailor suits stroll on the sidewalk arm in arm, laughing. A woman in overalls bicycles past, balancing a brass trophy on her handlebars. Two little girls with pink backpacks sit on the grass, licking vanilla ice cream cones. An old woman with a wicker basket on her head waits at the bus stop, cooling her neck with a silk fan. An antique tractor chugs beside a canal, followed by a man in a safari suit pedaling a rickshaw. Fishermen squat on a stone pier, smoking. Ahead of us, vintage white and grey sedans coast along the wide, pale avenues. Flanking them, at a gracious distance, are green and pink apartment blocks, old but spotless—with window boxes full of flowers.

I feel disorientated and confused. It's not just because I'm somewhere I've never been before. It's because something is missing. Something crucial, that I rely on to gauge where I am, to locate myself within space. Something ever-present.

Then I realise what it is: advertisements. Those visual flashes that sell you things—on your mobile screen, on news stands, on the backs of taxis—blinking from gas stations, winking from the hopping bags of people walking by. The logos you see when you sit next to someone on a park bench or stop beside them at a traffic light, registering, without even realising, the brands they're wearing—those images have vanished. Capitalism has been turned off. The visual noise is gone.

The overwhelming effect is of total calm. Instead of fast-food ads on the bus stops, there are landscapes. Instead of billboards in the streets, there is hand-painted propaganda art. Instead of flashing logos in the public squares, there are monuments. No looming screens with naked women selling perfume, no paparazzi snaps of stars with cellulite in the stands. No McDonald's, no Sony, no Nike, no Apple, no Coke. Instead of neons marking the buildings as the property of IBM or BHP, there are big red banners with bold white slogans, under smiling portraits of Kim Jong Il. And yes, the air is deliciously clean.

Pyongyang is unexpectedly beautiful. It's an open-air museum, a giant socialist theme park. To me, it's Disneyland.

I glance at Lizzette, wondering if she shares my wonder. But she's poker-faced behind her Ray-Bans. I remind myself that the journalists who've been here before us have dismissed Pyongyang's beauty, focusing on the deprivation and fear tucked behind its facades. The window boxes filled with flowers are fake; the backs of the buildings are burnt-out shells. The pyramid-shaped hotel in the distance is just for show—an unfinished symbol of Kim Jong Il's hubris, with nothing inside. The two million people living here are the lucky ones, weeded out from the sick and the crippled and the ideologically deformed, allowed to exist in this huge Potemkin village for the benefit of prying foreign eyes—while the rest of the country lives in abject horror.

I try to match this picture with the one outside my window. Is it really all a front? On the other side of this glittering boulevard, is there a barbed-wire wasteland full of mud huts and misery? What would happen if, like Jim Carrey in *The Truman Show*, I made the driver do a U-turn? Would the laughing schoolboys and contented women at the bus stops suddenly not be there? Would the streets be empty, with extras lined up behind barriers, waiting for the order to walk happily around the block all over again, the next time a van of foreigners drives past?

Somehow, I don't think Lizzette and I are that important. Our agenda is not the same as that of the journalists who've come here for a new twist on the North Korean horror story. I decide to keep an open mind.

The van cruises onto an overpass. Under the concrete pillars, I catch a glimpse of a thousand small children, squatting in perfect lines in the baking dirt. They flip heavy cardboard squares above their tiny heads, as a guard barks orders on a megaphone. The cards flip from yellow to red . . . then the image is gone.

"God—they're only in kindergarten!" I say, before I can stop myself. Ms. K turns to us, surprised.

"We saw children under the highway," explains Lizzette. "It is very hot," I add. "In Australia at midday, children go inside."

"Yes!" Ms. K beams proudly. "They are practising for the Arirang Mass Games. It is a great honour. They love it."

The children squatting in the dirt did not look as if they loved it. They looked hot, and for six-year-olds, unnaturally still. Seeing and believing are clearly two different things in Pyongyang. I rephrase my decision: I will keep my mind as open as it *can* be in North Korea.

KUBRICK WHO?

THEY DO THINGS AT CHOLLIMA SPEED around here. Chollima is a mythical winged horse that inspired Kim Il Sung's postwar slogan *Let us rush with the speed of Chollima!* The slogan got Pyongyang rebuilt in record time. Chollima is also the mascot of North Korea's soccer team, which has been mysteriously absent from the *Pyongyang Times* ever since it lost 3–0 to Côte D'Ivoire at the 2010 World Cup.

Ms. K gives us exactly three Chollima minutes to pay our deposit at the Yangakkdo Hotel, dump our bags with the concierge, and regroup in the lobby, an expanse of green marble as big as an ice rink. The usual markers of global travel are there—a jewellery and souvenir shop, a gallery, a cafe, a business centre—but none of it appears to have changed since 1992. The gold watches are Seikos, the souvenirs are dusty, the business centre has an old computer under a red velvet drape, and the gallery is filled with pictures of Kim Jong Il back when his *Eraserhead* hair was fashionable, looking at flowerbeds and mountains, surrounded by his minions.

I wait next to a narrow, wall-sized aquarium, staring into the eyes of a huge turtle. He bumps his shell against the glass, trying to get a better view. On the other side of the glass, waitresses in miniskirts dust red banquettes in the cafe. The turtle studies me closely. According to Ms. K, he has been here for twenty years, as long as the Yangakkdo.

He gives me a resigned blink, full of the jaded ennui of someone who's seen two dictators come and go, and floats to the bottom of his tank. I decide to call him Simon Sheen—the name Shin Sang Ok chose for himself when he escaped Kim Jong Il's gilded cage and fled to LA.

"Anna, let us go to the Pyongyang Film Studio!" Ms. K calls from the revolving doors. A leggy girl in white denim slouches next to her. Eun is our interpreter. Her name means "grace," and she resembles it physically—languid and slender, with flawless white skin. But her manner is affected—a studied kind of worldliness. Eun's father is a diplomat, and she went to high school in Cairo. I compliment her on her leopard-print heels—did she buy them here? "No," Eun sighs. "My dad got them in Shanghai." Does she like fashion? I ask, wondering how much she knows. "Yes, I like it a lot." So what does Eun think of Pippa Middleton's bridesmaid's dress—the one which briefly made her bottom the star of the tabloids? Eun looks confused: "What wedding? The one of Lady Di?" Eun left Cairo in 1998: that's when her knowledge of the outside world stopped. She has no idea William and Kate just tied the knot, let alone Camilla and Charles. She has never heard of Net-a-Porter, The Sartorialist, Lady Gaga or the fact that fake fur is back in vogue. I make a mental note to sneak in a wedding pic of Wills and Kate for Eun, if Ms. K invites us back.

"On your left is Kim Il Sung Square," Ms. K says loudly, as if she can sense what I'm plotting. We're driving past a Sahara of concrete, flanked by huge buildings. I recognise it from the news—this is the famous square from which Kim Jong Il broadcast his parading soldiers every time the US or South Korea did something to annoy him. Today, it's empty. A few women stroll in the distance, under pretty pastel parasols. A massive cutout of a man holding a bugle sits silently against the sky above a slogan: *Let us carry out this year's military tasks!* To his right and left are two huge halls, all gilt and marble, with more slogans: *Let us uphold our great Party by changing our sadness to courage! Let us make 2012 full of proud victories of our strong and prosperous nation as per our Comrade Kim Jong Il's departing teaching!* From the Grand People's Study House, an Asian palace as big as the Vatican, Kim Jong Il's visage smiles down at the deserted square, full of papal love.

Kim disappears from view and a grassy hill appears, crowned by a rearing bronze Chollima. The horse stands forty-six metres high and is exquisitely cast. This is not the cheap patriotism my country trundles out each Australia Day—all corkboard murals, nylon banners, and flags made in China; North Korean symbology has been built to last. Its artists may have limited subject matter, but their execution is brilliant. We enter a roundabout and glide around an ostentatious white granite riff on the Arc de Triomphe. This one, Ms. K tells us with pride, is ten metres higher than the one in Paris. Lizzette nods, impressed, but I'm starting to feel nervous. The Pyongyang Film Studio is the most powerful propaganda factory in North Korea—and, if you don't count Hollywood, the world. I doubt they tolerate slothful Western idiots who haven't done any homework. I pull out the copy of *Great Man and Cinema* Johannes gave me in Beppu, trying to get myself into a suitably reverent frame of mind . . .

23 frames

This is what happened when Comrade Kim Jong Il examined one film.

The creators appreciated the film's scenes and music, deeply enthralled by them. But Comrade Kim Jong Il said quietly, "Stop projecting." The creators wondered why, looking at each other.

Comrade Kim Jong Il asked the director if any shots were cut off in the editing. The director was at a loss, because he had examined every scene, shot by shot. Comrade Kim Jong Il asked the composer. "Have you sensed anything different?" The composer answered that he had not. "That's not true. I am sure several shots were cut off. Find them," said Comrade Kim Jong Il, and left.

The creators ransacked all night the piles of film that had been cut. At daybreak the director ejaculated abruptly, "I've found it!" He was holding a 23-frame strip of film.

The creators doubted it was the right one, because it was only one second. But they had no choice but to put the 23 frames back in the film.

Comrade Kim Jong Il visited again. When the projection was over, he lightly slapped his knee and said in joy, "All right! You found it! Thank you. The scene now exactly harmonizes with the music."

This was really beyond imagination, for any man without a keen sense of detecting the minute flow, that flashes away like lightning.

GREAT MAN AND CINEMA

When I look up fifteen minutes later, Pyongyang's statues and boulevards are gone. We're bumping along a narrow road dissecting a cornfield, bordering what looks like a nineteenth-century village. Farmers idly herd cows out of our path. Women in straw hats pull reeds from the mud. A man ploughs the field with an oxdrawn cart. It is unbelievably clean and completely pre-digital: no ads, no plastic bags, no technology. We swerve around a pack of bicyclists, scattering chickens in our wake. Pyongyang has more environmental cred than Amsterdam, if you ignore the fact that its lack of cars and commitment to urban farming are due more to the limited means of its citizens than to any climate-driven ideology.

The road degenerates into a patchwork of concrete and dirt, and a loud beep causes our driver, and everyone else on the road, to swerve in alarm. A brand-new armour-plated Range Rover glides past, the van shuddering in its slipstream. Ms. K points at some cinematography students filming further down the road, as if the SUV isn't there. I ignore her and peer into the tinted windows, trying to catch a glimpse of Kim Jong Un. Is he in there with his new pop-singer girlfriend right now, drinking tequila and playing Angry Birds on his iPad? Or does he travel only after the 7 p.m. curfew, in army-protected cavalcades?

I whisper to Eun: "Your Great Leader Comrade Kim Jong Un, where does he live?" She shrugs. I try again: "What about your Dear Leader Kim Jong Il, where was his palace?" Eun glares at me, as if it's obvious: "I don't know." I'm astonished. Kim Jong Il's palaces were legendary among the leaders of the developing world. They enjoyed lavish banquets and drunken dances with the girls of Kim's Joy Division, sometimes in the nude. How can the North Koreans not know where their Leaders live? Before I can push Eun further, Ms. K says something in Korean, and Eun looks pointedly in the opposite direction. The Range Rover disappears in a cloud of dust. Maybe it was only one of the generals from North Korea's military parades. Hell, maybe I never saw it at all.

The cows and bicyclists return to their pre-industrial crawl, and we round a wide bend. Rising up to meet us, above the chickens and tethered goats, is the magnificent gate of the Pyongyang Film Studio. Kim Il Sung beams down from the arch, like Rapunzel at the top of her tower. A girl with a Kalashnikov slung sexily on her hip presses a red button on the wall. I've dreamt of this moment for a long time. The gate slides open. We're inside.

The compound is huge, full of square buildings and wide roads—like the MGM back lot, but bigger. In the central courtyard, a massive bronze statue of Kim Jong Il holds a camera, flanked by adoring children. Facing him are the two buildings that Shane Smith penetrated in *North Korean Film Madness*: the cinema museums of Kim Il Sung and Kim Jong Il. On the wall of Kim Jong Il's museum is a mosaic as big as a football field, celebrating the contribution of North Korea's filmmakers to the nation's flowering soul. Even Sunmo's work did not prepare me for this: it is the most beautiful propaganda art I have seen.

From a distance, the mosaic is an explosion of colour, with film crews pointing cameras at the horizon like bayonets. Behind the crews, men and women in shirtsleeves wave revolutionary banners, surrounded by clapping workers. Rising above them are charging soldiers, yelling at an invisible enemy. And bursting through a halo of clouds at the top, like a North Korean Jesus, is Kotpun the flower girl—cradling her basket of glorious red blooms. It would be kitsch if it weren't so exquisitely done. The grandeur is breathtaking. I walk closer to examine the tiny hand-painted tiles and realise why I feel so uplifted. It's the first mural I've seen without a Kim in it. I sit in the grass, dazzled.

Ms. K cuts my reverie short, calling from a stone building next door. She looks irritated behind her tight smile: lounging on lawns and asking for the Kims' addresses are not part of her itinerary. I promise myself I'll shoot the mosaic next time and follow her up the steps. The entrance is hung with movie posters of bosomy heroines and granite-jawed men: a Pyongyang take on Bollywood. Above them is a slogan, which Eun translates in a bored monotone, ignoring the enthusiastic punctuation: *Let us create masterpieces in our own way, portrayals by no means inferior in any aspect!!!*

We enter to find a large mural of Kim Jong Il rocking his Mao suit, with babes in flowing gowns hanging off him like groupies at a Liberace concert. Then we climb a marble staircase and step inside a spacious room. A stunning collection of mid-century furniture is spread over the parquetry floor. It looks like Eames, low-slung and elegant—but this stuff really was made in 1953: the last furniture, perhaps, to make it over the border. Two unusually solemn Kims look down from one wall, facing a beautiful trompe l'oeil of swans in a misty green pond. I register all this in a few seconds, then forget it, as I see, sitting in the middle of the room, Kotpun's brother from *Flower Girl*. After four decades, he still looks like Harrison Ford—but the *Patriot Games* version, rather than Han Solo. His name is Yurim. He is the most famous actor in North Korea.

Yurim unfolds his long legs and stands. He is painfully shy. He smiles and ushers us to our seats. We bow and shake hands with the leading lights of the North Korean film industry, all over fifty. Mr. Pak is short and suave, with magnificent white hair. He is the North Korean Scorsese—known for searing political thrillers. Mr. Ri is scruffy and blunt, built like a wrestler. He directs military-action pictures: the North Korean Oliver Stone. Next is a composer with a high forehead and bright eyes, Mr. Pei. For his music on the drama *My Happiness*, Kim Jong Il made Pei a People's Artist—the North Korean equivalent of winning an Oscar. Last to greet us is Ms. Yun, an ageless, soft-skinned beauty. Despite the heat, she's wearing a lacy suit and thick white stockings. Ms. Yun is also a People's Artist: the North Korean Meryl Streep. She blushes, as shy as Yurim.

Lizzette spreads some Guylian pralines on a low table, which the filmmakers politely refuse. There is a dignity, and a sharp intelligence, behind their pleasantries. They watch closely as I pull Kim Jong Il's *The Cinema and Directing* from my handbag. I can sense their quiet approval that the book is well thumbed. Nervous, and speaking slowly so Eun can translate, I begin: "Thank you for having us. I am here because I have a problem in my country. Many companies are coming from overseas. They are drilling for gas and destroying our land."

The filmmakers nod but say nothing. I continue: "I want to make a documentary, in which you instruct my actors and me how to follow your General Kim Jong Il's filmmaking rules. Our goal is to produce, at the end of the documentary, a ten-minute drama, in which a humble Sydney gardener inspires her village to stop the evil miners destroying her park." I smile at them hopefully: "I don't know enough about your films to write the script. I need your help!"

Silence. The filmmakers look at me, poker-faced. No one moves. At the back of the room, a man in a black Mao suit has entered. He sits next to Ms. K, takes a gold pen from his pocket, and gazes blankly at the wall. Clearly, I'm not going to get a response from him either. The silence stretches on. I keep smiling, until my jaw hurts. Finally, Mr. Pak takes a long drag on his cigarette and exhales. He says something quietly to Eun, and everyone giggles. She turns to me: "Senior Comrade Pak says you used to be an actor. But you were stiff as a stick. So now you direct."

I look at Ms. K. She's chuckling behind her hand. Clearly, the self-deprecating remarks I made to her on Skype in Beijing got through North Korea's firewall. I grin bravely at Mr. Pak: "I am not a good director either, when it comes to making a film in your style. Your General Kim Jong Il says one must 'aim high in creation' when choosing the seed. But I am not sure what my seed is . . ."

Mr. Pak cuts me off, speaking directly to Eun. "Tell her this: with plants, you need good-quality seeds to bear good-quality fruit." Eun obliges, and he warms to his theme: "With animals too, good breeding produces superior beasts. In filmmaking, the seed is what the creators want to say. It's the nucleus of the film. She doesn't know what her seed is, because she's trying to do too much. Her documentary is already complex—but on top of that, she wants to fit her gardener drama into ten minutes. It's too ambitious."

Mr. Pei nods gloomily. Mr. Ri slumps in his chair, overwhelmed by the impossibility of my task: "Yep, it's way too ambitious." I look at Lizzette, stymied. This is worse than pitching to the ABC. The North Koreans are the epitome of artistic ambition: they produced thousand-actor extravaganzas like *Sea of Blood* at Chollima speed. How can they be daunted by my little film? Then I remember that *Sea of Blood* is three hours long. Lizzette comes to the rescue, smiling graciously at Mr. Pak: "In our country, it is very expensive to make a drama. We must hire a proper crew and pay the actors high wages. We cannot fund anything longer than ten minutes."

The filmmakers stare at her, mystified. There is no such thing as a producer in North Korea. What does Lizzette do? "I go to investors, asking for money," she explains. "Then I visit set every day, to make sure the director is getting everything shot on time. After that, I work with distributors to get the film shown." Mr. Pak nods: "Ah. You're like him." He points at the Man in Black, a little dismissively: "He follows our progress, on behalf of our beloved Party. We're funded by the state, so we are free to create. We don't have to worry about money, or do what investors tell us. That sort of thing must never, can never, and will never happen in our country." He leans back, satisfied—and lights another fag.

Lizzette and the Man in Black exchange a wary look across the chasm between them: the Western producer with whom the buck stops, and the North Korean Party official, an ideological rubber stamp for films green-lit by Kim Jong Il. I wonder who approves Mr. Pak's budgets now, with the sports-focused Kim Jong Un in charge. Someone must: Mr. Pak has just come from the seaside city of Wonsan, where he's making a film about a coal miner. Our request to visit his set has already been met with a flat no from Ms. K: the mine is "too dangerous" for us to enter. I suspect the real reason is that Mr. Pak's cast of miners is real, and Ms. K doesn't want us seeing the conditions in which they work.

I turn to Mr. Pei, hoping he'll be more collaborative. Composers have to be, unlike directors; it's part of their job. "I know you've written many number-one songs," I say. "We hope you will do us the honour of writing a song for our drama." He nods enthusiastically: "I'd love to. You must hear my work, before you go." But Mr. Pak ashes his fag, shooting Mr. Pei a dark look: "We will decide if we can help her, if and when she sends us a script."

Everyone nods and clams up again. At the back of the room, the Man in Black scrawls something with his gold pen. I realise why Mr. Pak is being so cagey: Lizzette and I are not the only ones being monitored. He flips up his cuff and looks pointedly at a seventies Rolex. I hold his gaze. It's a Confucian power play; as the respected elder, Mr. Pak has final say. I have a nightmarish flash of myself back in Sydney, trying to write a Kim Jong Il–style script that will earn this patriarch's approval. Even if I email it to Nick to give to Ms. K, there's no guarantee it will get to Mr. Pak. And if it does, and he likes it, the Man in Black might not. I need to win Mr. Pak over now, in front of his colleagues, or our project is kaput.

Mr. Pak pops a praline into his mouth, thoroughly bored. I look at Eun, desperate, but she avoids my eyes. We all sit there, listening to Mr.

Pak chew. Then, from the back of the room, Ms. K speaks up: "Anna, did you know our Dear Leader General Kim Jong Il once called Senior Comrade Pak 'the white-haired director'? After that, he never dyed his hair again." Bingo! Mr. Pak is the director who searched all night for the missing twenty-three frames! I feel as if George Clooney just walked into my cafe—here, in front of me, is Kim Jong Il's favourite filmmaker. Ms. K has thrown me a lifeline: I haven't been treating Mr. Pak with the respect he deserves. I shoot her a grateful look, and turn to him with new reverence: "I understand, Senior Comrade Pak, that you worked closely with your Dear Leader Kim Jong Il, on over seventy films . . ."

Mr. Pak immediately relaxes and beams, a different man: "Our Dear Leader was someone who, once he placed faith in you, trusted you till the end. The fact he remembered me, even in his dreams, is the greatest honour anyone can receive." He picks up my copy of Kim's manifesto, taking care not to cover the Leader's name with his hand: "This book is a weapon for filmmakers in our country. Every time I make a new film, I go over the Dear Leader's words again, to see if I've strayed from the right path. When I was arrogant, he taught me to see the error of my ways. It is all thanks to him that our film industry made great strides, and our nation is strong." The filmmakers nod happily, and Mr. Pak glows with pride: "We might be a small country, but no one can look down on us because we have nuclear weapons. We've even launched satellites into space. All of this is thanks to the Dear Leader, who, with his iron-like will and great passion, gave his whole life and body to achieve it. That's why we still mourn him, and the agony of his loss remains un-erased in us to this day."

Mr. Pak strokes the book, misty-eyed. It's bizarre to see someone remembering Kim Jong Il with such love, after the drubbing he got in Seoul. Then again, Kim treasured his filmmakers, giving them watches, cars, and high-rise apartments so they could create. When they were between projects, he sent them to the USSR and East Germany to improve their skills. I suppose a benefactor like that would be missed. I address Mr. Pak in a suitably awestruck tone: "Is

it true your General Kim Jong Il had an extensive knowledge of foreign films, including American ones?" He nods solemnly: "He was a
genius, unrivalled by anyone. We watched many together: *The Patriot,
Sound of Music, Jaws, Schindler's List, Star Wars, Gladiator, Avatar*, a film
called *God* something . . . what was that one again?"

Mr. Ri helps him out: *The Godfather*. Mr. Pak nods: "Yeah. That
was quite good, wasn't it?" The Man in Black is writing furiously now.
It's not a good idea to speak positively about capitalist movies: North
Koreans living near the DMZ have been shot for hot-wiring their TVs
to pick up South Korean soaps. I know Mr. Pak is going out on a limb
for me, but I'm too curious to stop: "What other directors do you like?
Kubrick? Fincher? Tarantino? Hitchcock? Ephron? Woody Allen?"
Each name draws a blank, except for Hitchcock, who Mr. Pak concedes
made the greatest horror films in the world. I guess it's no surprise that
he hasn't heard of Stanley Kubrick, given the director's obsession with
imprisonment, torture, and rebellion. *A Clockwork Orange* might just
show the North Koreans how to escape it, once and for all.

James Cameron, on the other hand, is top of Mr. Pak's list. No
surprise there, either: *Titanic* is the biggest socialist-propaganda pic
Hollywood has ever produced—the cloth-capped Leonardo DiCaprio
even looks like Lenin as he saves the *Titanic's* working-class passengers
from the aristocrats in first. And *Avatar* is the most anti-capitalist, with
its corporate stooge, Parker Selfridge, cynically bombing the beautiful
Pandora to mine it for unobtanium. I decide that James Cameron is
safe ground: "Is it true you made your own version of *Titanic*, with
exactly same plot?" Mr. Pak bristles: "*Souls Protest* was made *before
Titanic*," he says. "It's about how Koreans were killed by the Japanese
bastards at the end of colonial rule. It's not technically as good as
Titanic, of course—which was made only to make money. I made *Souls
Protest* to bring the Japanese crimes to light." He looks at me coolly:
"Maybe James Cameron copied us?"

Lizzette and I share a look. *Titanic* came out in 1997, and according
to Johannes Schönherr, Kim Jong Il's alleged line-for-line-rip-off, *Souls*

Protest, was made in 2001. Mr. Pak mutters crossly at the others in Korean—and I change the subject: "James Cameron cares about green issues. So do I, which is why I am making my film. Do people in your country also care about the environment?" Mr. Pak is too annoyed to answer, but Ms. Yun leans forward, her voice a reverent whisper: "Our Beneficent Leader Kim Jong Il cared deeply about it. Once a year, he planted trees with his bare hands in the hills. He also closed down many coal mines that were too near the farms. He even stopped Mount Myohyang being mined for gold, so that its beautiful nature could be preserved."

The filmmakers smile, relieved to be back on hallowed turf. I make a show of looking admiringly at Kim Jong Il on the wall, struck by this new proof of his brilliance. I feel like a dirty hypocrite—until I remember my daughter and the gas mine I've come here to stop. I turn to Ms. Yun with new confidence: "Do you have coal seam gas in your country?" She frowns and looks at the others. They shake their heads. "Have you heard of climate change?" I press on, drawing out each syllable like a kindergarten teacher: "Glo—bal—war—ming?"

Mr. Pak butts out his fag, deadpan: "We don't live on the fucking moon."

Everyone bursts out laughing—even the Man in Black. Mr. Pak points at me, delighted: "Hasn't she heard of our slogan *From each according to their ability to each according to their needs, for the good of the nation?*" More laughter. Clearly, I haven't. Mr. Pak pats my hand, as if I'm three years old: "She needs to learn about our ideology, before she comes here asking us questions!" The men slap their knees, in stitches. Ms. Yun gives me an apologetic look, but even she can't stop laughing.

I grin sheepishly, like the capitalist idiot I am, and feel relieved. The ice has been broken. Mr. Pak looks at me warmly, and stands: "Let's eat!"

One Summer Night

Comrade Kim Jong Il worked with the film crew for seven hours without rest. That evening, he had a simple supper with them, thus encouraging them to push ahead with their work on location vigorously.

GREAT MAN AND CINEMA

A banquet is spread on a low table: crisp potato pancakes, skewered meats sprinkled with sesame seeds, kimchi, and lots of beer. There are also several bottles of what looks like sochu, or Japanese vodka. The North Korean version, *soju*, as Lizzette and I are about to find out, is considerably more lethal, at 1.5 standard drinks a shot.

We join Nick and the filmmakers on long leather couches. The banquet is a disturbing image in a country where an alleged eight million people are starving. Even more eerily, we are consuming it inside a fake Swiss chalet. The mansion has soaring gables and white latticework: one of the many houses, churches, and halls that Kim Jong Il had built for his European film set. We drove through three other film sets to get here: a 1920s-era street full of Chaplin posters and Suntory ads, for films about the Japanese occupation; a South Korean street lined with bars, brothels, and beauty parlours, for films set in wartime Seoul; and an ancient North Korean village, with thatched huts and a Buddhist temple, for movies about feudal Korea. I am sure the stone fortress we passed on the way to Europe is the same one Kenpachiro Satsuma's Godzilla smashed in *Pulgasari*. But I'm also sure if I mention this to our North Korean friends, I'll get an early pass back to China.

"Geonbae!" says Pak, holding up a shot glass of *soju*. I clink my glass with his, and everyone laughs. "No, no," Pak admonishes: "You are much younger than me. You need to clink underneath my glass—unless you are actually an old lady who has had lots of plastic surgery." I try again, and Pak cheekily keeps lowering his glass, so that we end up under the table, trying to out-youth each other. Then we drain our drinks, and everyone claps, and I clink glasses with the whole table—taking extra care to let Ms. K clink her glass under mine. Nick gives me an encouraging wink, pulls out a harmonica, and lets rip.

I recognise the song. It's the kindergarten tune that Chun the TV entertainer sang so enthusiastically in Seoul. Pak, Ri, and Pei sing along, already flushed pink with *soju*. Yurim and Ms. Yun hum rather more sedately, as the only people still drinking tea. Then Nick throws down the harmonica and launches into a new song in an excruciating falsetto. I'm shocked: it appears to be a blistering parody of the melodramatic opera songs in *Flower Girl*. Nick flings his arms wide and warbles like a drag queen version of Kotpun, and I look nervously at the Man in Black. Any second, he's going to tell Nick to stop, shut down Koryo Tours, and boot us all back to Beijing. But the Man in Black is swaying along with the others, mouthing the words in melancholy ecstasy. Ri rips off his shirt, leaps up, and throws his arms around Nick, and everyone joins in for the chorus, singing as loudly as they can, tears streaming down their faces.

A waitress brings out more bowls, and everyone immediately wipes their eyes, sits back down, and devours the contents in silence. "Cold noodles," says Eun, solemnly. "Pyongyang *naengmyeon*: our national dish." I peer inside my bowl. A twisted hunk of vermicelli sits in grey water, surrounded by faded vegetables and what may be a boiled egg. Droplets of grease glimmer on the icy broth. Everyone turns to me, and I realise I've hit that moment every traveler dreads—the one where you eat a live monkey's brain, or drink freshly masticated cassava, to belong. Lizzette dresses her noodles with mustard in stoic silence, and I follow suit. Then I shakily lift up the noodles with cold steel chopsticks, shut my eyes, and slurp.

An explosion of salty, sweet, spicy, and sour fills my mouth. It's delicious. I look at Pak, astonished. He grins complacently, as if to say: *Of course it's delicious. What were you worried about?* Then Ri charges our *soju* glasses for the fifteenth time and pushes his bowl aside: "So an American, a Frenchman, and a Russian are on a plane," he slurs. The filmmakers chuckle: Ri has wheeled this one out before. "The plane crashes on an island. The natives want to eat the foreigners. But they plead for their lives." Lizzette and I smile, a little unsettled. Is this some kind of North Korean tourism metaphor?

Ri puffs out his chest: "'All right,' says the chief, 'we won't eat you, on one condition. You must name one thing we do not know.' The Yankee goes first: 'I bet you don't know what TV is.' The chief answers: 'Of course we do. It is a box with pictures and sound, that tells you stories.' SPLASH! The Yank is thrown in a huge pot and boiled for supper."

The filmmakers cheer, delighted: that's one very dead American. Lizzette and I nod gamely, playing along. "The Frenchman goes next," continues Ri. "'I bet you don't know what wine is,' he says. The chief laughs. 'That's easy. It's a beverage made from fermented grapes, and when you drink it, it makes you sing with joy.' SPLASH! The Frenchman lands in the pot." The filmmakers think this is hilarious. They toast Ri and gulp down more *soju*. Ri leans forward: "Last, it's the Russian's turn." He frowns drunkenly under his eyebrows, doing a passable Boris Yeltsin: "'Do you know what a Soviet Central Party Sub-Committee Meeting is?' the Russian asks. The cannibals scratch their heads. 'That's too hard to explain to anybody,' says the chief. And the Russian goes free!"

I pinch myself. Did I just hear a plastered North Korean man in a singlet tell an anti-Soviet joke in the middle of Pyongyang? Around me, everyone has cracked up, and it's clear that I did. Well, if they're breaking taboos, I'll break one too, I decide—and pull out a pack of Benson & Hedges. It's a habit I fell back on when my marriage collapsed, and I swore I wouldn't do it in front of the North Koreans. But my nerves are shot, and every man at the table has been chain-smoking since we sat down. I'll show them a female director can party with the best of them.

I rummage in my bag for a lighter—but Pak beats me to it. He flicks open an old brass Zippo and whispers in my ear: "Women are like cigarette smoke: when you try to stroke them, they disappear." I realise with a shock that he's flirting with me—in Japanese. I glance at the Man in Black, but he's eating his noodles. If he can hear us, he's not letting on. Pak continues happily, in the forbidden language of the hated enemy: "Do you miss your family?"

I wince before I can stop myself. I miss them both. But only one of them is family now. I wonder if my daughter is coping without me, and how she is getting on with her daddy's athletic, and singularly unmaternal, girlfriend. "It's always hard, going away," I say, hoping Pak doesn't notice my pain.

He studies me closely, his skin moist in the heat. His voice is soft with concern: "Making films is like climbing a mountain, Anna. You must look after your legs. If you cannot put one foot in front of the other, you cannot direct." I nod and exhale, wondering if I've translated him correctly. I've been told many things about directing over the years—but looking after your legs isn't one of them. "Thank you," I say, and mean it.

The table erupts with laughter at another of Ri's jokes—something about David Beckham and the South Korean president. It's clear who's just landed in the cannibals' pot. Pak stretches back lazily, placing his arm behind my shoulders with practised ease: *"Eiga no kazoku wa eiga no kazoku desu yo, doko demo,"* he says. "Filmmakers are family. Wherever you are." I look at the laughing faces, and I know that he's right. This could be a post-shoot party anywhere in the world. I can feel Pak's hand, millimetres from my skin: "To the world we want to say that we love nature, and we love humanity. People who make these kinds of films are one big family."

I look into Pak's eyes and feel a shiver of recognition. He's giving me a message. He wants me to take it back out and share it with the world. *We are all family.* Pak holds my gaze, making sure I understand. Then he buries his face in his noodles and drinks up the last drops of broth.

BLUE DANUBE BLUES

I'M ON THE PROWL—BUT NOT FOR eligible men. There aren't any. So far, I've met a Swiss prospector, a Chinese developer, and a Canadian missionary. They all wore wedding rings, so I'm keeping my virtue intact and prowling for information instead. After twenty-four hours of total isolation from the outside world, I'm hungry for answers. The Swiss man, who is here to explore the northern mountains for the minerals used in mobile phones, was really quite cute. In the eighteen-minute ride down to the lobby, he gave me a useful tip: if I want to know just how closely we're all being watched, I should go to Floor Five.

I peer through the doors of Restaurant Number One, where Nick, Lizzette, and Ms. K are eating cucumber salad for breakfast. The restaurant is white and stark, as brightly lit as a TV studio. Maybe it is a studio, feeding images back to Floor Five from a camera hidden in the chandelier. Certainly, Nick is keeping the conversation weather-related. I decide to pass on breakfast and head for the lobby.

Simon Sheen the turtle knows I'm up to something. He gives me a loaded look as I slip past the bellboys and head for the entrance to Floor Five. Ms. K and Eun are living there until we leave, a fact I discovered last night when we said our goodbyes. As we got in the elevator, they disappeared behind a large potted plant—and up a hidden staircase. Ms. K was drunk and did not look like she was about to do after-hours surveillance.

But this is North Korea: in 2009, it imprisoned American documentary makers Euna Lee and Laura Ling, accusing them of sneaking over the Chinese border to "conduct a smear campaign." In 2010, Korean-American businessman "Eddie" Jun Yong-Su was arrested for committing a "grave" but undisclosed crime; two years later, Christian missionary Kenneth Bae was charged with plotting "to overthrow the government" and sentenced to fifteen years, hard labor. More recently, officials arrested an eighty-five-year-old US war veteran, Merrill Newman, on his Air Koryo flight, minutes before it left for for Beijing. The sightseeing trip Newman had just enjoyed down memory lane became a two-month ordeal, during which he was held by armed guards and interrogated. Newman's captors only released him when he read out a hand-written confession on national TV, apologizing for the "US invasion" and Korean war.

I duck behind the potted plant and start up the stairs. It is pitch black: the hotel obviously reserves its electricity for guests. I know I'm putting our project in jeopardy. But I feel a heavy responsibility: my documentary, if I am allowed to make it, will be seen around the world. I need to know exactly where the truth sits between the gulag state of the newsfeeds and the bizarrely functional society I've seen so far. If we really *are* being surveyed 24/7, and Pyongyang is hiding suburbs of starving people, the North Koreans are better at deception than I would have guessed.

I arrive at the head of a long corridor with thick crimson carpet and a mirrored ceiling—it could be the set from *The Shining*. Smooth grey doors run down both sides at perfect intervals. Above each one is a number in a slanted, seventies sci-fi font. The place is dead quiet. I tiptoe down the carpet and press my ear to a door. All I can hear is the faint hum of air-conditioning, and somewhere beyond that, the muffled creaks of the Yangakkdo's metal skin, expanding in the heat. Suddenly, a door at the end of the corridor opens. There's a hot gust of air and a sound I recognise: the loud hum of industrial fans—the kind that TV tape rooms use to stop monitors overheating.

Before I can peer inside, the door shuts. A young man in a crisp white shirt and thick glasses walks towards me. He stops. "You are lost," he says matter-of-factly, in the clipped accent I'm coming to know so well.

"Not really." I smile. "I was just wondering if this is some kind of film equipment place?"

He nods benignly, as if guests ask him this every day: "The business centre is on the ground floor."

I jiggle the handle of one of the locked doors: "Maybe you can help me? I just want to see."

He watches politely as I try one door after another. I suddenly feel embarrassed: what if there is nothing behind the doors but hotel rooms? That would make me a stalker—or worse, a thief. I stop and give him an apologetic smile. He doesn't smile back and points at the stairs: "The business centre is on the ground floor."

I'm eyeballing Simon Sheen again, back where I started. He gives me a jaded blink: *What did you expect?* I decide to cut my losses and film the lobby. No one seems bothered by my camera down here; the bell-boys move their mop buckets so I can line up a shot of the revolving doors, and the lady in the bookshop smiles as I snap off rows of Kim Jong Il instruction manuals, on everything from ostrich farming to ike-bana. I ask if she sells Dear Leader pins, and she waves her hand frantically in front of her face, as if I've just asked for a crucifix in a mosque: "No, no, not possible!" Clearly, capitalist infidels are not allowed to wear the pins—they are holy objects, not souvenirs. I apologise, feeling like an idiot for asking. She nods kindly and pulls out a tray of Juche Tower badges. They are much tackier than the Dear Leader pins, and wonderfully kitsch.

I buy some badges for my actors, along with the new Kim Jong Il biography *A Great Personality*, a sombre tome called *Japan's War Crimes*, and a brightly coloured cookbook, *Best Recipes of Pyongyang*.

The recipes are too fascinating, both gastrically and economically, to pass up. "Aspic jelly of ox trotter," the Cook's Association of the DPRK assures me, is one of the "speciality foods of Pyongyang where the immemorial history and brilliant culture are prouding themselves." The picture displays a congealed, translucent meatloaf. Made from ox feet, tongues, tendons, and tails, "aspic jelly of ox trotter" requires the diligent Pyongyang housewife to "cook slowly, skimming fat and scums until the meats become tender" before seasoning the whole thing with salt to release its "nutritive value, good taste, and various medical properties."

Quietly thankful I didn't eat breakfast, I wander off to explore the banquet halls. They are huge, clean, and empty. Banquet Hall Number One has a mural of snowy mountain peaks that I recognize from the happy snap Kim Jong Il took with Madeleine Albright when she visited in 2000. On her last day, she gave him a basketball signed by Michael Jordan and wore a gold brooch of the earth—which the North Koreans interpreted as a hopeful sign that the Americans wanted peace. The Albright basketball now sits on a velvet cushion in the International Friendship Exhibition, alongside gifts from Gaddafi, Arafat, Castro, Ceausescu, Mao, and Stalin. There's a bear's head from Romania, a crocodile suitcase from Cuba, a gem-encrusted sword from Palestine, an armoured train carriage from China, an East German tank, and a bulletproof Soviet limousine.

I am sure the bellboys polishing the floors outside Banquet Hall Number One have been to the International Friendship Exhibition many times: North Korea is full of museums, which children visit from kindergarten onwards to learn about the outside world. The propaganda displayed in the Three Revolutions Exhibition, the Victorious Fatherland Liberation War Museum, and the Museum of American War Atrocities is reinforced by KCNA, the state-run TV channel, and the "walled garden" of the North Korean intranet, which blocks the World Wide Web. If I were an ordinary person raised in Pyongyang, my understanding of the world might go something like this:

Kim Il Sung saved us from the imperialist Japanese in 1945. Before that, we were horribly oppressed by feudal overlords. Then, in 1950, the Americans invaded and tried to oppress us all over again. They killed 2.5 million Koreans, subjugating us to their corrupt capitalist ideology. But Kim Il Sung and his guerrilla fighters fought back valiantly and drove them out.

Our cousins in the South were not so lucky: they fell under the spell of materialist greed and became the lackeys of America. As a result, they live in abject poverty, and our nation is tragically divided. Thanks to our superior socialist system, we live purposeful, hard-working lives. But our hearts are filled with bitter grief at the families and friends lost over the border. We wait for the day when we can liberate them, and share the joys of Juche.

The Americans are sore losers who can't admit they lost the war. Every year they threaten to attack us again. If our Dear Leader hadn't built nuclear rockets to make us a global superpower, America would invade and destroy us, just like it has invaded sixty-nine sovereign nations since 1776. The Yankees are toxic warmongers, and we are the only people in the world not to bend to their will. Every July 4 is "Independence from America" day.

As for the Westerners who come here, with their shiny gadgets and unkempt clothes, they too will one day see the light. The way they look at us, with condescending pity, is irritating. But we know we have nothing to envy. Capitalism creates masses of illiterate poor who are mercilessly exploited by the obscenely rich few.

We do not ask the Westerners any questions. People who have done so have disappeared. So we just smile politely and treat them as our guests.

The waitress in Restaurant Number Two smiles on cue when I walk in with my camera. Restaurant Number Two is identical to Restaurant Number One in every detail: white and square, with a pretty woman in a pink *hanbok* to take your order. The *hanbok* is a traditional Korean gown shaped like a parachute. The floor-length skirt creates the illusion that the wearer is floating. The waitress glides towards me like a North Korean hovercraft and asks what I'd like for breakfast. I say I'd like a photo of her to show my daughter, and she sweetly obliges.

I walk next door. The Korean Barbeque Restaurant is hidden behind a fortress-like gate with antique iron hinges. The gleaming photos of *bulgogi* and *bibimbap* look appealing—but the door is locked. I try the glass exit door, leading out to a vast courtyard. The view of Pyongyang, spread across the river at the bottom of the steps, is spectacular, but the door, again, is locked. The Yangakkdo's guests may already be marooned on an island, but clearly, if we want to explore the gardens, we must exit through the lobby. I guess that's so the bellboys can ensure a minder comes too. I jiggle the rusting padlock, hoping to get a closer look at the smoke gushing from a pipe to the west of the city. The smoke has smothered the buildings in a thick white haze. Perhaps Pyongyang's air is not so clean after all, but I won't be able to smell it to know for sure: the lock doesn't budge.

I move on to a spiral staircase and descend into an underworld of vice. A bank of poker machines lines the wall, facing a floor-to-ceiling photo of Pyongyang, circa 1971. It's like looking at New York without the Twin Towers: the trademark Juche Tower, with its glittering flame, is disconcertingly absent. Kim Jong Il built the tower in 1987, at his virile, propaganda-producing peak. He followed it up in 1992 with the soaring Yangakkdo. It is a myth that North Korea is completely off limits to the rest of the world: for Chinese tourists and properly accredited foreign entrepreneurs, it's always been open for business. Kim designed the Yangakkdo as a honey trap for Beijing holiday-makers on a budget. His goal is reflected by a gaudy sign hanging under a disco ball next to the pokies: Good Luck Casino. North Korea's tourist invasion won't start for another two months, when the weather cools down. But trade is booming: the Chinese developer I met in the lift last night is tearing down the Yangakkdo's putt-putt range to build a brand new casino, bigger than Caesars Palace.

I snap some selfies beside the casino sign, to prove to folks back home that the lust for filthy lucre is alive and well in Pyongyang. Then I walk over to what looks like another restaurant. Surprisingly, these doors swing wide open—and I enter a low room, done up like a Hawaiian cocktail joint. Two girls in LaCroix T-shirts lounge at a well-stocked bar, drinking Coke. One of them is playing Candy Crush on her tablet; the other is watching a Chinese dating show on TV. I could be back with Monica in Seoul, in some neon-lit dive in Itaewon. The girls glance indifferently at my camera and return to their screens. I suddenly feel horribly homesick. I want to pull up a stool and drink pina coladas with them. I want to play Candy Crush, check my Facebook, and see what Lady Gaga wore to the Emmys. It may be breakfast over here, but my jet-lagged body is clocking midnight.

"Good morning, *tongmu*," I say to the girls. Before they can answer, a middle-aged Chinese man in a towel pads out from behind a screen at the back of the room. A girl in a Minnie Mouse tank top and tight denim shorts follows. He leaves without a word, and she walks to the cash register to place some grimy yuan inside. I don't need to read the kanji signs on the wall to know that one of them, for sure, guarantees a happy ending.

BACK OUT IN PYONGYANG'S SIN-FREE STREETS, it's rush hour. Our driver toots aggressively, pushing through swarms of bicyclists and pedestrians to get to Ms. K's first stop for the day. Riding in air-conditioned comfort as sweaty commuters scurry out of the way brings back uncomfortable memories of my chauffeur-driven childhood in the Philippines and Myanmar. But there is a difference: in Pyongyang, the people are not servile or cowed. They are annoyed. They are showing us the same disdain the Iranians used to show my mother and me when we put on *Chadoors* and braved Tehran's traffic to get to the bazaar. To the North Koreans, we're not cashed-up tourists, but the despicable exploiters of an enemy state.

We stop at an intersection, and people in colour-coded uniforms cross the road, looking like extras from Gattaca. The scene is perfectly designed, a neatly delineated hierarchy of roles that reminds me of the Pentagon corridors I've filmed inside, where each officer wears a colour specific to his status. In Pyongyang, the soldiers wear khaki, the labourers brown, and the Party officials grey or black. A petite woman stands inside a chalk circle in the middle of the intersection in a buckled blue dress and high-heeled boots. She points a baton in swift, graceful movements, conducting the traffic. The thin chalk line is the only thing between her and the army trucks thundering around her, missing her by inches.

Much has been made of Pyongyang's traffic ladies: critics say the regime uses them to save electricity. But I think they perform another function. They are as mesmerising as ballet dancers; their elegant choreography makes you feel instantly calm. Thanks to the traffic lady, Pyongyang has no road rage. *Peep!* goes the traffic lady's whistle, and we jolt forward. She has the vermilion lipstick and arched eyebrows of one of Sunmo's World War II starlets. Just before I left Beijing, a report went viral about a North Korean traffic lady who had been executed for sneezing on the job. She was shown in what appeared to be a Pyongyang courtroom, crying like a baby. Now I'm actually here, I still have no idea if the report was fake or real.

My inability to separate reality from fiction continues once we stop at the sweeping lawns of Mangyongdae, the birthplace of North Korea's founding father, Kim Il Sung. A tour guide in a *hanbok* and Madonna mic floats up and starts a monologue about Kim Senior's childhood, pointing at a gleaming hut: "Here, in this humble home, the Great Leader learnt the hard working conditions of the Korean people, and made up his mind to build a new country, free from pain." The hut looks like it was built yesterday. I feel like the knight in *Monty Python and the Holy Grail* when King Arthur's posse arrive at Camelot: "Camelot!" says Arthur reverently, and the knight growls: "It's only a model." The guide points at a crumpled terracotta pot, preserved from the day Kim Il Sung's grandma went to the market and discovered she was too poor to buy a proper one. The pot, the hut, and the tools inside it are all oddly spotless. "Is it real?" I blurt out. The guide

The entrance to the Pyongyang Film Studio, watched over by Kim Il Sung.

North Korea's top filmmakers view my Sydney video—and a Macbook Pro—for the first time. Seated (left to right) are composer Mr. Pei, directors Mr. Pak and Mr. Ri, actress Ms. Yun, and cinematographer Mr. O.

The workers of the Pyongyang Film Studio wave to us outside the Kim Jong Il Film Museum.

Producer Lizzette Atkins and me with (left to right) Mr. Pak, Yurim, Mr. Ri, and two filmmaker colleagues.

Mr. O shoots a scene (without sound) in the April 25 Military Film Studio.

The actress, who did her own makeup, lit up the screen.

Mr. O, Mr. Pei, and their colleagues watch rushes in the April 25 Military Film Studio.

The April 25 Military Film Studio projectionist.

Me, cinematographer Nicola Daley, and our North Korean film crew inside the Taekwondo Palace, Pyongyang.

The massive *Flower Girl* mural at the Pyongyang Film Studio—standing beside it, my head came up to the first step.

Reading Kim Jong Il's propaganda rules in the Three Revolutions Exhibition museum, Pyongyang.

The Australian cast of *The Gardener*—(left to right) Kathryn Beck, Elliott Weston, Susan Prior, Matt Zeremes.

The entrance to the Ponghwa metro station, Pyongyang.

The Tang Tap monument celebrating the Worker, the Artist, and the Farmer, Pyongyang.

The *hanbok*ed guide photographs Nicola, me, and our North Korean crew at Mangyongdae, Kim Il Sung's birthplace.

The Juche Tower and Arirang Stadium, viewed from my room on the forty-seventh floor of the Yanggakdo Hotel.

A detail from the *Sea of Blood* mural, which celebrates Kim Jong Il's invention of the three-camera shoot.

Mr. Ri and his crew shoot a scene on the captured American spy ship, the USS *Pueblo*.

Mr. Ri shows a nervous actor how to act.

Reading *The Cinema and Directing* in Kim Il Sung Square, site of North Korea's military parades.

stops mid-sentence and blinks rapidly, as if there's a glitch in her programming. Then she rearranges her face into a rigid smile: "Yes, this is original site."

We walk back to the van, passing groups of women squatting in the grass, clipping it with scissors. They carefully place the green blades in flat straw baskets. Soothing music pipes from speakers hidden under the bushes, but that doesn't hide the horrific possibility that these women are collecting the grass for food. The lawn is already perfectly manicured; what else could they be doing? "It is to feed the rabbits," says Ms. K simply.

Best Recipes of Pyongyang doesn't contain a single recipe for rabbits. I surreptitiously press the record button on my camera, feeling like every other journalist who has snatched illicit footage for proof of starvation. "What rabbits?" I ask Ms. K, trying to distract her from what my hands are doing.

"*The* rabbits," says Nick loudly. It's not clear if he's using our code word, or if he just thinks I've got a hearing problem. Either way, subject closed.

Hunched in the back of the van, I hide my camera under the scarf and keep on rolling. I'm not enjoying the double game I'm playing. On the one hand, I have to behave so that we're invited back. On the other, I'm in a country where yes means maybe and maybe means no. So far, when we've raised the subject of trip two, Ms. K hasn't even offered a maybe. And the images flashing past my window are too extraordinary to miss. Every frame counts if I'm not coming back. We cross the Taedong River, and I angle the lens down to the water. Canoes and iron barges move slowly up and down its glassy surface. Astonishingly futuristic skyscrapers rise up on the left bank, facing the Juche Tower on the right. Further up the river is the huge dome of the May Day Stadium, where the Arirang mass games are held every year—the ones the children we saw yesterday were practising for. At this distance, the stadium looks like a concrete crème brûlée.

The van pulls up at the Hana Music Information Center, a marble trapezoid bizarrely resembling Darth Vader's helmet. Inside is a stunning woman with dewy skin and almond eyes. The minute she sees us, she wells up with tears: "Our Dear Leader Kim Jong Il visited us here on December 11, 2011," she says. "We were the last people to see him alive." I'm not sure if Ms. K realises that in taking us here, she's giving us a worldwide scoop. When Kim died eight months ago, the BBC ran grainy footage of North Koreans crying at a Pyongyang escalator, claiming it was the last place the Dear Leader had been seen in public—but it seems the BBC was wrong.

The woman pulls a remote control from her *hanbok* and activates an LCD screen on the wall. Slides of an unusually frail Kim Jong Il play in silence: trying on the Hana Center headphones, inspecting the Hana Center DVD machine, standing with the Hana Center workers on the steps, supported by his minions.

The woman looks at us sadly: "The Dear Leader took off his glove to inspect our computer." A close-up of a tattered glove appears on the screen, haloed in gold as if it's the Shroud of Turin. "The glove was old, with a hole in one finger. Our Great Leader was so modest, he did not even think to buy new gloves. We were so filled with gratitude, we sang for him, with all our hearts and souls. When we heard that he passed away on his train the next day, we could not believe it." The woman starts to tremble, racked with grief. She seems utterly genuine. "There will never be another Leader like him again, in the entire history of the world," she sobs, her voice rising in a tremulous crescendo. "He is the greatest and most noble Leader that ever lived." The slideshow ends, and a sentence appears, decorated with roses: *"My first love is music— Kim Jong Il."* The words reflect back at us, upside down, from the polished floor. I line up a shot, but Ms. K stops me. The Dear Leader's name, when inverted, cannot not be filmed.

The woman dabs her eyes and guides us to a padded door. Inside is a tiny cinema with red velvet seats. The seat in the middle of the front row is covered in a silk slip. "This is the very seat the Dear Leader sat in on that day," says the woman gravely. We sit on either side of it, and the lights start to dim. "This is the last music he ever heard," she says, and curtains silently part on the wall, revealing the Vienna Philharmonic, playing—of all things—a Strauss waltz. The orchestra sits on the flower-bedecked stage of the Musikverein, where Austria's famous New Year's Day concert is held each year—ever since the Nazis established it in 1939.

After twenty minutes of watching conductor Franz Welser-Möst coaxing his bejewelled audience into a synchronized clapping frenzy, I've had enough. The parallels between Hitler and Kim Jong Il are already horribly apparent—but now I have to endure identically clapping Austrians behaving as if they're in the Pyongyang mass games. I look hopefully at our guide—maybe she'll let us go? But she ignores me, staring at the screen in rapture. Clearly, you don't walk out on the last song the Dear Leader heard. Especially not when it is by a favourite composer of the Third Reich.

Two hours later, our ears still ringing to a Viennese 3/4 beat, we're back in the van. Ms. K has cancelled our last stop, at the Juche Tower: the lift isn't working, and we're running out of time. If we go there now, we won't make it back to the hotel before the 7 p.m. curfew. That's when civilian vans and cars have to be off the roads, and the army trucks take over. I slump in the back, annoyed. The Juche Tower is Pyongyang's Statue of Liberty: the lift takes you as high as the flame. It would have been the perfect vantage point from which to shoot panoramic wides of the city, with its Cheshire Cat portraits of Kim Jong Il. They won't be there much longer: the propaganda workers of the Mansudae Art Studio have already been instructed to paint one thousand new portraits of Kim Jong Un.

The traffic lady conducts us through the lights, and we waltz around her with the bicyclists in perfect formation, like Kubrick's gliding satellites in *2001*. I have the irritating sensation that I'm still stuck in "The Blue Danube." I don't know if it's the fact that I dislike waltzes almost as much as musicals, or if it's the strange, searing pain in my stomach. But either way, I'm fed up with being polite. We pull onto the overpass heading back to the Yangakkdo, and there, in the baking dirt, are the children again, flashing their placards. I whip out my camera and shove it against the glass, grabbing every frame. I don't care if Ms. K notices.

Sure enough, she clocks me in the rear-view mirror, and frowns. Nick calls out from the front: "Anna, that's not a good idea . . ." but I just grunt and keep filming. The kids have gone, and now I'm brazenly capturing whatever I can: ladies on bicycles, soldiers in flatbed utes, those maddening mugshots of Kim Jong Il, smiling his Pepsodent smile.

Ms. K mutters something to Nick. He mutters back. I keep on filming. "Rabbits!" Nick calls out again. I ignore him. The tension in the van would make the DMZ feel like a yoga retreat.

"Nick," says Lizzette, a little too brightly, "do you think we could have a quick coffee?"

GREY MULLET SOUP

GREY MULLET SOUP OF THE RIVER TAEDONG

Ingredients: Grey mullet. Soy. Water. Grey mullet soup is considered nutritious and special dish. It is hearty enough to be served to a honourable guest. You will fully feel the nostalgia whenever you enjoy the Pyongyang dishes not only on the festive days but with your family, relatives and friends.
BEST RECIPES OF PYONGYANG

NICK, LIZZETTE, AND I SIT IN the revolving restaurant at the top of the Yangakkdo. Nick and Lizzette are eating grey mullet soup. I can't manage anything stronger than lemonade. The dreaded Pyongyang belly has got me. I boiled water for my coffee this morning but forgot to use it to brush my teeth. Now, after our day of fake mud huts and Strauss, I am sick and faint, struggling to stay upright between dashes to the loo. Nick has thoughtfully chosen the banquette closest to the Ladies. If it weren't for the Imodium tablets, I'd be passed out in my room.

Ms. K is not with us, thanks to some deft diplomacy by Lizzette. It's our first time alone with Nick since we got here. After two days of doublespeak, we are desperate to debrief. Diarrhoea is not the only thing causing me pain: I'm frustrated with the constant surveillance and the orders not to film. Pyongyang is the most photogenic set I've ever stepped inside, but every time I pull out my camera, I feel like a criminal. A thousand extraordinary images have already passed me by. Now they are lost forever. It hurts.

Nick urges me to be patient. Ms. K is playing her cards close to her chest, but she wants our film to happen. She's not protecting North Korea; she's protecting our chances of getting back in. It's vital she knows she can trust me. Listening to Nick repeat what he said back in Beijing, I feel like a recalcitrant child. I should rein in my ego, stop being a diva, and simply cooperate. But the more Ms. K tries to stop me, the more I want to shoot. I guess that's why I make documentaries and not drama: the thrill of capturing the illicit is in my blood.

I sip my lemonade and look down at Pyongyang's impenetrable sprawl. Like everything else in this topsy-turvy place, the revolving restaurant is not what it seems: the only things moving are the windows. This creates the illusion that you are spinning around the city, but the view never changes. Then again, I could be wrong: we might be rotating, but so slowly I can't tell. One guidebook I've read says the restaurant really does revolve, but stops before it reaches the part of the city the regime doesn't want you to see. That would be the starving part, the ugly part—the part that, so far, I have seen nothing to indicate exists.

I remember the resolution I made yesterday, to keep an open mind. Nick knows his country better than I ever will: this precious window of unmonitored face time is my one chance to grill him. I start with the hostess on the Air Koryo flight: why was she interrogating me? Is she a spy? Next, what are the pipes that belch smoke all over the city every morning? Then there's the anti-Soviet joke Mr. Ri told at the banquet: if he's cynical enough to bag the Russians, surely he can see through the propaganda he's being fed at home? And why was Mr. Pak openly speaking Japanese, if he believes the official line about the imperialist enemy? I move on to the women we saw on the lawn: are they so hungry, they have to eat grass to survive? And finally, what about those six-year-olds under the overpass, who looked like they hadn't moved since yesterday? Surely being made to squat in the baking dirt for hours on end is not "training," but child abuse?

Nick smiles, and beckons a waitress comrade over to order tea. Lizzette looks uncomfortable but says nothing. She must be as hungry for answers as I am. The comrade walks off, and Nick turns back to us, totally relaxed: "I get asked those questions by everyone I take in. I know it's hard to understand, but the girls on Air Koryo are innocent. They are proud to be the first North Koreans most foreigners meet. They want to make a good impression, and they're peachy-keen to practise their English. That hostess wanted to be your friend, Anna. As for the pipes, that's 'the nine o'clock haze.' It's steam from the thermal power plant that heats up the city. It's harmless. Mr. Ri told the Soviet joke because it always gets a laugh. It's been perfectly acceptable to criticise the Russians ever since they stopped giving aid. That doesn't mean Ri is a subversive, and neither is Pak. They meant everything they said. Pak speaks Japanese because he is old enough to have lived under the occupation, when everyone was forced to speak it. He's also made a few movies in Japan, through a North Korean friendship group called Chongryon. Like anything else here, provided you do it in the right context, speaking Japanese won't get you shot."

Nick waits for me to take all this in. My head's spinning a million times faster than our table, as I try to match his rational explanations to my paranoid thoughts. They just don't fit. "What about the rabbits, then?" I ask, stubbornly. "And the labour camps? I mean, not every bad thing we've been told about this country is a lie, even if we haven't seen any evidence of it. The UN has figures to prove it! Thirty-three percent of people in North Korea don't have enough to eat! And those poor little kids, under the overpass . . ."

"Shhhhh," says Lizzette, looking around the deserted restaurant. "We can speak about this in Beijing." She's right. The restaurant is probably wired to Floor Five.

Or is it?

I can feel my bearings slide from under me, as Nick looks at me with concern: "Ms. K was hurt you didn't believe her about the rabbits. People do eat them; they gather grass all over the city to feed them. And those kids do love practising for the mass games. This is a poor country, sure. There is starvation, but not at the levels of the '90s famine. In Pyongyang at least, people lead normal lives. They may not have air-conditioned gymnasiums, but they pride themselves on their ability to use every inch of space. You've seen the vegetable plots people grow beside the roads. It's the same with the mass games. It's normal to prac- tise under an overpass; the gymnasts I filmed practised backflips on the concrete. North Koreans are raised to be resilient. If you come back in September, when the games are on, you'll see for yourself."

Lizzette nods, on Nick's side: "The main thing is, don't alienate Ms. K. You've already won over Mr. Pak. Don't push it."

But I'm not giving in, yet. My fever is raging, and I'm in a bellig- erent mood. I'm the Commander of the Creative Group, aren't I? Why should I have to obey these tycoon Western producers? Kim would approve. If Ms. K is listening in from Floor Five, so be it. I fix Nick with a sweaty gaze, and raise my voice: "What about the traffic lady? The one who was executed for sneezing on the job? And what kind of fac- tory produces 'steam' in the middle of a city, for God's sakes? Exactly what aren't we being shown? How evil is this place, really, between the horror stories on Fox and the saccharine barrage they've fed us since we got here?"

Lizzette lets out an exasperated groan. Nick doesn't answer. The comrade is back with his tea. She lays the cups on the table with swift, deft movements, frowning with concentration. "Oi," says Nick, teasing her, "I know what you're thinking: That tongji Nick, always making me work. When will he stop ordering more bloody English tea!"

It has the desired effect: the waitress gives him a glorious smile, utterly charmed. Then she turns to me, painfully shy: "Madam, would you care for an alcohol-based beverage?"

"Wow, you've been studying!" says Nick, and the girl nods,

delighted. She's guileless, just like the hostess on Air Koryo. I feel awful for having been so rude. I run to the loo and lock myself inside the cubicle, trying to still my raging brain. I've been looking at this place through First World glasses, I tell myself: of course they can't afford gymnasiums. I have a flash of the local school I attended as a child in Manila—we held assemblies in the dirt, made toys out of rubber bands and did athletics in the car park next to a stinking canal. And we were happy. If you ignore the Kims and look at this country as a Third World economy, the lives its people lead start to make sense. Perhaps you really can take the North Koreans at face value, I decide. Perhaps, unlike Westerners who have the luxury of cynicism, able to find the catch in every transaction, North Koreans really do believe what they say. Their propaganda has certainly taught them to believe it, just as democracy has taught us to look for the lies.

I return to the table, shaky but purged. I smile politely at Nick's waitress. "Can I please have a bourbon and Coke?"

She shakes her head, affronted: "No. We do not have Coke in our country."

And there's the disconnect again: in the basement of this very building is a tropical bar, with hookers, iPhones, and Coca-Cola on tap. Does this girl know about it, or not? Or in the world she has been trained to inhabit, is it possible for Coke to exist in one place, and not in another? I order water, and she walks away. "She's sweet," I say to Nick, trying to be conciliatory.

He nods: "Most of them are."

We watch the sun set over the city in silence, and I shelve my other questions until we get out. The buildings slowly slide into blackness. The only thing still visible down there is Kim Jong Il's face on the Grand People's Study House, glowing greenly in the void.

"Look, this is a nasty place," says Nick, softly. "That's undeniable. But most people out there are like you and me. They love their kids and just want to get through the day."

When we get back to the forty-seventh floor, Ms. K is waiting. She gives me an old DVD player and a stack of discs. She has scrawled the titles in black text: they are Mr. Pak's and Mr. Ri's latest movies, plus some classics starring Yurim and Ms. Yun. At least five have been made in the last three years. I thank Ms. K profusely. This is pay dirt: I have in my hands twenty-two films that no one, not even Johannes and his underground cinema friends, has seen outside North Korea.

Lizzette and I shower and throw on the Yangakkdo's thin terry-towelling robes. I dose up on Imodium and hook the DVD player to my boxy TV. We climb into the narrow beds for a slumber party, Pyongyang style: no room service, no bar fridge, and no sleep. Ms. K has not said if we can take the films with us when we leave, which means that if we want to know what North Korean filmmakers have been doing for the last decade, we have to watch everything at Chollima speed—tonight.

I slide in the first disc, a 2009 movie by Mr. Ri called *Two Families of Hangdong*. I've pegged the tough-looking Ri, with his crumpled combat gear and permanent fag, as an action man. But I'm wrong. *Two Families* is a witty satire about married life: the North Korean *Husbands and Wives*. It follows two women living in the same Pyongyang apartment block. One has a successful husband, happy kids, and a sparkling flat. The other is a poor but beautiful singer, struggling to raise her son in the absence of her deadbeat husband. When he does come home, they fight—and the whole apartment block joins in, advising them how to fix their marriage in group-criticism sessions run by the block's bossy chairwoman.

Gradually, the wives' fates shift: the happy wife's husband fancies the singer and starts to neglect his work. Meanwhile, the deadbeat husband reveals he's been working on a top-secret project to help North Korea cut its dependency on foreign oil. He unveils his invention and becomes a national hero, praised by Kim Jong Il himself. The singer realises she's been wrong about her husband and embraces him in their newly furnished flat. Next door, the once-happy wife has driven her husband to drink, thanks to her relentless nagging to keep up with the

Joneses. The message is clear: he who sacrifices personal happiness for the good of the nation will be rewarded; he who pursues his own selfish ambitions is doomed. But *Two Families* is not heavy-handed; it is lightly acted, simply shot, and surprisingly funny.

One down, twenty-one to go. So far, so good. This is no more gruelling than watching back-to-back episodes of *Seinfeld*—and a lot more novel. I pick up *The Country I Saw*, by the white-haired Pak. It's a box set: part two was made this year, part one twenty years ago. The prequel stars a humble Japanese professor who teaches North Korean politics in Tokyo. Determined to find out what has become of North Korea since he fought there in the war, the professor travels to Pyongyang. There he meets a mysterious stranger (Yurim), who guides him through the country's miraculous postwar prosperity. Yurim seems familiar, but the professor can't work out why. Then he realises Yurim is one of the soldiers he brutally interrogated during the war. The professor is astonished: Yurim has not only forgiven him, but wants to share with him the utopian joy of Juche. The professor returns to Tokyo and broadcasts North Korea's brilliance to the world.

Part two is a different beast: better shots, tighter editing, and a plot that is more political thriller than history lesson. Pak continues his theme of North Korea seen through a stranger's eyes—this time with the professor's daughter. She's also an academic, but her world is more dangerous than her father's. South Korean spies on motorbikes are constantly harassing her and her elderly mother outside their Tokyo apartment, and a rival academic is attacking her for being too "pro–North Korea." But the professor's daughter knows injustice when she sees it: George W. Bush has just labelled North Korea a failed state and is preparing to destroy it, like he destroyed Iraq. The professor's daughter must uncover the truth about North Korea's nuclear program to counter America's propaganda, before it's too late.

Dramatic scenes of pursuit and espionage follow—some shot in the places we saw today: the Yangakkdo lobby (as Tokyo airport), the lawns of Mangyongdae (as a Japanese golf course), and Kim Il

Sung Square, where the professor's daughter learns about Juche. As she runs through the revolving doors of our hotel, chased by South Korean agents, you can see Simon Sheen bumping against his glass, and the bellboys in crazy nineties tracksuits and blond wigs, looking like extras from a Wes Anderson movie. The professor's daughter flees to Tokyo and gives a passionate speech supporting North Korea's nuclear program, intercut with detonating American nukes: "The Dear Leader proved that the DPRK was invincible," she says to her awe-struck students. "Kim Jong Il no longer had to go to the world. The world came to Kim Jong Il." Cue the photo of Madeleine Albright and Kim Jong Il shaking hands in Banquet Hall Number One, like Tweedledum and Tweedledee. A crane soars triumphantly against a red dawn, and the credits roll. Conclusion: nukes, good; America, evil; the UN nuclear-disarmament program, hypocritical bullshit.

I lie back, exhausted. Pak hasn't just laid on his propaganda with a trowel; he's used a cement mixer. Here's the story of North Korea's nukes, from the other side of the looking glass. But watching it in the same country Pak made it in, only six months ago, I find myself in his shoes. Why shouldn't the North Koreans defend themselves, when their enemy is a nuclear superpower itching to avenge itself for an embarrassing and unresolved war? Why shouldn't the North Koreans do everything in their power to stop the US from imposing its free-world "democracy" on their country, if it means that multinationals can come in and plunder their pristine hills for riches and take them all back out? How would I feel if the leader of my country, no matter how much of an arsehole he was, was strung up by foreigners and shot? The Kims may be bastards, but they're the North Koreans' bastards. And if America can maintain close to five thousand active nuclear warheads, why can't the North Koreans even have one?

I am feeling indignant on Pak's behalf. His kindness has made me want to defend him, just like Dennis Rodman defended Kim Jong Un when he returned from their first "basketball diplomacy" playdate in 2013. "People respect him and his family," Rodman told *ABC News*'s disbelieving anchor. "I sat with him for two days. And he wants Obama to do one thing: *Call him*. He said, 'Dennis, I don't want to do war.' He loves basketball. Obama loves basketball. Let's start there. The kid's twenty-eight years old. He's not his dad. He's not his grandpa. He's very humble, man. He loves power, because of his dad. But you know what, dude? He's a good guy too. I don't condone what he does, but he's my friend."

Rodman was slammed, of course. Just as I will be, when I try to humanise the North Koreans in my film and make the case for cultural diplomacy over military threats and sanctions. Then I remember why: North Korea is evil. It oppresses its people. It puts them in gulags. Nothing it does can be justified. The problem with that theory is that, so far, I've seen no evidence of oppression. And I've had the same access as many of my journalist colleagues. "Remember, the people in Pyongyang are the lucky ones," Lizzette says gently, and I know she's right. We'll never meet the twenty-two million others, living beyond this deceptively beautiful city in God-knows-what-kinds of hell. But we can go to their villages—through these films.

I grab another, hoping it's been shot outside Pyongyang. We're in luck. *Urban Girl Gets Married* is the opposite of Pak's atom-bomb thriller: a frothy rural rom-com about star-crossed lovers. Girl meets Boy; Girl hates Boy; Boy woos Girl; they fall in love. Think Meg Ryan and Tom Hanks in *You've Got Mail*, or Julia Roberts and Richard Gere in *Pretty Woman*—but this time, it's the man who is poor. The heroine of *Urban Girl* is an uppity Pyongyang dress designer, forced to work on a communal farm as part of her company's annual community-service trip. The hero is a humble duck herder, who thinks the heroine's airs and graces are hilarious. As she shovels shit in the rice paddies, his ducks keep stepping on her beautiful drawings and splattering her dresses with mud. She hates him and his hideous ducks on sight. He thinks she's adorable.

The film is kitsch and fun, with poppy synth music and crazy freeze-frames. The airbrushed village is pristine and pre-digital, like the one

the Pyongyang Film Studio. No one is fat; no one is starv-
ryone is happy. But the film is too saccharine to sit through in
full: there's only so much choreographed group singing in paddocks
you can take without gagging. We fast-forward to the end, feeling like
naughty schoolgirls. And sure enough, the heroine is now wearing a
peasant smock and singing a tune of socialist joy to the duck herder,
flanked by a brass band of her delighted Pyongyang colleagues. She's
decided to work beside him in the ditches. He's taught her that pretty
frocks are too bourgeois for a true daughter of Juche. *"Tra la la la,"* they
all sing, *"we're all happy socialists with nothing to envy; the Dear Leader is
the greatest leader in the world; tra la la, look at the plump potatoes we grew,"*
etc., etc., the end.

It's now 4 a.m., and we're giggling like maniacs. It's a propaganda-
induced hysteria: the first phase religious cult members go through
when being brainwashed to reject reality. Thankfully, we have an
escape route—the eject button. In a few hours, we have to meet Ms.
K's boss. We need to be alert for the meeting, because he's going to
decide if he'll let us back in. So we shelve our guilt and fast-forward
the remaining films. We're not missing anything by not watching them
in real time—the subtitles are appalling. Besides, when an average
North Korean propaganda film is sped up, it plays almost as fast as a
Western one. I insert something called *Pyongyang Nalpharam*, praying
for another comedy. But it's better: a fantasy-action pic, starring a tae
kwon do–fighting princess and her nemesis, a long-haired vixen who
looks like an Asian Angelina Jolie. Quentin Tarantino would love this
one—it's the North Korean *Kill Bill*.

The plot's too convoluted to work out. It has something to do with
preserving the Korean martial art of tae kwon do, against a corrupt feudal lord who is trying to make judo the national sport. Suffice to say,
the princess and the bad girl kick the living daylights out of each other
in many picturesque settings. There are slow-mo punches to the head
and lots of convincing gore. There's also a wet T-shirt scene, in which
the princess kills the bad girl in an icy mountain stream. Then—out of

the blue—there's a line-for-line rip-off from *Spartacus*. The lord's soldiers ambush some monks in a paddock, looking for their ringleader. "Which one of you is Hyong Pil?" says the soldier's captain. A monk steps forward. "I'm Hyong Pil," he says. Then another joins him: "No, I am Hyong Pil." Then a third: "No, I am Hyong Pil." And so on. The camera zooms in to the real Hyong Pil, overcome with gratitude as he realises, like Kirk Douglas's rebel slave Spartacus, that his noble brothers would rather sacrifice themselves than betray him to the oppressor. I have no idea what happens next; we've already hit eject.

We're enjoying our propaganda crash course now—fast-forwarding the films like lunatics and expertly predicting the plots. *My Happiness*, the World War II drama scored by Mr. Pei, is a turgid buddy film about two nurses who befriend each other in the trenches and go on to live melancholy but comfortable postwar lives. There's a lot of gazing into the Taedong River at dusk and rippling dissolves to various American war atrocities. The subtitles don't work at all, but even at quadruple time, you know when the obligatory Dear Leader speech is being made: it is always done in one shot, with the actor gazing out a moonlit window, or staring at the Dear Leader's portrait, or addressing his rapturous comrades. Pei's song is the most engaging thing about *My Happiness*—that, and the novelty of watching a big-budget war movie that stars two women.

We whizz through three more war movies, full of explosive battle scenes. *Wolmi Island* is spectacular. One sequence shows an army cook standing on a raft in the middle of the boiling sea, dodging real torpedoes fired by three massive frigates. Another shows the sixteen-year-old Ms. Yun singing to North Korean soldiers in a bunker as they prepare to sacrifice themselves to the Yankee wolves. The scene is gorgeously lit and moving. When the captain puts on a record to accompany Ms. Yun's dazzling voice, it's like watching the end of *Gallipoli*, when the brigadier plays Albinoni's "Adagio in G Minor," just before young Archy runs over the trenches and is killed. Ms. Yun sprints through exploding bombs to save the hero, only to discover he is already dead.

You want to cry with her. "Tongji!" she says. "Comrade! Wake up!" But it's too late. Ms. Yun is shot through the heart—another casualty of the imperialist warmongers.

After Ms. Yun dies, a North Korean actor in a ragged red wig appears, attempting—and failing—to portray an American soldier. His exaggerated scowls and bad makeup turn what has until now been a riveting drama into a sketch from the British World War II comedy *'Allo 'Allo!* Bleeding to death on Wolmi Island's rocky cliff top, the Yankee writes a letter to General MacArthur. A clipped North Korean voice reads out his words, underscored by surging music. I swear it is the same voice that called me in Sydney. "The Korean people are the toughest people I've ever met," it says, in its coolly detached tone. "We cannot win against them. They will defeat us." The soldier then dies a slow and appropriately horrible death.

By the time we slide in DVD twenty-two, we're beyond tired. The endless speeches and relentlessly happy peasants have turned our critical faculties to mush. All we can do is insert, fast-forward, laugh, and eject. "Oh look," I say, "another group song."

"Ah," says Lizzette, "there's red-wig guy again. He still can't act." And every time someone places their hand on their heart and looks to the heavens to deliver the Dear-Leader-is-the-love-of-my-life speech, we heckle them mercilessly: "The Dear Leader saved me! The Dear Leader never sleeps! The Dear Leader is a big fat Hennessy-gobbling tosser, but when I have nothing to eat, I just *have* to sing about him!"

The laughter is a release, like therapy. It's keeping us sane. On the screen, Yurim stands in the International Friendship Exhibition, gazing at a glass-encased boar's head as if it's the Holy Grail. And I'm on the floor now, rolling around, in stitches: "Reckon that's a gift from Idi Amin, or Pol Pot?" "Nah—that's from Putin. Shot it himself. Hope Kim sent back some cold noodle soup!"

The phone rings.

I look at Lizzette. I didn't think the room had a phone. It keeps going—a low, insistent growl. I scrabble around until I find it, wedged between an ashtray and the curtain. It's Ms. K. She sounds annoyed. "Anna," she says. "Please watch the films." Ms. K hangs up—from Floor Five.

Oh, *shit*.

DRINKING THE KOOL-AID

IF MS. K KNOWS WHAT WE did last night, she's not saying. We're walking out of the hotel, past the casino building site. The hedges are divided every ten metres by stone plinths, carved with slogans. "What does that one say?" I ask Ms. K, working hard to be a dutiful, Kim-loving guest. She stops and translates each time, as if it's her civic duty: *"Let us love our machines like the anti-Japanese guerrilla fighters loved their weapons!"* she says. *"Let us dedicate our love to the road our Dear General has taken!"* We move on. After five minutes of being told to *"aim high in creation!"* and *"contribute through our arts to bring a faster victory!"* we arrive at our destination.

The performing arts centre looks like a huge and particularly expensive shipping container. In this iron-clad fortress, Johannes Schönherr and the other foreign guests of the Pyongyang International Film Festival spent most of their time. It was considerate of the architects to build it within walking distance of the hotel, I decide. Or totally paranoid. Did they want to make the foreign guests comfortable, or did they want to keep them all on the island, away from the real Pyongyang? After last night's phone call with Ms. K, I still have no idea what's more likely. I decide to be Buddhist about it and accept both options.

We step inside the largest foyer we've seen so far—which is considerable, given most of Pyongyang's public buildings appear to have been built for giants. The absence of electric light transforms the space into a massive cave. It's so gloomy and vast, you can't see where the floor ends. A magnificent marble staircase curves down three balconies into a grand hall. A chandelier the size of a Sherman tank floats above a grand piano. There are towering mosaics of Kim Il Sung everywhere, looking robust in various bird-filled settings. And every surface is coated in a fine veil of dust. Perhaps the place lies dormant for two years, until the next festival's foreign guests arrive. But I'm not asking Ms. K about it. We have twenty-two hours left in North Korea, and they may be our last.

Ms. K guides us into a shadowy vestibule zebraed by strips of daylight leaking from under the doors. We continue along a gradually shrinking corridor until we arrive at an old brown door. Ms. K knocks, the door swings open, and there, in a beautifully cut black suit, is the composer Mr. Pei. He ushers us in, delighted.

The room is hot and narrow, with a peeling linoleum floor. At one end, thick velvet curtains are wedged open for light. Ripped vinyl chairs line each wall. There is an old upright piano at one end and an analogue mixing desk at the other. All the chairs are empty, except for one: the Man in Black nods at us curtly, then stares blankly at the wall.

Mr. Pei tells us that ever since we met, he's thought about nothing but writing a song for our film. All he needs are the lyrics and he can start. I nod confidently, realising I have absolutely no idea what the lyrics will be. I don't even know who will sing them. All I know is that the song must not be one of Kim Jong Il's aggressively happy peasant ditties. It must be melancholy and beautiful, and in a minor key. "Excellent," says Pei. "That's a good start. Send me the words later." We all sit, and Pei inserts a four-track cassette into the mixing desk. The speakers crackle to life. Ms. K turns off the fans, and the music starts.

I am terrified, after last night's movie marathon, that Pei's music will be sentimental and cloying. But it's extraordinary. Within two minutes in that hot room, I am somewhere wild and grand, a place of sweeping hills and jagged peaks—a land of people who think with their hearts and act with their souls—a surging, tempestuous place, full of passion and sorrow and joy. The track grows mournful, and a flute strokes our ears, soft as water. Then it swells again, pushing forward urgently, underscored by drums that beat like blood, and an insistent samisen, sharp and low.

I grin at Pei. I'm in love with this thing. It's as cinematic as Ennio Morricone's work, as powerful as a rock concert, as intense as love. I'm tapping my feet, but I want to march; I want to wave triumphant banners with the hordes of soldiers now singing jubilantly above the thundering drums. And then I have an awful thought: Pei's mixing desk isn't digital. This isn't something he can copy onto a USB drive. I grab my camera and point the mic at the speakers, mortified that yet again I'm rolling without Ms. K's permission. *I'm sorry*, I mouth at her. *I need a copy*! She just gives me her half-happy, half-rueful smile and says nothing. Pei watches me ride the sound levels, thrilled. I guess no one has ever taken his music out to the West before.

The track builds to a shattering climax. *"Pyongyang Nalpharam!"* sings the choir, and I realise what we were missing out on when we fast-forwarded the North Korean *Kill Bill*. Kim Jong Il was right: a film without music is no film at all. I have a new respect for North Korean soundtracks. I must find a way to watch *Pyongyang Nalpharam* again, in real time, before I go. The track ends, and two more play: a cheesy ballad full of eighties synthesiser with a screeching soprano that could crack glass, and an elegant orchestral piece with an Asian chord structure played by classical Western strings.

The tape clicks off, and Lizzette and I clap loudly. We mean it. It was brilliant.

"Which one did you like?" Ms. K asks coolly.

I play along: "I like them all."

Ms. K narrows her eyes and speaks more softly—something she does when things aren't going according to plan. "You must choose one. They are by three different composers. Whoever you choose can work with you."

I look at Pei, alarmed. I thought all the tracks were his. He looks straight ahead, stiff with pride. His high forehead is beaded with sweat. The Man in Black takes out his notepad and turns to me expectantly. It's a test, and a cruel one. I have no choice but to be honest: "My favourite was number one." Pei's face crumples. I've seen Western composers react the same way when I cut a song or ask for a rewrite. Composing is the most emotional thing you can do. Rejection cuts to the bone.

"That composer is in the country," says Ms. K simply. "But if you like him . . ."

"No, no," I say quickly, hoping that by "country," Ms. K doesn't mean a gulag. "For our drama, I think something Korean but played by Western instruments, like violins, would be better. Something that blends our two worlds. Something like track three. I love that too." I smile at Pei, praying that track three is his. If it isn't, and he wrote the cheesy stuff in the middle, my Kim Jong Il–style film will be a parody, whether I like it or not. Pei dabs his forehead with a soggy tissue. His hands are trembling.

"Track three was written by People's Artist Comrade Pei," says Ms. K, and I can tell that she is pleased.

"Mr. Pei, please write us a song like that," I say, and he flushes with joy. We lock eyes, and I speak in English, knowing that while he can't understand my words, he understands me perfectly. I'm talking and humming, and he's nodding and humming back, and somehow, we're in perfect sync. Maybe it's because we both play the violin. Or maybe it's simply what Pak said, back at the banquet: filmmakers, no matter where they live, are family.

Ms. K hurries us back through the slogan-filled hedges for our ten a.m. with her boss, and my good mood evaporates. What if she was just going through the motions with Mr. Pei and has no intention of letting us back in? What if she's leaving it to her boss to tell us our film is not going to happen? If they watched us heckling the DVDs from Floor Five last night, all bets are off. They'll send us back to Beijing, and the short clips I've shot will be all I ever have of North Korea. Ms. K's rigid smile hasn't shifted all morning. She'd be brilliant at poker.

I follow Ms. K into the Yangakkdo's revolving door, imagining playing Texas hold 'em with her back in Sydney—with my rowdiest friends and a bottle of bourbon. Maybe then her veneer would crack. She'd tell us what arseholes we were for slagging off the Dear Leader's films. I'd tell her how mean she was to make me choose a song in front of Mr. Pei, and she'd joke that if I hadn't chosen the right one, she'd have made me drink ten bowls of grey mullet soup. Then we'd get drunk, she'd clean up the pot with a royal flush, and we'd share stories from our lives, woman to woman.

It's a fantasy, of course. Ms. K has drunk us under the table every night since we arrived, but her polite formality has never changed. She's kept conversation to a minimum and observed every detail. I hate to think what she's seen. "This way," she says, leading us up to Floor Five along the same corridor I snuck down yesterday. Today, her shirt is a riot of frangipanis. I stare at their optimistic colours, hoping they are a sign—just like the North Koreans hoped Madeleine Albright's earth brooch was a sign America wanted peace.

"Now Comrade Pei is writing a song, can I come back to film him play it?" I ask Ms. K, forgetting I'd sworn not to ask her anything. She ignores me and knocks on a door. A crew-cut man opens it, wearing a crumpled brown suit. He smells of alcohol. He ushers us into a tiny room dwarfed by an ostentatious mahogany table. Ms. K takes a seat beside him and a bird-like person in a waist-length orange muu-muu. Lizzette and I squeeze in to face them on high-backed chairs. The usual Kims look down from the wall. The drapes are closed.

"I hear from Comrade K you have enjoyed your time here," says Ms. K's boss, flashing us a friendly smile. There is no evidence of surveillance monitors in the room, or even the power points needed to run them. Just this tipsy man, his eccentric sidekick, and Ms. K—who pulls a leather folder from her briefcase. "Here is a tally of expenses for your stay," she says, sliding some documents to Lizzette. Lizzette slides back an envelope fat with euros, and Ms. K's boss shunts it to muu-muu. She rips it open and rapidly counts up the bills, licking her finger with little darts of her tongue.

"We are very grateful to you for having us," I say to Ms. K's boss, trying as discreetly as possible to nudge a duty-free bag of Johnnie Walker and SK-II Essential Power Cream under the table towards him, with my boot. Maybe I'm being too discreet: Ms. K's boss studies me slowly descending in my chair with cool fascination, as if I've developed a nervous tic. Perhaps he thinks this is a form of Australian business etiquette and is waiting for it to pass. I bend down and shove the bag hard, until it collides with his loafer.

When I pop up again, he's still smiling, but his eyes are cold. "Comrade K has worn out her shoe leather running around showing you things," he says. "It would take a lot of work to make your film possible."

Lizzette smiles: "Should you invite us back, our investors will finance our trip at the appropriate level."

Ms. K's boss chuckles, and slowly looks us up and down. "I'm surprised you're awake," he leers. "I hear you were up all night, watching our films."

I gulp. After my time in Seoul, I am keenly aware that the Koreans, unlike the Japanese, value honesty over politeness. If Ms. K's boss has seen footage of us bouncing on our beds and mocking North Korea's greatest directors, he won't appreciate a lie. I hold his bloodshot gaze: "We watched as many as we could but didn't finish them. I would love to take them to Australia and give them the attention they deserve."

Something like relief flickers in Ms. K's eyes, and her boss turns solemn: "We have a saying, in our country: *eight hundred* ryang *of gold will buy a house, and one thousand* ryang *a neighbour, but even one thousand* ryang *cannot buy a comrade. Your wife and children can be with you in times of peace, but only your comrades can share life and death with you in times of adversity.*"

We nod and stay silent. That's one thing the Koreans do share with the Japanese: important pronouncements are usually preceded by a heavily symbolic aphorism.

"The workers of the Pyongyang Film Studio and Korfilm support your project," Ms. K's boss continues. "Comrade K tells me it will forge a positive bond between our countries. I am sure she will do everything necessary to make sure it is a success."

Ms. K turns slightly pale. Her boss slaps the table. "Next time, let's make it a heavier envelope!" he barks. And before we can respond, he's swept out the door, with the duty-free bags, the euros, and his sidekick in tow. Ms. K, Lizzette and I look at each other, stunned. We're going to make a movie.

> Trust nurtures People.
>   GREAT MAN AND CINEMA

When people want to celebrate something in Pyongyang, they go to a funfair. These places are featured in horror-themed galleries on the web: Cool Things in Random Places shows the Kaeson Youth Park to be an abandoned wasteland with mangled bumper cars, a broken Ferris wheel, and rotting roller-coasters frozen on their tracks. The very idea of a "North Korean funfair" seems oxymoronic—until you go to one.

Driving through the twilight to the Kaeson Youth Park, we're high on beer and relief. Ms. K has secured a permit letting us out after curfew, and the tension between us has been replaced by warm camaraderie—and excitement. Now we're making a film together, we're a team. Ms. K sits with Nick in the front of the van, chatting happily about their North Korean rom-com *Comrade Kim Goes Flying*. The movie has just been invited to the Toronto Film Festival. The last time a North Korean film screened in the West was 2007, when the coming-of-age drama *A Schoolgirl's Diary*, which Kim Jong Il script-edited, played in Paris. It was labeled *"un film intéressant et . . . décalé* [offbeat]," and quickly forgotten. The Toronto invite is a huge honour for *Comrade Kim's* cast and crew—despite the fact they won't be allowed to attend. It's also made Nick an even bigger celebrity in Pyongyang. Now, a new North Korean script is doing the rounds, about how Nick and Ms. K got *Comrade Kim* made. Nick asks Ms. K what his character should be called. He likes the sound of "Eddie."

"No! Too casual," admonishes Ms. K, always protective of Nick.

She prefers the more dignified "Robert."

Eun and Lizzette sit behind me, talking about men. Lizzette has survived two marriages, both of which she ended amicably to preserve a stable environment for her kids. Eun, gorgeous, privileged, and single, is torn between two boyfriends. She defers to Lizzette's experience, hungry for advice: "One of them is handsome but boring. He's in the country doing farm work with his science brigade, so I'm dating the other one. He is successful, already a Party member. But he is too short. I can't decide."

Lizzette suggests Eun visualise her ideal husband, then see if either man fits.

"I guess I would first marry a Party official, then a soldier, then a university graduate," Eun sighs. "If he is tall and handsome, that's a bonus. For men, it's simple: they just go for someone pretty."

Eun's got prettiness in the bag, Lizzette reassures her. She can go with whomever she likes.

Eun takes this in. Then she leans close and whispers: "The problem is, the scientist always laughs at my jokes. The Party official expects me to laugh at his jokes, but he is not funny."

I tell Eun that a man who finds you funny without being threatened is a precious thing. The fact the scientist is also a hottie should seal the deal: a shared sense of humour will take any marriage a long way; there's no reason why it can't be the woman driving the laughs.

Eun nods thoughtfully, weighing up a future of guaranteed luxury as a Party official's wife against good sex in a home where she calls the shots. Then she arches gracefully back in her seat, content: "I still have time. I'm only twenty-six. We don't have to get married until at least thirty-one."

Lizzette shows Eun photos of her daughter, the same age as Eun—and Eun listens, riveted, to glittering stories of the daughter's peripatetic career as a fashion designer and chef. I absorb the friendly chatter around me and curse myself for having been so paranoid. The cameras on Floor Five are obviously a myth: our North Korean minders were never out to get us. The hostility I sensed was all inside my head. Ms. K may be daunted by the work she has to do for our film, but she's always been behind it, just as Nick said. And Eun's not aloof, she's distracted: by boys. These dignified, generous people, so often demonised as brainwashed idiots by the West, have decided they can trust us. Now we must show them they're right.

Outside, the sunset suffuses the pale avenues with a soft pink glow. Everything is rosy, including my gaze: the city looks as innocent as a Rodgers and Hammerstein musical. In front of the Grand People's Study House, little boys shriek with delight as they chase a soccer ball around roller-skating girls. Under poplars by the river, people squat over sizzling barbeques, drinking beer. On the steps of a postcard-perfect temple, a family takes happy snaps, their toddler twins in pride of place at the front, wearing lacy white socks. My three-day materialism detox has flushed out my cynicism: I feel like an anthropologist who has stumbled upon a unique and undiscovered tribe. Remove the gulags and Kims from the equation and Pyongyang is how the West might have evolved if we too had never had the web, video games, fast food, globalisation, beer barns, or crystal meth.

I don't care what they will say back home: I've fallen in love with this city. Its fluttering flags, its laughing children, its enthusiastic slogans fill me with joy. This is the set for my next film: a month from now, I'll be capturing it with the best camera our budget can buy and sharing its strange beauty with the world. Maybe I'm just deliriously happy I've been allowed to come back—but Pyongyang is beautiful to me. I find its old technology nostalgic, its lack of commercialism appealing. I like the fact that even in this rigidly totalitarian nation, people have found ways to have fun—and what they've found is more humane than the conversation-stopping gadgets back home. I like that they meet in parks to sing songs, get drunk, and swap stories, to talk to each other. And I love the fact that when people in Pyongyang want to see a movie, they still go to the cinema, to see films that are actually shot on film.

"There are no scary rides here, only fun ones," asserts the neatly permed guide of the Kaeson Youth Park, as people scream on the Turbo Twister behind her. With so much else to fear in North Korea, I guess being flipped upside down and flung through space at 250 kilometres per hour, with nothing but a metal bar between you and certain death, really does constitute harmless fun. The funfair looks nothing like the pictures on Cool Things in Random Places: it is a neon-lit wonderland of fast-food joints and futuristic joyrides. Kim Jong Un revamped the park shortly after he assumed power six months ago, gifting it to the people of Pyongyang in gratitude for their loyalty. Now, up to seven thousand men, women and children come here every night, paying a small entrance fee to enjoy the state-of-the-art rides that Kim Jong Un personally imported from Italy.

"Our General Comrade Kim Jong Un came here in January 2011, and rode every ride to make sure our People would be safe," the guide says proudly, and points at a space-age roller-coaster hurling people around a loop in bullet-shaped tubes. It's difficult to imagine Junior 2.0 squeezing his tubby frame inside one of these things: they're as narrow as bobsleds and streamlined for speed. The rider has to lie face-down and hold on; centrifugal force does the rest. Shrieking people shoot past in a blur, their screams hanging in the air. Lizzette's keen to get on, but I am terrified and Eun doesn't want to get her white denim dirty. They settle on the twenty-five-metre Tower Drop instead, and I make a pathetic excuse about wanting to film them, staying safely on the ground.

"It is important for ladies to wear pants, or they might be embarrassed," the guide says gravely, as Eun and Lizzette strap themselves onto a platform next to twenty giggling North Koreans. A park worker in a yellow and brown uniform flicks a lever, and they slowly ascend to the top of the tower. The park must look spectacular from up there: a pulsing galaxy of neon in the middle of the city's lightless sprawl. I'm sure Lizzette is enjoying the view—but all I can see of my fearless producer now are her tiny white sandals, dangling against the starry sky. The park worker nudges his lever forward with the concentration of someone landing a plane, and the platform plummets towards us through eight storeys of accelerating terror—screeching to a halt a few metres from the ground. Before Lizzette and Eun can stop screaming, the worker shunts them all back up again for another death-defying plunge.

"Would you like some ice cream?" the guide asks afterwards, leading the shaky Eun and Lizzette into a milk bar fitted out like Arnold's diner from *Happy Days*. More comrades in yellow and brown polish spotless counters as families stand around eating the "meat with two breads sandwiches." Hamburgers aren't the only things on offer here: there are also hotdogs, popcorn, shoestring fries, and corn dogs on sticks. The ice cream display case is empty apart from two perfect pink spheres, each on a white paper doily. A beaming comrade walks up with two empty cones, as if she's been waiting for us all night. Suspecting this may well be the case, we dutifully order the ice cream. It tastes the way most of Pyongyang looks: pleasant and oddly familiar, yet utterly alien. I can taste strawberries, lemons, and detergent. I wish I'd ordered a hamburger.

Ms. K and Eun pull on disposable surgical gloves and pick up their burgers. I look around and realise that the Pyongyang approach to fast-food hygiene is communal: everyone, from the burger flippers and waitresses to the customers, is wearing the gloves. Families eat and chat at high tables, the plastic gloves bunching at their wrists. There are no chairs. "Why is everyone standing?" I ask.

Eun shrugs as if it's obvious: "The Dear Leader Kim Jong Il, when he designed this restaurant, took away the chairs. He said 'fast food' should be eaten fast. Otherwise, everyone would sit around for a long time talking, and others would not have a chance to enjoy." Lizzette and I share a look, and Ms. K flushes with embarrassment. She's seen enough McDonald's in China to know that wearing latex, standing, and eating at Chollima speed is not the normal way you down a burger.

Back in the fair's main boulevard, the crowd is heaving. We rub shoulders with a laughing throng of soldiers, schoolkids, and workers—all having the time of their lives. Throbbing speakers blast an odd fusion of Korean folk and Hawaiian surf rock as twenty-year-olds promenade past in aviators and leather jackets, somehow managing to make their khaki uniforms look sexy. Further up the park, parents squat in circles talking, as their children play tip. "Boo!" I say to one ruddy-cheeked five-year-old, and he stops, frozen in terror. His playmates freeze behind him. The smallest grabs her sister's hand and starts to cry. To these kids, I am a pointy-nosed American, the devil incarnate. My ancestors bombed their ancestors until Pyongyang was a pile of ashes and there was no one left.

I bend down to the little boy's level. "*Je ireum-eun Anna.* Do you know Australia? Kangaroo!" I jump up and down in circles like a mad woman. The boy stares at me, fascinated. Then he bursts out laughing. The others join in, nudging each other. This mumsy foreigner is clearly ridiculous. I grin and bounce while the children shriek with delight, and I'm filled with the heartwarming truth that no propaganda is strong enough to repress a child's impulse to laugh. The boy beckons me over to the games arcade, pointing excitedly at an eighties Speed Racer by the wall. Two little girls jiggle steering wheels from leather bucket seats, manoeuvring 2D Maseratis around an animated track.

"This is the same game our Dear Leader Kim Jong Il played with General Comrade Kim Jong Un, when he was just six years old," the guide says, and barks at the girls to get up.

The girls let me take their place without a word, too stunned by my foreignness to protest. I race a yellow Lamborghini round the chequered flags of the Monaco Grand Prix, oddly chuffed that Kim Jong Il once gripped this same wheel. Behind me, there's the crack of a rifle—and I turn to see the delicate Eun obliterating laser-projected targets with the precision of a sniper. I pick up a rifle to see how I compare, and soldiers, workers, and grandmothers all crowd in to watch. Marksmanship is highly valued in this country: according to *Kim Jong Il: A Life*, Kim was an expert gunman, able to hit targets from a galloping horse at the age of five. His mother, Kim Jong Suk, an unassuming woman whom Kim remodelled in the history books as a kick-arse, Jap-slaying "revolutionary immortal," taught him how:

> One day, Kim Jong Il saw his mother in a shooting stance with a pistol in hand, while inspecting the rifle range for the guards, and he said he would like to try his hand at it. She extracted the cartridge from the pistol, showed him how to aim and pull the trigger, and then said: "You must not start shooting without a definite target. You must have a noble aim before you start shooting. The day I shot my rifle for the first time during the armed struggle against the Japanese, I made up my mind to fight for the revolution to the end under the General's leadership and destroyed many enemies. You must grow up quickly and safeguard your father with this pistol and hold him in high respect."

Young Kim took these words to heart, determined to serve Kim Il Sung as faithfully as his mother—who, as all North Koreans know, used to warm the General's wet socks against her holy bosom and line the soles of his boots with her hair. Kim practised every day in their guerrilla camp on Mount Paektu—until finally, "with everyone watching him, he aimed at his targets and pulled the trigger. *Bang, bang, bang!* The three shots hit his three targets. Kim Il Sung hugged his son and exclaimed, 'Excellent!'"

With this story in my mind, and the eyes of Pyongyang's fairgoers upon me, I cock my rifle for Queen and country and pull the trigger. *Bang, bang, bang!* I miss fifteen targets in a row. Everyone thinks this is hilarious. "We spend at least five years in the army," says Eun, not bothering to hide her disdain. She passes her gun to a woman my age with a baby on her back, who blasts each pinprick with bored efficiency. Shooting is too much like work around here: the real fun seems to be coming from the corner. I hand my rifle to a cackling grandma, who reassures me that not everyone can be a crack shot, and walk over to join a mob of people whooping with delight. A broad-shouldered Party official is belting the crap out of a leather bag. His admirers cheer as the machine above the bag bleeps and bings with the strength of his blows.

I stare at their ecstatic faces—the young and old, the hopeful and beaten, the intelligent and dull—and remember that in the distant galaxy I've come from, North Korea is seen as a religious cult. The mass devotion of its citizens to the charismatic Kims is difficult to explain any other way. Here with the happy punters of the Kaeson Youth Park, it's easy to forget that mass devotion can be fatal.

In 1978, when charismatic American cult leader Jim Jones asked over nine hundred members of the People's Temple to drink a lethal cocktail including valium, chloral hydrate, and cyanide, they did so willingly. Some believed they'd be reincarnated; others thought that "revolutionary suicide" was preferable to being sent back to America. On the "death tape" recorded on the day, Jones told his followers: "You can go down in history, saying you chose your own way to go— and it is your commitment to refuse capitalism, and in support of socialism." The poison had been flavoured with Kool-Aid so the children wouldn't be alarmed. Nursing mothers went first, using syringes to squirt the Kool-Aid into their babies' mouths. Older children and adults drank from cups. By the end of the Jonestown massacre, 918 were dead: the greatest single loss of American life in a non-natural disaster until the 9/11 terrorist attacks. One survivor said there was no panic while the Kool-Aid was handed out: people looked as if they were "in a trance."

Jones had persuaded his people to follow him to death by convincing them their goal was holy, just as the Taliban convince suicide bombers they'll be rewarded with seventy-two virgins in heaven, or General Tojo convinced the Kamikaze their greatest glory was to die for the emperor. Kim Il Sung, another charismatic leader, convinced his guerrilla fighters they were sacrificing themselves to protect the very people I am playing arcade games with now.

I extract myself from the laughing crowd and head for the park entrance. Under oak trees strung with fairy lights, people are still pouring in, although it's almost midnight. Beside the gate is a mural of Kim Il Sung. Several people stop to bow before queuing for tickets. They appear to be doing so willingly: there are no officials monitoring the crowd. I watch a family line up under Kim's painted feet and remember the strange discovery I made while researching doomsday cults in the 1990s: people like to follow charismatic leaders. There's a freedom in surrendering one's will to the pack, in eradicating the ego for a belief—no matter how twisted—in the leader's vision of a greater good. The alien worshippers, polygamous survivalists, and apocalypse warriors I interviewed all had the same glassy-eyed reverence when speaking of their leaders. Their devotion seemed a touch crazy but ultimately harmless. Then I stumbled on the Aum Shinrikyo cult on the slopes of Mount Fuji and saw just how dangerous devotion to a charismatic leader can be.

As we shot the Aum's darkened compound, cult members in white jumpsuits started rising up from behind mangled car bodies and shuffling towards us, like zombies. Their shaved heads were wired with electrodes—which were transmitting the brainwaves of their blind leader, Shoko Asahara. We later found out that Asahara was meditating in a bunker beneath us, surrounded by the emaciated corpses of followers who'd resisted his methods. We asked the Aum several questions, but they did not answer. They seemed incapable of individual thought. Asahara had used LSD, hypnosis, and starvation to transform his followers from harmless suburban misfits looking for something to believe in to full-blown terrorists. Two weeks after we filmed them, the Aum fatally gassed Tokyo's subways with sarin.

But people don't follow charismatic leaders just because they are crazy. Sometimes, they do it to belong. In 1961, Yale psychologist Stanley Milgram conducted a famous experiment in which a group of ordinary Americans knowingly tortured an innocent man. Milgram's participants believed they were helping him assess the effects of pain on the ability to learn—and willingly zapped the man with increasingly powerful electric shocks whenever he failed to correctly answer a quiz. What they didn't know was that they were Milgram's subjects: the shocks were fake, and the man was an actor. Milgram was testing the effect of authority on the human impulse to obey. When the man failed the last question, Milgram instructed his participants to administer a 450V shock, which they knew could be fatal. They hesitated. But the majority pressed the button.

Milgram's participants, the Aum Shinrikyo, and the People's Temple had all drunk the Kool-Aid. They believed what they were doing was right, because a charismatic leader had told them so. Their reward was blissful abnegation—a total surrender of responsibility to the moral authority of the group. You don't have to look further than a fundamentalist sermon in Texas, or a climate-change rally in Sydney, to know that drinking the Kool-Aid, in its more benign forms, does have a unique kind of collective appeal.

I stand at the gate of the Kaeson Youth Park, watching punters lick orange ices and melt into the night, and ask myself the question only a capitalist infiltrator could ask: is North Korea one massive Jonestown? A nation of people so brainwashed they would willingly commit mass suicide for the Leader if asked? The idea seems plausible enough when you watch these people on TV in the West, marching like remote-controlled robots. It's not too hard to make the leap from their deliriously reverent faces to the electrode-covered zombies of the Aum.

But driving back to the hotel with our Pyongyang minders, the comparison feels dehumanising and cruel. For the first time, Ms. K is sitting next to me in the back of the van. She rummages in her bag and pulls out all the DVDs Lizzette and I failed to watch, plus a stack of new ones. "To help you write your script in Sydney," she says and places them in my lap. I gasp with gratitude, and she pulls out one more. "My uncle was a director," she says, in that open, friendly tone she normally reserves for Nick. "He made many films. This is my favourite." She places the DVD on top of my pile. The cover shows ancient trapeze artists in brocade robes, flying against a soft green sky. I thank her, and she shrugs. "Don't lose it," she orders. But her eyes are warm.

Outside, the city is quiet and still, as deserted as a mausoleum. The Reichstag-like buildings float past like ghosts, their dim silhouettes caught by the blazing spotlights trained on portraits of Kim Jong Il. His face is the only thing still lit in the misty night.

The driver slides a cassette into his tape deck. The tune is soft and sweet, some kind of lullaby. It makes the buildings look beautiful instead of eerie, as if they're part of our own private soundtrack.

I look over at Ms. K, and she smiles. If she has drunk the Kool-Aid, then so have I.

So far, it doesn't taste of cyanide.

PART 3

THE SHOOT

Comrade Kim Jong Il stressed that officials and creators should always remember that truth is the lifeblood of an artwork—and that especially films, a visual art, should describe life truthfully in every detail.

GREAT MAN AND CINEMA

PITCHING GENERAL ELECTRIC

WHEN I ARRIVED IN BEIJING AFTER three days in Pyongyang, the first thing to hit me was the smell. Capitalism smells of plastic. Sterile, hot off the production line, and ready for use. I looked around with my new ad-free eyes, astonished how often I was being told to buy something. Shiny people waved mobile phones and deodorant on every wall I passed, girls in hot pants gave out Red Bulls on the escalators, and in the ultimate multi-brand attack, a Mini convertible sat in the middle of a park, covered in Coca-Cola stickers—as boys in Apple shirts displayed the car's stats on their tablets, distributing free Cokes from the trunk. The whole tableau was framed by a retro poster, showing heroic young things rising from the back of the Mini, thrusting Cokes in their fists against a blood-red sky. It was clever and fun, a slick nod to communist chic. I would've enjoyed the irony if I hadn't just come from North Korea. Instead, it made me feel faintly sick.

The world had been busy in the time I'd been away. Psy's hit "Gangnam Style," with its frat-boy humour and sexy chorus, had crossed every cultural barrier on the planet to become the first YouTube video to reach one billion hits. As Psy galloped across Seoul's glittering vistas, touting his horse-and-champers lifestyle as a sugar

daddy from the posh hood of Gangnam, the Western media was poring over revelations from North Korea's most famous chef, Kenji
Fujimoto. Astoundingly, Fujimoto, the man I'd spent months trying
to track down in Japan, had been in Pyongyang the whole time I was
there. I wasn't surprised the North Korean news hadn't run anything
on Fujimoto's visit: if the regime didn't want its people to know their
Leaders lived in palaces, it sure as hell wasn't going to advertise the fact
those palaces once contained a Japanese man who was paid €45,000
a year, owned two Mercedes, regularly flew to Okinawa to buy fresh
abalone for Kim Jong Il, and woke up after one debauched night with
Kim's Joy Division babes and North Korea's most famous singer, Om
Jong Yo, to find his pubic hair shaved and a wedding ring on his finger.

Fujimoto described his secret meeting with Kim Jong Un and
his new girlfriend to the fascinated world. The fact the young Leader
even had a girlfriend had only just been discovered when an attractive
woman was photographed beside him at a concert, holding a Louis
Vuitton bag. Now Fujimoto, who'd escaped a decade ago and written
three tell-all books about the decadent excesses of Kim Jong Il, was
back in Pyongyang to sing the praises of Kim's son:

> I jumped up to hug him, shouting "Comrade General" and instantly
> burst into tears . . . He hugged me back, the first hug in eleven years.
> I said, "Fujimoto the betrayer is back now," and I apologized for
> all I did and all I disclosed about him. He said, "OK, don't worry
> anymore."

Of Kim's new girlfriend, Ri Sol Ju, Fujimoto enthused: "She was just
so charming. I cannot describe her voice, it's so soft. . . . She said to me,
'Welcome to the Republic. Our Comrade the Supreme Commander
missed you the most.'" The *Asahi Shimbun* ran a picture of the manly
Kim Jong Un cradling the sobbing Fujimoto in his arms.

Fujimoto's peace-making mission had an ulterior motive: he still
had family in Pyongyang. When he fled to Japan in 2001, Fujimoto left

behind kids and a wife, Om Jong Yo: the singer he'd woken up married to after that Cognac-fuelled night in the palace. Now he needed to make sure they were safe. During his reunion with Kim Jong Un, the chef promised: "If I go back to Japan safely, the reputation of Supreme Commander Comrade General would soar enormously"—and went on to talk him up to every news channel who'd listen. Pyongyang had "changed drastically since the Kim Jong Un era started," he asserted, describing seeing "plenty of goods in shops. That's already a big difference. There was nothing there ten years ago." Humbled by the graceful hospitality of the new Leader, Fujimoto was "surprised how gentle a person he is."

"Gentle" is no longer a word that springs to mind now that Kim Jong Un has murdered his powerful uncle, Jang Song Thaek, for being "despicable human scum"; assassinated Jang's children and grandchildren for guilt by association; and allegedly gunned down an old girlfriend, Hyon Song Wol, and members of her Unhasu Orchestra and Wangjaesan Light Music Band, for "making porn." But at the time, the Pyongyang Kool-Aid was fresh in my veins, and I naively accepted Fujimoto's claims. I googled the report about North Korea executing a traffic lady for sneezing and discovered it was just another YouTube hoax. This fuelled my desire to defend the North Koreans from ridicule; I thought it unfair their Leader should be attacked in the same way as his father, before he'd had a chance to prove himself. The country I'd seen was vibrant and full of optimism; I imagined it was only a matter of time before it would open up, like China, under the technologically savvy Kim Jong Un.

The odd sensation of viewing my world through a North Korean lens, and finding it lacking, intensified in Sydney. I took my daughter to Luna Park on the sparkling harbour, and all I could see were bulges of fat hanging over cut-price jeans, as junk food–munching families waddled between substandard rides. I watched twentysomethings queuing outside Apple for the latest iPhone and felt pity for these aspirational patsies of capitalism spending their wages on something designed to be obsolete within a year. I drove past American sailors, fresh off the US frigates at Woolloomooloo, pawing their way through Kings Cross as if they owned the joint, and envied the North Koreans for having the cojones to kick them out. At a Taylor Swift concert, I watched two scowling teenagers bark at their father to photograph them in front of the stage and was appalled by the fake smiles they turned on for the shot, only to snap back to rudeness once their glamorous update was online.

The trash in the streets, the drunks on the beaches, the tarts on the billboards, the beggars outside Gucci—all of it coalesced in my mind as a righteous new mantra: This Would Never Happen in Pyongyang. On TV, Chevron flogged "natural" gas as the answer to global warming, assuring viewers that "we have more in common than you think," while unseasonal bushfires raged in the Blue Mountains. The blazes had been triggered by a routine military training exercise—a fact that baffled Defence as much as everyone else, given October is normally quite cool. But when the firefighters said global warming was to blame, the media shut them out of the debate. Prime Minister Tony Abbott, a God-bitten conservative who had called climate change "a load of crap," tore down the former government's price on carbon as "socialism dressed up as environmentalism," and I yelled at the screen: *"This Would Never Happen in Pyongyang!"* Socialism stood for free healthcare and education for all. Even in North Korea, the population was 99 percent literate. I was outraged that Abbott—or anyone else—could think it was a slur.

The affluenza that had made Sydney one of the world's most expensive cities also infected my private life. My ex, keen to establish a new life with his girl, was harassing me to sell our house. As I sat in my study watching North Korean propaganda movies, he'd turn up and wave bank documents in my face. We brawled like toddlers: I'd scream and refuse to sign; he'd punch holes in the door. *"This Would Never Happen in Pyongyang,"* I'd mutter, as I covered the holes with paper, images of happy North Korean couples strolling by the

Taedong River fresh in my mind. I knew divorce was stressful—but that didn't explain how the gentle, sensitive man I'd loved had become so aggressive. Then I discovered a psychiatrist had diagnosed him with temporary depression and stress. I hid behind my mantra and ignored his pain, disgusted by Big Pharma's hold on the First World. Depression is a luxury the North Koreans cannot afford, I told myself callously. When North Koreans are stressed, they get on with things, or they don't survive.

I would have had a breakdown if my life hadn't been so absurd. It was as if the capitalist universe could sense I'd defected and was putting me through its version of a North Korean boot camp to hook me back in. In one of those ironic real-life twists that happen when you're making a documentary, while I was battling my ex and writing my Kim Jong Il propaganda script, I was also being courted by General Electric—who wanted some propaganda of their own. The marketing suits in New York needed a local filmmaker to produce a video about GE's new Gorgon gas mine on Western Australia's Barrow Island. The money was excellent and the brief was simple: create a feel-good documentary about the mine. I normally would have run a mile from such a gig: Barrow was home to the rare osprey and the even-rarer bettong, a cute little burrowing kangaroo. Now, their pristine breeding grounds were about to be ripped apart by a massive gas plant, extracting three hundred terajoules of gas per day and producing fifteen million tonnes a year.

The clever folk on the GE PR team had done their homework: they knew gas drilling was increasingly on the nose in Australia, thanks to the horror stories coming out of Queensland. Rather than assuage the public's fears with big-budget ads, their strategy was to commission homespun, documentary-style testimonies: the kind of authentic branding that would make Gorgon seem unthreatening and folksy, in a market glutted by spin. The construction blueprint for Gorgon indicated it was going to wipe out half the island, but the opportunity to contrast GE's propaganda with Kim Jong Il's socialist version was too delicious to pass up. So I Skyped New York and pitched for the project.

Tom, Mark, and Brigita listened from their elegant boardroom, impressed. I would show the miners of Gorgon wandering around the island on their days off, enjoying the fragile delights of ocean, beach, and bush. Then I would crane up over their contented faces, revealing the futuristic yet harmoniously integrated mine nestled among the trees. Reassuring vox pops from Gorgon's down-to-earth engineers would take us out, explaining how General Electric had found a way for mining to coexist seamlessly with nature. Cue the GE logline over the crystal-clear waters of Barrow—one of the most unspoilt (for the purposes of this video, anyway) islands in the southern hemisphere— *GE creates things that make the world work better*. Ramp up relaxing music, fade to white.

My pitch got me to the shortlist. When I disclosed that I was an environmentalist and couldn't possibly make the film unless I cared passionately about Barrow's natural beauty, I could see Brad mentally writing out the cheque. This was exactly the kind of authenticity money couldn't buy. I'd struck my Faustian bargain: the gig was in the bag. I signed off with a final request, and the PR team were all ears: "I'm about to go to North Korea to make a film about Kim Jong Il's propaganda techniques," I said. "Would you mind if I included my work for General Electric in the final cut?" There was a nervous cough in Manhattan, on the other side of the world. Brigita said she'd Skype me back. The gig went to some music-video makers in Melbourne.

"This Would Never Happen in Pyongyang," I thought with a grin, pleased to have lost a pitch for the first time in my life. I went to celebrate in the local pub and discovered that the beautiful old art-deco bar had been ripped out and replaced by the flat-screen TVs of developers hungry for the corporate dollar. The cacophony of rugby games and SUV commercials was a neurological assault—but that didn't matter: the patrons were all wearing headphones and texting people who weren't there. *"This Would Never Happen in Pyongyang,"* I sighed into my bourbon, wondering what my North Korean friends would make of it all. Would they look at this homogenised, increasingly soulless city

of mine and conclude that the system I live in is sick? Would they see it as proof that capitalism creates a moral vacuum, producing people so wedded to consumption they've forgotten how to connect? Once my North Korean friends had gotten over their Western-gadget envy, would they still want to defect?

Perhaps not, I decided, as I escaped to cosmopolitan Potts Point for dinner. My closest friend and I were meeting the ABC producer who had given me Kim's manifesto for my fortieth birthday. I couldn't wait to see her: she was the only person I knew who had been to North Korea. She was politically more conservative than me, but even if she hadn't drunk the Kool-Aid, she was morally obliged to humour me—it was partly thanks to her, after all, that my life was stuck on this crazy trajectory now. We sat down to delicate trays of tapas and toasted each other with Margaret River champagne. Then I began to share my rose-tinted views on North Korea. And everything turned to shit.

The producer was disgusted I could dare defend anything about the place. Her work with a source deep inside the gulags had left no room for positivity. The cruelty she'd been told about was horrific, and North Korea was beyond evil. Case closed. My friend gracefully tried to change the subject, but I rankled. Sure, the regime was brutal. But did that justify writing off the entire country? Didn't slamming North Korea's prisons smack of hypocrisy, when Australia locked up refugee children on Manus Island and Nauru, and the USA ran torture chambers in Guantanamo, imprisoned terror suspects without trial, and had the highest incarceration rate in the world? With one-quarter of the globe's prisoners on US soil, and one in three African American men destined for jail at some point in their lives, was North Korea the only gulag state? And what about America's culture of violence, where you were more likely to be shot than killed in a car crash, and violence in PG-13 movies had tripled in the past twenty years? How could anyone condone the US and its allies attacking North Korea, when America had invaded fifty sovereign nations since World War II, and North Korea was yet to invade one?

The producer shot me down with one word: freedom. We had choice; they did not. "Yeah, choice to consume crap and be brain-washed by ads and destroy the planet," I kvetched. But the producer wasn't buying it. And nor was my friend. It's always a mistake to play the quid pro quo card on North Korea: you can't win. I slunk back into the night to find a hundred-dollar parking fine on my windshield and a junkie slumped in vomit under the fender. *"This Would Never Happen in Pyongyang,"* I grumbled, as I shook the junkie awake.

One block down, someone was shattering the pre-dawn calm with a leaf blower. I remembered the old woman in Pyongyang, silently sweeping the sidewalk with her ancient stick broom.

I couldn't wait to go back.

THE EXPLODING
SOUND RECORDIST

THE RED HOTEL IN BEIJING IS a fleapit of broken antiques and grimy wallpaper. I'm not bothered: our budget is going on the screen. I have a state-of-the-art Sony F3 HD camera with a PL mount, a 5D DSLR for stills, and three beautiful ground-glass Zeiss lenses. In the cubicle next door, my cinematographer Nicola Daley is programming the hard drives. In ten minutes, we'll meet Sam, our sound recordist, to pick up the lights. We've been planning for weeks now. Our visas are waiting at the North Korean embassy, our batteries are charged, and we have tools for every conceivable emergency. This time tomorrow, we'll be on Air Koryo, bound for ten days in Pyongyang.

I sort through my stuff, wondering if I should risk taking in a copy of the *Inner West Argus*. The community newspaper has an article about the Sydney Park gas mine on the front page. It also has full-page ads for Dan Murphy's vodka and brothel listings with colourful shots of naked Asian babes and pneumatic blondes called Tiffany and Cheyenne. I'm sure this makes the paper "offensive foreign literature." But I slip it into my suitcase anyway—under my battered copy of Kim Jong Il's manifesto. I've hidden the film files on my laptop in folders with innocuous labels, like "Healthy Lunch Boxes" and "Holiday

Gymnastics." I've also printed a sanitised blurb about our project, with the Koryo Tours logo stamped on top, in case any North Korean guard wants to know what we're doing. The royal wedding stamp of Wills and Kate I'm smuggling in for Eun is tucked in with the Band-Aids in my first-aid box.

The film's official, Ms. K, has been emailing me regularly from Korfilm to coordinate the shoot. But she's only vaguely aware of the video I've made to show the North Korean filmmakers. It features my actors and the gorgeous park we're trying to save and is full of images of comfortable Sydney homes and pretty beaches, with sparkling exteriors of happy crowds. These are not the kinds of images the North Koreans usually see of the West, and I've chosen them deliberately. The regime has just arrested a Christian missionary for distributing Biblical pamphlets, and I know it will take a dim view of my thinly veiled attempt to counter the anti-Western propaganda Mr. Pak and his colleagues have been fed. I hide the video in a folder called "Self-Saucing Puddings" and stick a backup copy on a USB stick, concealed in the lid of a pen.

I knock on the wall to let Nic know it's time. As we head down to the lobby to meet Sam, I am filled with the soothing conviction that there is nothing that can go wrong. I'm more prepared for this shoot than I've ever been in my life.

Sam is a Beijing-based Canadian who records international "posh docs" for National Geographic and Discovery. His website shows him in headphones, laughing and tanned, standing in exotic tropical locations surrounded by bikini-clad women. I hired him online after receiving a glowing recommendation from a soundman I worked with in Hong Kong. Despite Sam's party-boy persona, he has been nothing but efficient for the past four weeks: hiring mics for our camera, sourcing battery-operated lights for Pyongyang's power outages, and answering every email. In short, doing everything a soundman and fixer is supposed to do.

We step out of the lift, excited to be meeting our new collaborator in person. The lobby is empty, apart from a dirty figure in a hoodie, slumped in the corner. I check my watch: Sam must be late. When I look up, the hoodie is staggering towards us, pinprick pupils blazing in his chalky white face. "Let's get this trip to butt-fuck-nowhere on the road," he slurs and holds out a trembling hand. Sam, not to put too fine a point on it, is shit-faced. Nic and I pack our gear into his van, relieved that he's had the foresight to hire a driver. Our first stop is the North Korean embassy, and all the way there, Sam keeps up a fast-paced babble about how he wants to get drunk in the Yangakkdo's revolving restaurant, trash his room, and swim naked in the pool. When he asks Nicola if she brought her leopard-print bikini so they can have "an awesome time together," it's clear we have a problem.

In the embassy, we fill out forms under the cool gaze of a North Korean visa officer, and Sam can barely hold his pen. When I ask if he's brought a passport photo, he explodes. "*What* photo? You never told me I needed a fucking photo! Your whole outfit, lady, totally sucks. You got retards working for you in Australia. They're fucking hopeless. You're lucky you got a professional like me on board. No one ever told me about a photo. Fuck. Fuck. Fuck!" Sam stomps up and down, frothing at the mouth. He's having a full-blown meltdown, right there in the North Korean embassy—with armed guards outside, an increasingly inquisitive visa officer, and the Dear Leader smiling down from the wall. I calm Sam down enough to get him out of the building. He stumbles off to find an instant photo booth, agreeing to come back in half an hour.

I go back inside to find Nicola and the visa officer locked in a solemn face-off. I apologise as best I can for Sam's behaviour: "He was anxious he might not get everything you need in time. And he has been very . . . sick." The officer looks at me, poker-faced. Then, to our amazement, he stamps visas into all of our passports—and breaks into a huge grin. I guess no one's behaved like that inside the North Korean embassy before. We skip out, eager to tell Sam the good news. But Sam and the van have vanished. With mounting horror, we list everything we left in the van: two expensive cameras, three North Korean plane tickets, all our travel documents, €55,000 in cash, and both our mobile phones. We have no choice but to stay where we are, and pray.

Two hours pass. The heat is horrific. Every time we try to sit under a tree on the kerb, the armed North Korean guard waves at us to stand. Just when we've decided the whole shoot is doomed, the van trundles back with everything inside. Bar Sam. We plead with the driver to take us to Sam's house, and he refuses point blank. It costs me a lot of money, and a long argument involving handdrawn stick figures and a Chinese dictionary, to persuade him not to dump us back at the Red Hotel but take us instead to the gear-hire place, so we can pick up the lights.

I spend the rest of the afternoon leaving urgent messages on Sam's voicemail. North Korean movies are post-dubbed, which means that no one in Pyongyang knows how to use a lapel mic, let alone a boom. With visas taking over four months to secure, it's too late to find another sound recordist. We grab a coffee with Nick Bonner at Café Egypt, and he shares our alarm. He's not going in this time, and won't be there to protect us if anything goes wrong. I have a mental flash of Sam, high on God knows what, hurling himself from the top of the Yangakkdo to take a dip in the Taedong River, or dropping the F-bomb in front of the soldiers at the DMZ. Reluctantly, I agree with Nick that it is probably not wise to take a soundman on drugs into North Korea. Unless I can work some miracle, I am about to make a silent documentary in Pyongyang.

One hour before our flight, Sam still hasn't made contact. Nic and I push three huge trolleys of gear up to the Air Koryo check-in desk, praying they'll let us use Sam's baggage allocation for the sound equipment we've had to hire. As we're loading boxes onto the belt, Sam finally calls: to inform me, helpfully, that he isn't "the right man for the job." He is sober and full of remorse. Just before Nic and I got to Beijing, Sam explains, he received disturbing personal news from Canada and went on a three-day bender to cope. The fact he's on an antidepressant called Paxil didn't help: when mixed with alcohol, Paxil can make you psychotic. I hang up, cursing Big Pharma for damaging another crucial relationship in my life. I feel sorry for Sam; he seems decent. But thanks to him, I am going to a country that doesn't record sync sound—without a sound recordist.

I'd sue Paxil if I thought it would make a difference. But somehow, I suspect the fact that Sam was about to shoot in North Korea had something to do with his meltdown. It's that kind of place.

A PERFUME
NAMED KIM

Our country is the three thousand Ri golden tapestry-like land linked with the same mountain range.

KIM JONG IL: A LIFE

I SHOULDN'T BE SURPRISED: IN THE three hours it's taken us to fly to Pyongyang, the formidable Ms. K has solved our sound problem.

Mr. Wang is stocky and assured, with a shaving plaster stuck to his chin. He has agreed to be trained as our boom swinger, and is the fourth member of our North Korean crew. He shakes our hands brusquely and introduces us to the other three: the handsome gaffer Mr. Q; the taciturn driver from my last trip; and gum-chewing Sun Hi, our pretty new interpreter. Ms. K explains that Eun is too busy with the Pyongyang International Film Festival, and I am secretly relieved. Sun Hi has none of Eun's too-cool-for-school languor. She's alert and vibrant with a cheeky glint in her eyes. With her purple mascara and strappy sandals, Sun Hi could be just another K-pop-loving girl in Seoul. I wonder if she'd like the Wills and Kate stamp I smuggled in. "I am excited to make your film; it is crazy good!" she says, beaming, and I know she'll love the stamp. As the men load our gear into the van, I decide to find a way to give it to her.

The city has subtly transformed in the two months we've been away. The Cheshire Cat Kim Jong Il portraits have gone, replaced by freshly painted murals of Kim Jong Un, rocking his "youth ambition" hair. In the distance, behind the gleaming tenements, cranes are erecting a new building. The slogans are new too: *Generalissimo Kim Jong Il is eternally with us! Let us follow our Young Comrade General Kim Jong Un One Thousand Miles!* Our van, on the other hand, is the same as before: battered but clean, with no discernible branding and no air-conditioning. Pyongyang's pretty boulevards flash past in the stifling 113-degree heat, and I feel oddly grateful for my Kim Kardashian perfume. It was an ironic gift from my ex: props for having secured an access-all-areas shoot inside the most anti-capitalist industry in showbiz. He and I are still battling over money, but as parents, we've built a fragile peace. I have a flash of him guiding our laughing daughter through Maroubra's crashing surf, hugging her new boogie board. And I'm flooded with thanks that through all our torment, he's remained a kind and loving dad.

The van cruises under the glittering flame of the Juche Tower and onto Tongdaewon Street. The *Mad Men* extras are out in full force today: crew-cut men in beige stroll along baking pavements with lacquered women in twinsets cooling themselves with pink silk fans. Nic and I sit wedged between our North Korean minders, sweating. I twist open my perfume and give my neck a surreptitious spritz. Sun Hi, who's been studying me closely ever since we got in the van, squeals with delight. "Oh!" she says, gazing at the word *Kim* on the bottle. "You have a perfume named after the Dear Leader!" Nic and I share a look. How do you explain Kim Kardashian to someone who has never heard of reality TV?

"Would you like to try?" I ask Sun Hi.

She giggles and dabs a little on her wrist. "That's nice!" she says blissfully, and before the driver can stop her, she squirts him behind his ear. He makes a big show of being thoroughly affronted, as his macho status demands. Then he wafts the air theatrically towards his nose, and orders Sun Hi to squirt him again. She does so with gusto, and everyone laughs. If this is how a North Korean film crew behaves, I'm sure we're going to get on. I'm also sure that if they knew of the trashy celebrity culture that spawned the Kardashians, they wouldn't be laughing.

"Senior Comrade Pak likes your film script," says Ms. K. For the past month, Ms. K has emailed me every two days telling me to hurry up and deliver. The pressure of writing for her has made working for a Western producer feel like a cakewalk: each time I reply to Ms. K to buy more time, I know my emails are being examined not just by her, but also by every Party official and cadre connected to Korfilm. I wonder what they've made of my bizarre attempt to reproduce the key tropes of the North Korean propaganda movie in the middle of Sydney. I have faithfully included a suffering working-class heroine, people randomly bursting into song, sentimental nature metaphors, two chaste star-crossed lovers, and an evil capitalist who comes to a sticky end. The only thing I've left out is a speech celebrating the Dear Leader.

"Did you like the script?" I ask Ms. K, wondering if she has an issue with the glaring absence of Kim Jong Il.

She gives me her most enigmatic smile: "Thank you for working very hard on it."

Ms. K, pragmatically, is leaving the feedback to others. She's scheduled plenty: starting with a three-hour "artistic criticism session" with North Korea's top filmmakers. If my script is the hamfisted turkey I suspect it is, I'm sure that Mr. Pak and the People's Artists Ms. K has thoughtfully assembled will waste no time bashing it into shape.

The Gardener
A short film in the style of Kim Jong Il

SC 1—POND—SYDNEY PARK—DAWN

A majestic pelican floats in a pond. Karen (40s), in overalls, plants flowers.

KAREN *(voice-over)*: The pelican is a noble bird. Celebrated from ancient times as a symbol of motherly sacrifice, the pelican will gouge her own chest to feed her blood to her young. Once, I had to be like the pelican . . .

The pelican flies into the sky. Zoom in to Karen, watching in wonder. Gentle music surges.

SC 2—KITCHEN—HUMBLE ERSKINEVILLE COTTAGE—DAY

Karen sews a button onto the jacket of her railway-worker husband Al (48). At the table, their pretty daughter Sally (20) does maths on an iPad.

AL: You'll get square eyes.

KAREN: Now, now, leave her alone.

AL: Not my fault she got your brains and my looks . . . She'll scare off the boys!

Sally glares at Al. Karen kisses her daughter softly.

KAREN: Ignore him, hon. Love you.

Karen follows Al, giggling, down the corridor. Sally, despite herself, smiles.

SC 3—ERSKINEVILLE VILLAGE—DAY

Al grabs his guitar from the porch and strolls with Karen through the village, singing.

AL: Why do I love this village, why do I love this town? Come with me and I'll show you the way, show you what I see now. Laneways of smiling faces, backyards, we skip away, to the beautiful park we dream of, easy like a summer's day.

They round the corner. Karen is suddenly playing a piano accordion. The

Flower Seller, the Grocer and the Pharmacist wave at them happily, joining in the chorus.

SHOPKEEPERS: We love this village, we love this village. We love this village, we love this town!

Karen and Al reach the train station. Karen waves Al off, then stops. A gleaming new sign is stuck on the wall: NEW FUEL FOR THE VILLAGE: GAS!

KAREN *(troubled)*: Gas . . .?

SC 4—TAE KWON DO COMMUNITY DOJO—NIGHT

Sally does a perfect tae kwon do pattern. Students spar in the background. Mitch (30s), slick hair, gleaming new outfit, watches.

MITCH: "Heaven Earth" pattern with axe kick. Nice. Teach a humble white-belt?

Sally studies Mitch, instantly attracted. Hiding it, she shows him the pattern.

SALLY: Where are you from?
MITCH: Up north.
SALLY: To do what?
MITCH: It's complex. You won't understand unless you're an engineer. What do you do?

Mitch reaches out, gently, to move a wisp of hair from Sally's face. She almost lets him touch her—then—WHACK! She grabs his arm, throws him on her back and dumps him on the mat.

SALLY *(coolly)*: I'm an engineer.

Mitch gazes at Sally, in love.

SC 5—ERSKINEVILLE TOWN HALL—NIGHT

A Needle Energy banner sits on a stage—showing a small gas well, surrounded by flowers. Riccard, Needle's suave South African CEO, addresses Karen, Al, Sally, and Villagers.

RICCARD: CSG. Clean. Sustainable. Green. Smaller than a tennis court, a Needle well delivers natural gas straight to your home—raising its value as you sleep! To make your transition a happy one, please welcome community liaison officer, Mitch Pounder.

The Villagers clap. Sally looks up, delighted, as Mitch takes the mic.

MITCH: Thanks, boss. Ladies and gents, I've only been here a short time. But I've already fallen in love with your wonderful village—and the beautiful people who live here.

Mitch looks flirtatiously at Sally. Sally blushes. Karen puts up her hand.

SALLY *(whispering)*: Mum. Don't. Please . . . !
MITCH: Yes, ma'am?
KAREN *(standing)*: I hear coal seam gas is destroying the farms.

The Villagers look at Karen, surprised. Sally, mortified, shrinks into her seat.

KAREN: There's a farmer up north whose soil is turning to salt. His kids are getting nosebleeds. There's methane in his water, and he's not getting any answers! I'm just a gardener; I'm no expert. But are you selling us something we don't need?

The Villagers murmur, alarmed. Mitch is smoothly reassuring.

MITCH: Thank you, ma'am. I hear your concern. There's a lot of anxiety about fracking—delicious word, isn't it? Fracking.

Sally giggles. Riccard hands a jar full of clear fluid to Mitch.

MITCH: This is frack fluid: 95 percent sand; the rest is just guar gum and water. We're only building a test well here—we'd never frack anywhere before a proper safety report is done. But you know what? It's completely safe.

Mitch drinks the fluid.

VILLAGERS *(impressed)*: Ooh.

Riccard grins and jumps off the stage.

RICCARD: He can be so scientific sometimes. Seriously, folks, I love your country. My grandkids were born here. I have koalas on my bush block. If I thought CSG was harmful in any way, I would not be here.

Riccard moves confidently through the crowd, giving Karen a malevolent look.

RICCARD: So let's forget the fearmongers and doomsday soothsayers. The fact is, you will all be warming your tootsies in front of eco-friendly, gas designer fires within a year. And this village—your village—will be the envy of the world.

The Villagers clap, won over. Karen looks at Al, troubled. He smiles and pats her hand.

AL: They're the experts, love.

SC 6—POND—SYDNEY PARK—DUSK

Karen bends in the reeds, pulling weeds. Muttering angrily to herself.

RICCARD (*off-screen*): SIS Drill One runs under here.

Karen, surprised, peers over the reeds. Riccard and Mitch study a drill map of the park.

RICCARD: Eight horizontal drills in total, running beneath the village back to the main hub. It's the illusion I find so beautiful—from the surface, a toothpick. Underneath, a five-kilometre river of gold.

Mitch and Riccard move closer. Karen ducks.

RICCARD: We'll start phase one now. We'll have everything extracted before they know we've begun.
MITCH: What about the safety report?
RICCARD: Stuff the safety report.
MITCH: But . . . that's chemicals, compressor ponds . . . that's a full-scale frack!
RICCARD: Fact one. Fact two? We're legal, remember? Those NIMBY idiots own five centimetres of the soil under their poxy houses. The rest belongs to me, the minister, and China. Got it?

MITCH: Got it.

The men walk off. We stay on Karen, grim with rage. Military music starts.

SC 7—HILL—SYDNEY PARK—NIGHT
Karen, carrying secateurs, strides up the moonlit hill. Determination in her eyes. Close-ups of secateurs, flashing back and forth. Dirt flying through the air. Sweat, forming on her brow.

SC 8—HILL—SYDNEY PARK—DAWN
The music surges as Karen, secateurs raised high, stands heroically against

the sun. We crane above her. In the grass, Karen's made a sign out of flowers: STOP CSG. A camera flashes. Karen blinks.

It's Riccard.

RICCARD: Very pretty. You're a vandal.

KAREN: You come here, you destroy our land, you send your profits overseas, and you call me a vandal? I'll shed my own blood before I let you harm one inch of this beautiful place!

RICCARD: Sweetie, that's not going to stop me.

KAREN: The people will, in their thousands!

RICCARD *(walking off)*: Invite me when they show up.

SALLY *(off-screen)*: Mum!

Sally runs over the hill. Riccard, amused, stops and photographs her. Sally clocks Karen's CSG sign.

SALLY: What is that?

KAREN: They're drilling under the park.

RICCARD: I've no idea what she's talking about.

KAREN: He's lying! Sally, he's —

SALLY *(interrupting)*: I'm sick of it, Mum! Your pathetic stunts, your stupid old ideas! Not everyone is evil!

MITCH *(off-screen)*: Shall I call security?

Mitch, running up to Riccard, sees the sign and laughs. Sally's appalled.

KAREN *(to Mitch)*: Tell her you're using chemicals! You're going to frack this park!

MITCH: I think your mother needs a nice warm bath.

SALLY *(quietly)*: She is not my mother.

Sally walks off with Mitch and Riccard. Karen is devastated.

SC 9—POND—SYDNEY PARK—"THE GARDENER'S SONG"—DAY

Karen, full of pain, walks through the park, singing. She passes a turtle on a rock. A kookaburra in a tree. A pelican in the reeds. Cygnets in the pond.

KAREN: A tender love binds creatures in the wild, the love of mother for her child. Her strength and care guides all from soil to sky, she works and fights so her babe may fly. I plant seeds in the spring, I water them in summer. I prune in the autumn, defend them in the winter.

Karen stops by the pond. As she sings, we see Al—sewing a button on his jacket, alone. And Sally and Mitch sparring together in the dojo, in love.

KAREN: I seed and water tending for my daughter even though she cannot see, the bond is torn that once linked her to me, I fight for her but must set her free.

Karen sinks in the mud and stares at her reflection in the pond. The water flickers red. Karen looks up. A gas plume shoots into the sky. The pelican flies off, screeching in fear.

SC 10—SYDNEY PARK—"TIME PASSING" MONTAGE—DAY

The park is dying. The needle mine shoots toxic flames into the dirty sky. A dead bird lies tangled in reeds. Dead fish drift in the pond. The flowers in Karen's sign wilt and die. Zoom out from Karen, alone on the hill, to a huge wide shot of the desolate park.

SC 11—MAIN STREET—ERSKINEVILLE VILLAGE—DAY

Sally walks through the village. The shopkeepers give her rotting tulips, some wilted corn.

FLOWER SELLER: For your mother.
GROCER: Tell her we miss her.

Sally, upset, crosses the road. Mitch is waiting. She brightens, grabs his hands.

SALLY: It's safe, right?

Mitch won't meet her gaze.

SALLY: Mitch . . .?
MITCH: I'm leaving. Come with me.

Sally stares at him with dawning horror. Then she lets go of his hands, and runs off.

MITCH: Sally!

Sally doesn't look round.

SC 12—HILL—SYDNEY PARK—DAY
Music surges as Sally, sobbing, runs up to Karen on the hill. They embrace.

SALLY: How can I make you forgive me?

Karen looks at Sally with quiet conviction.

KAREN: Help me to fight.

SC 13—ERSKINEVILLE TOWN HALL—DAY
Sally, Al, and Karen address the Villagers. They are sick and desperate.

SALLY: My mother once made a sign, alone. But in her heart, she made it for thousands.
AL: For the gardeners who toil in the park, the children who play in its valleys, the animals who depend on its water, we must finish what she started!

KAREN *(standing)*: We must fight not just for ourselves, but for farmers and workers everywhere!

The Villagers stand and cheer. Military music starts.

SC 14—HILL—SYDNEY PARK—DAY

A yellow "NO GAS" triangle appears over the rise, bobbing on a stick. Then two more. They are followed by Karen, Sally, and Al, singing as they march: NO CSG! Behind them, more Villagers appear. Riccard and Mitch look on.

RICCARD: It's meaningless. The media will forget it in a day.

A hundred more Villagers surge over the rise, singing lustily. Riccard, shrugging, walks off.

RICCARD: They've got no proof.

Mitch stares at Sally at the front of the crowd, singing proudly. She glares at him, defiant. He thinks hard. Then he runs after Riccard and grabs the drill map from his briefcase.

MITCH: Here's the proof, you prick!

Riccard punches Mitch hard and snatches back the map. Mitch staggers to his feet and Riccard raises his fist again—but Mitch blocks Riccard's arm, throws him on his back, and dumps him on the ground. It's the move Sally taught him at tae kwon do. Sally beams. Mitch runs up to her with the map. The lovers embrace. The Villagers cheer. We zoom out to a magnificent wide of the hill. Revealing a huge human sign, spelled out by one thousand villagers in the grass: STOP CSG. Riccard groans in the dirt, a broken man. Karen stands ecstatic in the middle of the crowd. As she speaks, the sign melts away—leaving her alone on the hill.

KAREN *(voice-over)*: That is the tale of how I, a simple gardener, united my village to defeat a powerful enemy. It is a tale repeating itself across the world as people rise up to defend what is theirs. Proving to the venal capitalists, once and for all—if you put profit before people, the People always win.

Karen strides up the hill. A pelican wings across the sky. Karen stops, watching it. Then she waves at us, and disappears over the rise.

THE END

DO YOU LIKE PORN?

MR. PAK ISN'T INTERESTED IN TALKING about my script. He wants to know if I like watching porn. Despite the fact we were late, arriving to find twenty of North Korea's finest filmmakers already waiting in chain-smoking silence, Pak rose to greet me like an old friend. "I missed you so much, I dreamt of the day I would hold your hand again," he said, and I held his hands, genuinely happy to see him. Now he's bantering with me in Japanese as Nic lights the Kims on the wall.

"I guess I like French films that have some erotic scenes," I say, relieved that Pak's colleagues can't understand us.

He shakes his head: "I do not consider porn film at all." "But French films are not pornographic; they are art," Sun Hi says, blushing, coming to my defence.

Pak darkens: "Pornography is not film at all!"

I assume Pak's vehemence stems from the fact that sex has been banned from North Korean movies since Shin Sang Ok defected to LA. That famous close-up of Choi Eun Hee's thigh in *Salt* is now erased from the national memory. But Pak surprises me: "I have shot over seventy films, but sadly I haven't got to do a single sex scene yet," he says wistfully, and I realise the old man is not anti-sex; he just doesn't like being contradicted. The Man in Black enters the room, and Pak snaps back to Korean: "Although sex is a natural thing everyone does, it's not good for children's education, so we don't show it," he says, loudly. "In our country, we only make films that can be watched together by everybody, from little children to old people." I nod, struck by the oddness of a film industry without a classification system. Then again, when propaganda is the main game, and families attend each new release together, I guess it makes sense.

I show Mr. Wang how to plug the boom into the camera and angle it towards a person's mouth. Mr. Wang watches closely, then points the mic in exactly the wrong direction. Pak abuses him in rapid-fire Korean, but Mr. Wang is unfazed: "Tell the Comrade Director I shall do my best for her at all times," he says and lights a cigarette.

Pak, mollified, turns his attention to Nicola. "Your cameraman, is she married?" he asks pleasantly. Nicola blinks and keeps working. Female cinematographers are unheard of in North Korea, which to Pak is logical: "The equipment is too heavy for them, and anyway, they can't leave their children for long." I counter that Nicola, while single and childfree, is one of the top documentary shooters in Australia and Britain, lauded for her work in Iraq. "She is a brave and fearless comrade," Sun Hi embellishes supportively. "In Baghdad, she filmed inside the American bastards' tank."

Mr. Pak gazes at Nicola with new respect: "Nicola, we must give you a medal for being a freedom fighter," he says, enjoying the irony.

I check the viewfinder. Our first shot is a brazen product placement for Apple. The designers of the MacBook Pro would probably be astonished to know that right now their computer is sitting on a coffee table in Pyongyang under a picture of Kim Jong Il, being scrutinised by North Korea's top directors, writers, and movie stars. I plug in a puck-sized speaker I bought in Beijing, and the North Koreans watch carefully, taking care not to appear too impressed by my state-of-the-art gadgets. Then I tell Pak to press Play, and he looks at me blankly. I show him where the space bar is and how to manoeuvre the mouse. Frowning with concentration, Pak reaches out a stiff finger and pokes the keyboard. The Man in Black opens his notebook, and the video I made in Sydney starts.

"Annyeong hashimnikka," I wave from a bench in Sydney Park. "Thank you for helping us make *The Gardener*." Bucolic shots of casually dressed Sydneysiders follow: walking their dogs, barbequing chops, playing frisbee with kids by the swan-filled ponds. My beautiful heroine, Susan Prior, appears, meditating under a gum tree. "What I like most about Kim Jong Il's manifesto is he says that acting is a noble profession," Susan tells the filmmakers. "Oh—and just because I meditate every day doesn't mean I don't have fun." The North Koreans smile at Susan, charmed. I wink at Nic. This is going well.

Next up is our evil fracker Riccard, played by heartthrob Peter O'Brien. He rides into frame on a Harley, skidding to a stop on the wave-pounded cliffs of Coogee. "I want to know what films from the West you've seen," Peter says, grinning, "particularly the ones that I'm in." The North Koreans lean closer, fascinated by the bad-guy montage of Peter—beating up cops, kissing men in nightclubs, and smoking cigars in a spa—in everything from the Aussie crime soap *Underbelly* to the UK hit series *Queer as Folk*.

The video switches to the leafy suburbs, and my star-crossed lovers appear. Matt Zeremes sits in a toy-strewn lounge room and asks the North Koreans to teach his five-year-old son "how to jump over trees, like your awesome kung-fu fighter in *Hong Kil Dong*." The filmmakers nod, delighted, and gorgeous Kathryn Beck strolls into view, reading Kim's manifesto in the sun-kissed streets of Bronte. "What I love about your movies is the sincerity of the acting," she says dreamily, looking out at the mansions fronting the beach. "I also want to know if you believe in extraterrestrials and life after death."

The North Koreans stare at her, baffled. Their confusion intensifies when my actors line up and wave, under the closest thing Sydney has to a North Korean propaganda mural, the wall-sized Martin Luther King *I Have a Dream* painting in Newtown. "Hello, North Korea, we have the Internet!" Matt yells over the traffic, and Pak frowns.

The video segues to Elliott Weston, the gardener's husband, drinking merlot in his kitchen and imagining working in Pyongyang: "If I was a People's Artist, and I could write and act in *whatever I chose*, I'd love to live in North Korea!" he chuckles. Elliott picks up a guitar and strums his Kim Jong Il–inspired song over sumptuous wides of Sydney Park. "*We live and work as one, with all the children laughing, and everybody's happy always,*" Elliott sings with Juche joy, and the camera zooms in to a black swan in a reed-lined pond: the perfect negative of the white swan on the wall behind the now very confronted North Koreans.

I close the laptop. Pak leans back and exhales. The other nineteen filmmakers look stunned.

"Did you like my cast?" I ask.

Pak ashes his fag, and we wait for him to speak. He takes his time. "We were quite impressed," he says at last. "People working in the West—actors and filmmakers—are like us. They are not bound by formality; they wear comfortable clothes." He pauses. "They don't groom themselves much." The filmmakers titter.

"I like the actors you've chosen," Ms. Yun intervenes sweetly. "Even though they live far away, I feel close to them, because we do the same job." Miss N, the athletic young actress Pak has chosen to instruct Kathryn, says she finds my actors very good looking. The other women nod happily, and Miss N continues: "I want Kathryn to know I have heard about extraterrestrials. But I don't believe in them. As far as life after death goes, in our country, we live eternal life politically. I'm not talking about the eternal life that Buddhism and other doctrines teach. Physical life has a limit: it ends some day. But, here, our people can live without worries, even if they just live for one day. As the saying goes: *A tiger leaves his skin behind him*. We know that if we devote our life to our Party, the future generations will remember us, and we will live forever. I think your script is also based on such a love, for the home town and the future."

Edith, a soft-spoken editor with a mannish look that would brand her as gay in the West, looks at me shyly: "I like that the director is female," she says, and I wonder if she is gay. Edith edited Mr. Ri's 2010 film *Do People Know You*, an intimate buddy movie about a Party chairwoman and her ambitious female manager. When the manager cuts the workers' pay to improve profits, the chairwoman sacks her and forces her to repair shoes in a shed until she learns to serve her people with love. The film ends with the two women embracing passionately on a hill—but with the regime's view of homosexuality as decadent and immoral, I can't ask Edith if the Sapphic undertones are intentional. Instead, I stick to my script: does she think that using the Dear Leader's techniques to film it will work? "What a ridiculous question," Edith snaps. "Needless to say, our Great Leader Kim Jong Il is a genius in filmmaking, and this is recognised by the world. I think your question is nonsense."

Edith shuts down in disgust, and Ms. Jang, a ringletted rom-com writer, fills in the silence. "I found your script touching," she says kindly. "I get positive feelings from it. I like the fact it portrays Karen's character through a pelican. I have never seen a pelican, but from your footage it looks a noble, righteous, and meaningful creature. Just like this bird, Karen will gather others to fight for her village. I also think the lyrics are well written. They talk about the change of seasons. And in the end, the image of the pelican, associated with motherly love, is linked to patriotism. I am not talking about straightforward patriotism here. I think anyone in the world who knows the meaning of justice and beauty will share the meaning of your film. I hope it is the beginning of a beautiful friendship between our two countries. Thank you for writing it."

I thank Ms. Jang, grateful to whoever it was at Korfilm who translated my cheesy screenplay into the poetry she appears to have read. Then I remember that cheese is an acceptable part of a North Korean propaganda movie, and allow myself to feel proud. The blunt Mr. Ri knocks me back to earth: "I disagree with Comrade Jang. The actors are okay, but your script is boring. It is a mistake to open with the pelican. It's so bloody dull! You should cut straight to the action."

Mr. Pei, the composer, joins the attack: "It was nice to hear Comrade Elliott sing an Australian folk tune," he says. "But I found the lyrics for the gardener's song too sentimental and over the top, especially with pelicans flapping around all over the place. So I took the liberty of changing them." He flushes with embarrassment: "Now I'm worried you won't like what I have written."

Over-the-top sentimentality is the one thing that unites every North Korean film song I've heard, I think crossly, but I nod brightly at Mr. Pei, reassuring him that I'll love what he's done.

Pak, enjoying the frisson between us, picks up my script: "Anna, that badge on your bosom is the message of your screenplay," he says, pointing at the No Gas triangle pinned to my dress. "I think that Karen is you, and the pelican is your heart." I nod at Pak, wondering what lethal blow this wily man is softening me up for. "The seed of your film is the same as *Sea of Blood*," he continues. "As defined by our Dear Leader, the seed of that masterpiece is: *We must convert a bloody sea of ordeals into a bloody sea of struggle.* In other words, you might be able to break one sprig of bush clover, but when you bunch them together, you cannot break them. In the end, the village people achieve victory and safeguard their home town. It is a beautiful story. For the same reason, your script is quite touching. I enjoyed it."

I smile at Pak, secretly cursing him for setting the bar so high. I've already seen the Kim Jong Il Film Museum, where a marble chart lists each of Kim's 11,870 "on-the-spot guidance" visits to film sets. An entire hall is devoted to one magnificent painting celebrating Kim's most famous visit, to *Sea of Blood*. That film is a monumental epic shot on three cameras (thanks to the Dear Leader), with thousands of extras, extraordinary battles, and exquisite lighting. There's no way I'll be able to replicate its grandeur and intensity. But it is comforting to know that Pak thinks my script is okay. In fact, I'm surprised how nice he's being about it.

Nic and I take the filmmakers outside and ask them to stand under the stunning mural of Kotpun from *Flower Girl*. The shot is designed to match the one of my Australian actors in Newtown, waving under the mural of Martin Luther King. The filmmakers obligingly line up in the grass, their heads nudging Kotpun's enormous sandals. "Hello, people in Australia," Pak calls to our camera, leading the filmmakers in a group wave. As Nic pans back and forth, he keeps up a running commentary, making everyone giggle. Sun Hi, for some reason, won't translate. It's only weeks later, when I hand the rushes to an intepreter back in Sydney, that I realise Pak has had the last laugh.

"Hello, Australia! Don't come and start another war again!" Pak is saying as he waves. "If you come back and invade us like you did in the '50s, there will be a *big* problem."

"We won't forgive you," Mr. Ri chimes in, waving enthusiastically.

"No way," adds the waving Ms. Jang.

"Forget it," giggles Mr. Pei.

"Oh God, her camera's coming back again," says Pak—and cracks an even bigger smile: "Hello, Australia! You'd better watch out! We may look happy to see Anna now, but . . ."

"Fantastic, thank you!" I call out, to Pak's delight. "Cut!"

YOUR DEAR LEADER, BOB BROWN

"OMG," I WHISPER TO NIC AS the man in the grey safari suit runs into the bushes with our passports.

Sun Hi, who is proving to be a keen student of Western slang, wants to know what the acronym means. "Oh my God," I explain, giving her a crash course in texting shorthand. "There's also ROFL—rolling around on the floor laughing—and if something is *really* funny, you ROFLMFAO—which means you roll around on the floor laughing your arse off." I leave out the "fucking"—Sun Hi looks virginal enough to be offended.

"ROFLMFAO," Sun Hi parrots happily, rolling the letters on her tongue. Then she grins: "Right back atcha, honey!" That's something I said to Nic when we were packing up after yesterday's shoot. Sun Hi, who is wearing the pink koala cap we gave her with a No Gas pin stuck proudly on the top, learns fast. "We are Team Gas!" she exclaims, and Mr. Wang and Q, who've attached No Gas pins to their lapels, nod supportively.

"Soon we will arrive at the April 25 Military Film Studio," says Ms. K, ignoring my anxiety about our passport-less state. "April 25 is the auspicious day our Supreme Generalissimo Kim Il Sung led the glorious People's Uprising on Jeju Island against the imperialist Japs. You must only film inside. No filming out the window. At all."

I nod, trying to block out the images of the language teachers, computer programmers, engineers, and other experts North Korea has kidnapped over the decades to upskill its people. I'm not keen to emulate the career paths of superstar South Korean filmmakers Shin Sang Ok and Choi Eun Hee, whom Kim Jong Il kept in the gulags until they agreed to work for him. Then again, as a jobbing documentary maker from Erskineville, I'm hardly glamorous enough to kidnap. Comforted by this thought, I focus on our shoot.

The April 25 Military Film Studio has none of the laid-back outdoorsiness of the Pyongyang Film Studio. The treeless concrete bunker is accessed by an imposing road barred from the public by a gate with a red star. A gun-toting guard scans a document Ms. K shows him and slides the gate back on rusting wheels. We drive up to the steps of the building, where the Man in Black is waiting with a clipboard. He barks angrily at Ms. K: we are exactly six and a half minutes late. The April 25 Military Film Studio only makes war movies, using an arsenal of real planes, tanks, battleships, and bombs to create epic battle scenes, all shot in camera. Judging from the way Ms. K is begging the Man in Black's forgiveness, it's clear this place runs its shoots—and everything else it does—with uncompromising military precision.

I apologise profusely, and the Man in Black ignores me and marches inside. We hurry after him down the usual gloomy corridors. It may be sunny outside, but inside this building—like everywhere else we've been—it's permanent twilight. We stop at the metal door of a large soundstage, without the On Air light you'd normally see in the West. The Man in Black slides the door open without knocking. In the middle of the studio is a softly glowing wooden hut, where a film shoot is in full swing. A beautiful young actress kneels in a tatami-mat room, speaking quietly to an autocratic, cross-legged man. Nic and I instinctively freeze: when you're in an enclosed space like this, the slightest sound can ruin a good take. But Mr. Wang and Q walk up to the hut, bang our boxes down on the porch, and unpack the gear. Then I remember—they're not recording sound.

"Cut!" calls an avuncular man in a porkpie hat, standing up from his camera to be introduced. Mr. O is the brilliant cinematographer of the most haunting North Korean movie I've seen, *A Broad Bellflower*. Mr. O and his director greet us warmly, their dark suits and ties the only things distinguishing them from their more-casual Pyongyang Film Studio colleagues. Q, Sun Hi, and Mr. Wang take off their shoes to climb inside the hut, and Nic and I follow suit. This is not for sound reasons: all Koreans remove their shoes before entering a house—even a fake one. The custom is as ancient as it is practical: it prevents dirt from getting in, and in this case, it protects the delicate tatami matting on the floor.

Mr. O is using a battered but lovingly maintained Arri 435 camera, with one assistant, one gaffer, and a focus puller. Everyone wears gloves. There are no metal light stands: the gaffer is angling the diffuser—a circle of opaque silk tacked to a thin wooden frame—by hand. The gaffer peers curiously at our Western version, a collapsible disc of space-age metallic fabric, which Q unfurls with quiet pride. We train our lens on the young actress, and I gasp at how she lights up the frame. Mr. O's minimal lighting suddenly makes sense: this woman is a human light bulb. She has the luminosity of a young Meryl Streep: an inner glow only the rarest actresses possess.

"Action!" calls the director, and the old actor looks at the woman firmly: "You must, in good conscience, live up to the expectations of the Party and work where the Party needs you," he says, and the director stops him immediately: "Don't lecture her. She hasn't done anything wrong. You're just being supportive of your daughter. Say it gently: 'You must be the patriot the fatherland expects you to be,' that kind of thing, but with affection." This simple direction transforms the propaganda into a touching scene of fatherly love. The actor repeats his take, and the young woman gives him a look of exquisite devotion. Mr. O looks up from his eyepiece: "That was terrific!" he says, beaming and flashing a row of gold-capped teeth.

Watching the woman's close-ups spool back in the April 25 Military Film Studio screening room, I feel like I've been teleported back to 1935. The only sound in the theatre is the nostalgic whirr of the projector, operated with grim authority by a soldier straight out of a Riefenstahl movie: short-haired and high-cheeked, with a dramatic slick of vermilion on her austere mouth. "It would be nice to have the sound of waves over that shot," muses Mr. O to the director, as dreamlike images of the actress and her father spool back in the muted dark: planting trees with soldiers, pointing binoculars at the misty sea, reading sepia books by Kim Jong Il on guano-spattered cliffs.

"What is your movie about?" I ask the director as the projectionist threads the next reel.

"The commander of a guardhouse, who protects an island in the East Sea," he replies. "We're making it so the commander can be a role model for the whole army. He's been admiring our General his whole life, from this remote island. He's determined to guard it until death." The projector cranks back to life and a magnificent seascape appears, drifting over choppy waves towards the desolate island.

"It is also about isolation," Mr. O says simply, confirming what I've sensed about him. Despite the propaganda he shoots, and his outwardly jolly manner, Mr. O has the soul of an artist—dedicated to capturing the pain and complexity of what it is to be human. *A Broad Bellflower*, when the Dear Leader speeches are removed, is extraordinary.

"Does the commander have an enemy?" I ask the filmmakers, wondering if their movie is being made in response to the naval military exercises that South Korea and its American allies conduct every year, just off North Korea's coast. "No," says the director, looking at our camera. "Although we are faced with the enemy in real situations, our movie does not show them. It just shows the lives of the soldiers guarding the island. There is a real dimension to it, in that we are under threat of the Americans attacking us. But our film is not about the actions we will take in response to their military exercises. It simply celebrates the determination of the soldiers to achieve battle-readiness."

I wonder if the director's careful explanation is designed to dissuade the Americans from analysing his film for clues in the future, clues that might make North Korea easier to invade. He turns to the screen, its silvery light illuminating his calm face, and I realize that invasion is the one thing that connects us across our otherwise uncrossable political divide. His invaders possess seventy thousand tonnes of nuclear firepower that could obliterate his country in an instant. My invaders have an arsenal of chemicals that could pollute our water for centuries. We are both making films to give people the conviction to fight.

But I also know the director would not be helping me now if the miners in *The Gardener* were Australian instead of South African. Without the bogeyman of a ruthless foreign invader, coal seam gas becomes a national enterprise—which is something that the North Koreans must support without question. If Kim Jong Un decided to frack the ancient forests of Mount Myohyang, the director and Mr. O—in public at least—would be unquestioningly behind it.

"I like the message of your film," the director says when the projection finishes, rising to shake my hand. "Unfortunately, I haven't had much opportunity to learn about Australian movies. But now you've visited us, I'd like you to communicate closely, so that we can make high-quality films together in the future."

"Filmmakers are family," I reply, touched.

The strange sense that we're all on the same creative page continues when we interview Mr. O and his designer, Mr. Kang, in a bare, low-ceilinged room bordered by rose bushes. Mr. O uses Nic's set-up time to examine our digital camera, and the fastidious Kang makes sure—just as a Western designer might—that our radio-mic wire does not obscure the Kim Jong Il pin on his perfectly starched lapel.

"Your movie is about preventing gas mining to preserve ecology," says Mr. O. "I like the gardener a lot. Setting her in beautiful scenery, you should use natural light to portray her as even more beautiful than she is in person. Just like the scenery, she should be shot in a fantasy-like way, with a neat and pretty silhouette. Don't just use camera techniques to do this. Use natural light, with lots of bounce light to make her eyes and skin tone come alive."

Kang is more guarded. He instructs me to make Riccard "exquisitely dressed, like a gentleman." North Korean film design appears to have evolved since Kim Jong Il instructed that the villain's costume should be "undesirable."

"Negativity is most of all expressed through the actor's skill," Kang confirms. "We don't just give the villain dark and cold colours because he is bad—and we don't use bright colours just because a character is a hero. If we did, it would feel too artificial. You also need to make your home village much more photogenic and clean than it looks. Perhaps Karen can have a plot of flowers in the middle of town, to act as a metaphor for the park."

Kang folds his arms, satisfied with his offering, and Mr. O chuckles: "Art directors are stubborn, aren't they? Once they decide something is perfect, but maybe not perfect from a director's perspective, there's conflict. But I trust Comrade Kang. So I let him take the lead." Both men are adamant that I should not use the fast-cutting that is trendy in the West. And both are absolute about the need to shoot on celluloid. "We are going digital, like the rest of the world," Mr. Kang says pointedly, glancing sideways at the Man in Black—who, as usual, is in the corner, taking notes. "But celluloid is indisputably more beautiful."

Mr. O nods. "We also use fast-cutting," he says, "but we prefer 'one cut per scene' to keep the emotional flow. This is how our Supreme General instructed us. I think in general, emotions are different from in the past. They are getting faster. Shooting and cutting are following the speed at which human emotions are changing. Older people, like me, like slower transitions."

I smile at this civilised man, agreeing entirely. Our feelings have sped up, along with our attention spans. The gentler storytelling he's advocating is more meditative—designed for viewers who still have time to imagine. And celluloid does have an organic beauty that even the most expensive HD cameras fail to replicate. I have no idea how to find film stock and processing labs in Sydney's aggressively digital post-production scene—but I'll try. And Kang's right too: Erskineville, on its bad days, is a grotty, junkie-infested dive, which would be vastly improved by some artfully planted flowers. The only thing I can't endorse is Kang's assertion that North Korean cinema is going digital. Everything we've seen so far places it firmly in the 1960s: the last decade of analogue.

"Your crew is working very hard," Mr. O observes, watching Nic adjust his light for a close-up. "I look forward to seeing your movie. I hope you can all keep the spirit up to the end!"

The Man in Black has left the room, bored by our technical chatter. Figuring this is as good a time as any, I pull out my smuggled copy of the *Inner West Argus*, unrolling it on the table. In this pristine room, it looks grimy and cheap. "This is a paper from Sydney," I say, pointing at a crumpled picture of protesters waving *No Gas* banners in Sydney Park.

"It is a small village paper," Sun Hi adds helpfully. "That's why it looks so humble. Those are her villagers, fighting the mine." Kang analyses the paper with the intensity of someone devouring a gourmet meal. Mr. O reads the headline in halting English: "*People Power vs Gas Mine!*"

"That's right!" I say. "But my script has no leader like Kim Jong Il. Is that a problem?" Sun Hi looks shocked by my dropping of the honorific, but dutifully translates. I am expecting Mr. O to give the same answer that Ms. Jang, the rom-com writer, gave yesterday: "People can only defeat a powerful enemy if they are led by someone as magnificent as Kim Jong Il and Kim Jong Un."

"But we don't respect our leaders like you do," I had protested, and she'd laughed at the absurdity of the idea.

"That's because they are letting gas destroy your farms. Given that fact, it is okay not to have a leader in your film," she said. "But is there really no great politician you look up to?"

Karen's grassroots leadership was clearly not enough: to be a true North Korean homage, my film needed a uniting figure of godlike proportions. "Well, there is this Greens senator called Bob Brown, but he's retired," I offered, and Ms. Jang's eyes lit up: "That doesn't matter. If Miss Anna likes him and he's against gas, then you must show the Dear Leader Bob Brown at the end of the film, standing with the villagers, surrounded by a golden light."

I thanked Ms. Jang, imagining the laconic Bob Brown in gold-framed Technicolor, beaming Kim Jong Il–style from Erskineville's dirty lampposts, and filed her idea away in my discards list—along with her suggestion I should rename my film *The Tranquil Pelican*.

Now, Mr. O has a new idea, and the audacity of it takes my breath away. "Rather than using a leader to say what you want to say, use people power," he says. "Show how powerful it can be. Even in our country, the true revolutionary hero is the People. People rally to protect the environment not just for the sake of it. They have a common interest, which is to use resources sparingly. This is the source of their power. If you can portray that in your movie, a leader isn't necessary." I ask Sun Hi to translate again, to make sure I'd heard her correctly. She does, and I did. Mr. O's cheerful smile hasn't changed, but he's just said the most subversive thing I've heard in North Korea: *The true hero is the People. A leader isn't necessary.*

We end the day with a tightly orchestrated ride on the subway. The entrance to Ponghwa Station is marked by a blazing portrait of a worker holding a Juche torch against the sky. The escalator ride down takes ten minutes: at 110 metres underground, the Pyongyang metro is one of the deepest in the world. It's also a useful bomb shelter, should the Americans ever decide to attack. I'm sure Kim Il Sung had this in mind when he designed the metro in the late 1960s: for the three hundred to seven hundred thousand citizens using it daily, Ponghwa Station is a glorious reminder that they live in a socialist paradise worth fighting for. The platform is a magnificent gallery of propaganda art, with lavish mosaics of fighters, workers, and the Leaders, all lit by crystal chandeliers. It leaves the extravagant St. Petersburg metro for dead. The shiny red-and-green carriages of the Chollima line slide up, and we step inside a wood-panelled cabin with the obligatory Kims on the wall. The cabin guard, a stout woman in a black suit with gold epaulettes, studiously ignores us—along with all eighteen of her passengers.

Exactly one stop later, Q and Sun Hi hurry us out—doing nothing to dispel the rumours that the remaining stations, which foreigners never see, are miserable cesspits, with none of the splendour dazzling us now. We step onto the gleaming floor of Yonggwang Station: an even more spectacular celebration of all things Juche. The staircases are marble, the chandeliers are gold, and from every wall, enormous Kims smile at the tiny passengers from exquisite mosaics. People wander around in the museum-like calm, peering at glass-mounted copies of today's *Pyongyang Times*.

In this web-free country, even the newsfeeds are works of art. Then the tranquillity is shattered by an explosion of laughter—as hundreds of children burst from the Chollima Line in a blur of red-and-blue sailor suits. They stream past us, lost in that chattering, school's-out-for-the-day excitement common to kids all over the world, and the guards and office ladies step out of their way with indulgent smiles.

I stand next to Nic as she films the children surging up the staircase, fingering a little strip of celluloid in my pocket. I found it under a rose bush at the April 25 Military Film Studio. It contains three precious frames of a young soldier, his eyes full of defiant pride. The children run past our camera, bursting with curiosity and excitement. And I remember Mr. O's words: *Even in our country, the true revolutionary hero is the People. A leader isn't necessary.*

MONROE HAD A VOLUPTUOUS FIGURE

FORGET THE FARMERS AND WORKERS: NORTH Korean artists are number one. Tang Tap is a monument to this fact. From its huge base, a sickle, hammer, and pen rise on stone pillars, the pen soaring highest of all. Creatives have always been valued by totalitarian leaders: Stalin and Lenin believed cinema was the most powerful art of all; Hitler, an amateur painter, lavished resources on Albert Speer and Leni Riefenstahl; Mussolini knew that a book and a gun made the perfect fascist; and Saddam commissioned lavish biopics to promote his own mythology—before the war with Kuwait diverted his funds. But none of them managed to blur the line between dictator and artist as successfully as Kim Jong Il.

"A cameraman should be able to use small things to portray a great thing," the Dear Leader wrote in his manifesto, and archival footage of Kim Jong Il expertly operating German film cameras shows he knew what he was talking about. Nic and I stand under the fifty-metre Tang Tap brush—a "small" thing the sculptors have managed to make truly great—and try to fit it into frame. The problem is, no matter what angle we film it from, it looks like a penis. The top is an elongated bulb, and the shaft is unapologetically phallic. We start to giggle. Q, curious, saunters over to check the viewfinder. Sun Hi is too horrified to translate, but Q knows why we're laughing. "I'm sorry, Mr. Q, I just can't fit it in," I say, sending Nic into new paroxysms with my unintentional double entendre.

"Yes," says Q pleasantly. It's the only English word he knows.

We try panning around the brush to solve the problem—but this turns it into a gigantic revolving dildo. A *hanboked* guide floats up to recite her propaganda spiel, and I turn the camera on her with relief, wondering what Tang Tap's Australian equivalent would be. Artists are seen as indulgent, taxpayer-sucking parasites in my sports-loving motherland. That's unless they're Kylie Minogue, Russell Crowe, Nicole Kidman, or some suburban crooner who's made it big on *The Voice*. The Antipodean Tang Tap would have a beer can, barbeque tongs, and a cricket bat—with the beer can indisputably at the top.

"Our Dear Leader designed this monument to commemorate the Workers' Party of Korea . . ." the guide starts to say—but Mr. Wang's mobile phone rings. He drops his boom, lights a fag, and squats down to have a chat. I shrug at Nic. I've already explained to Mr. Wang that whenever Nic's rolling, so is he, as our only source of audio. But Mr. Wang is proving extraordinarily dedicated to maintaining his social life.

Mobiles, surprisingly, are everywhere in Pyongyang. Until 2013, foreigners couldn't take them in, but the locals have plenty. Sixty percent of the city's 2.5 million citizens own a Nokia, Samsung, or smartphone clone, hooked up to 3G service Koryolink: a joint venture between Egyptian conglomerate Orascom and the Korea Post & Telecommunications Corporation. The phones are blocked from making international calls. As Mr. Wang chats and smokes, I watch people wandering around Tang Tap—reading books, waiting for buses, talking on their phones. The sun is shining and a pleasant breeze riffles the trees shading the square. Pyongyang would not be such a bad place to make movies, I decide, if you didn't care about script control. When Kim Jong Il made Tang Tap's brush higher than the hammer and sickle, he backed his symbolism with cash.

North Korea looks after its filmmakers assiduously, from the moment they enter the prestigious Pyongyang University of Film and TV. As students, they're given access to Western films that ordinary North Koreans never see. When they graduate, they're attached for life to one of Pyongyang's five movie studios, installed in apartments, and put on permanent retainers. Female writers, editors, and actors are given free childcare to cope with the demanding hours. Cinematographers and directors are sent on overseas sabbaticals to improve their skills. Scriptwriters on deadlines are housed in the North Korean equivalent of luxurious Western script workshops like eQuinoxe: tranquil writing cottages in the country with twenty-four-hour catering and no distractions. "We are given preferential treatment," actress Ms. Yun confirms. "The Party runs a special shop only for artists, so we can enjoy modern lifestyles. The shop provides us with everything from household goods to daily necessities. Thus, we can concentrate on making movies without any worries."

Back when Kim Jong Il was in charge and flush with funds, filmmakers who did well, either locally or on the festival circuit, were given gold Rolexes, cars, and condominiums. Those who became People's Artists never had to worry again. Ms. Yun is one of them: Kim installed her in a modern high-rise soon after she played the juvenile lead in *Wolmi Island*, and she now lives there with her children alongside famous musicians, playwrights, and opera stars. The artists are recognised wherever they go: "Often the fan mail is so high, it cannot fit under our beds," Ms. Yun says shyly. She insists that nothing's changed under Kim Jong Un, and that North Korea still produces thirty to forty feature films a year. The other filmmakers haven't said anything to contradict her; but the rueful look in their eyes, when I ask what life was like before Kim Jong Il slashed their budgets in the 1990s to fund the army, suggests a different story.

That afternoon, as Mr. Pak walks me around the Pyongyang Studio, pointing out the offices, restaurants, crèches, and a building where filmmakers distil their own beer, it appears that life, for a dwindling elite at least, is still cushy. "You know what beer is, don't you?" Pak asks playfully, the dappled light playing on his silver mane.

"Of course. It's our national drink," I say.

He fixes me with a look of intense curiosity. "Do you have many drunken people in Australia?"

"Being drunk is our national way of life," I deadpan. "That's why you won so many medals at the Olympics, and our swimmers bombed in the pool."

Pak grins. He has enough English to know that I'm teasing him. He's enjoying it. "DPRK came twentieth in the medal count. That's not bad for a small country, is it?" he says—and leads me over to the ghostly streets of Kim Jong Il's outdoor film sets. Now I've seen more than fifty North Korean movies, the plaster facades feel alive. "This village is modelled on the Yi Dynasty, from the 1400s," says Pak—and I can see the black-clad ninja skittering across the eaves of the ancient temple, ready to spring on the heroic Hong Kil Dong.

"From here are the Japanese streets," Pak continues, rounding a small hut to enter an urban streetscape circa 1931, covered in kanji. "This is what it was like under colonial rule. You can't find houses that look like this any more, so with his thoughtful consideration, our Great General built this for us in 1974." I stare at the shop fronts lined up in eerily silent rows. There's the wooden gate where the mother in *Sea of Blood* shot the Japanese commander dead; there's the cobblestoned square where the businessmen and prostitutes spat at Kotpun in *Flower Girl*. Hanging above the dusty windows are clumsily hand-painted ads, their once-vibrant colours faded grey. "Lion toothpaste," says Pak, pointing to one. "If you brush your teeth with Lion toothpaste from an early age, you will be healthy. That's what it says."

Pak helped design these streets when he was a young man and hungry to impress Kim Jong Il. He points out the buildings with proprietorial pride: the "Meiji textile mill," the "Fuji film shop," the "Suntory whisky bar," and a cafe advertising—of all things—the Japanese soft drink Calpis. "I didn't know they made Calpis in the '30s," I comment, and Pak looks affronted: "All advertisements are exact reproductions from the original time. This set covers imperial rule from the 1920s to the 1950s. We change the signs, depending on which decade we're filming." I ask Nic to film the tattered facade of the Eiga cinema, which has a Charlie Chaplin poster above its eaves. Pak, who's shot it himself many times, makes sure she's using a wide-angle lens to capture it at its most impressive. "The king of comedy," I say, managing to decipher the Japanese. "Do the Korean people like Chaplin?"

"Everybody likes Chaplin." Pak shrugs. "These are the movies that were popular then. Look—there's *Blackbeard the Pirate* directed by Raoul Walsh, starring Linda Darnell. And this one is Billy Wilder's *Seven Year Itch*." The posters are painted in sepia and mounted on warped wooden frames. Marilyn Monroe's luscious pout reflects back at us from a muddy pool in the gutter. We continue up the cobbled street, our footsteps echoing inside the empty, neglected buildings.

Hundreds of movies may have been made here in Kim Jong Il's heyday, but the place feels like a ghost town. It appears to have been dormant for some time. As if to confirm this, a beige cow appears from behind the "Asahi work boots" shop and walks slowly across the road, its neck bell swinging from side to side. "Oh look, a cow," Pak says nonchalantly—and walks off to chat with Sun Hi while Nic trains her lens on this surreal image.

The cow clanks its way past Clark Gable and on to "Mitsubishi electrical parts," followed by a man in a singlet and a line of skinny goats. We can hear Pak and Sun Hi chatting through the camera headphones: Mr. Wang has dropped the boom to take a call, but our Beijing radio mics are still in range. According to our Sydney translator, the conversation goes like this:

Pak: "Do you think Australian cows look like that?"

Sun Hi: "No, they have black-and-white ones. You know: milk cows, with spots."

Pak *(sighing)*: "Marilyn Monroe had a voluptuous figure, you know. She did movies mainly to exhibit her body. She was very famous."

Sun Hi: "Really?" *(Lowering her voice.)* "What nationality was she?"

Pak: "American, of course. There's a rumour she had an affair with Kennedy."

Sun Hi *(gasping in amazement)*: "Oh wow."

Pak *(annoyed)*: "Haven't they filmed enough of the cow?"

Nic and I look up from the lens to see Pak frowning at us, hands on hips. The afternoon is fading away, and Pak wants us to film the sets in a wide shot, in that brief window of magical light just before sunset, known to filmmakers the world over as "the golden hour." Pak hurries us round the corner to 1950s Seoul: a hotchpotch of bars and massage parlours, with billboards of wasp-waisted dames holding martinis and cigarettes. "Look, there's the 'brothers' bar,'" he says, and I'm struck by how innocent this take on Westernised vice is compared with the X-rated, drug-riddled free-for-all that Seoul's red-light district has become. "This is South Korea during the American bastards' occupation," Pak explains helpfully.

"You've made it full of brothels and bars and massage parlours!" I challenge. "Is that because you want South Korea to look decadent?" Pak laughs: "It's not all massage parlours—look, that sign says '*Samjung Trading, Daedong and Co.*' That is a chemicals manufacturer. There's the 'Office of Public Prosecution.' You need all sorts of scenes for movies about Korea under occupation. We needed to create a variety of shops, and due to the hostility between the two Koreas, we can't film in the South. Besides, you can't see old shops like this in Seoul any more, thanks to modernisation."

We stop under a shopfront displaying a torpedo-breasted woman reclining on a pink love seat. "That's not a massage parlour," says Sun Hi defensively. "The sign says: '*Female's true attractiveness comes from the breasts.*' It's a breast-enlargement cosmetic centre." She flicks her ponytail, pleased to have backed up Pak. I wonder what Sun Hi would make of her cashed-up sisters in Seoul, forking out thousands of won to pump their chests full of silicon, widen their eyes, and lighten their skin. I could ask her in front of Pak, but with Q hovering next to

Nic's viewfinder, it's too risky. Q may only say "yes" when spoken to in English, but he appears to understand a lot more. Probing Sun Hi about what she knows of plastic surgery, or anything else in South Korea, could compromise her in ways I don't want to contemplate.

I follow Pak across a small square to a shack decorated with coyotes and tumbleweeds. *New Popular Songs! Arizona Music Shop*, the awning says. Pak studies it fondly: "I saw a photograph of a shop like this in a coffee-table book on America once. That's why I chose it." He turns to me, serious: "Anna, I didn't intend to show that South Korea has an indolent lifestyle. We can't make them—or any other place—look bad just because they are the enemy. I'd like you to understand that clearly."

I nod, fighting the impulse to point out this is not what Kim Jong Il instructed in his manifesto. Pak seems troubled behind his urbane smile. I have several days of filming left with him, and I can't afford to blow it. So I walk to the shop next door, the "Migrants' Information Centre." The sign invites Brazilians, Germans, and Canadians to come inside for travel advice. I step in and peer at Pak through the plywood window, making what I hope is an acceptable joke: "Can Australians use this place? I want to migrate to the DPRK."

"She wants to move here. What should she do?" Sun Hi translates, not amused. Pak looks at me coolly. "She can go to Brazil," he says. And walks away. He knows I will follow him, this courtly man in his neatly pressed chinos who has taken me under his wing like a tae kwon do master might take on a promising but particularly irritating student: tolerating my banter, correcting my errors, and attending to my education with genuine solicitude. I leave Q and Sun Hi to help Nic shoot golden hour and join Pak in the shadowy glade behind the Arizona music shop. Below us is a thickly wooded forest, and beyond it a broad meadow flanked by the churches and chalets of Kim Jong Il's Europe. In the distance, the goatherd leads his flock towards a gothic abbey, its stained-glass casements glowing in the twilight. There's a sudden flash of colour as a window below the belfry swings shut—and

I'm sure I see a figure behind it, ducking into the shadows. Perhaps the Pyongyang Film Studio doubles as a shelter at night.

"It's hard to find thick forests like this," muses Pak, ignoring what just happened. "When I stay back late for work in the evening, I find the air here so fresh. It's different from the air in the city." I stand beside my North Korean mentor, breathing in the beautiful air. Pak has earned my respect, and not just because he wants my film to succeed. He doesn't miss a trick. Back at the studio, I asked him to hold a picture frame for a portrait, something I've done with all the filmmakers. The frame contains green cardboard so that we can superimpose images from North Korean movies in the edit. "Please stay still and stare down the barrel for fifteen seconds," I asked Pak, and he shot me a crafty look: "Are you using me to advertise products?" I promised I wasn't, and he held the picture with indulgent gravitas as Nic zoomed in and out of the frame: "God, I feel like a dead man being photographed," he said, with a martyrish groan.

Now, in the gloaming, the woods spread beneath us are full of mystery. The deepening affection I'm feeling for Pak is just as mysterious—both resonant and delicate. I am yearning to know how he became North Korea's favourite director, what his relationship with Kim Jong Il was like, what happened to his filmmaking friends who failed, or stopped working, or just disappeared. But Pak is not free to answer me, and I cannot question him at will. If he could answer, I suspect his stories would be horrific. Pak's serenity indicates that he, at least, has not destroyed others to get where he is. He has the air of someone who sleeps well at night.

Gazing at Pak's cherished forest, I'm reminded of places where I've spent some of the happiest times of my life: camping with my ex and our beautiful new baby, playing guitar with friends around languid summer bonfires, walking with our growing daughter through Australia's ancient bush. I slip into Japanese and the one thing we can discuss without retribution: "Sensei, are you married?" I ask.

He gives a tired smile. "I've been married so long, I've forgotten our wedding day."

"Do you find it hard, making films and maintaining a relationship with your wife?"

"No one wants to be married to a filmmaker," he sighs. "You betray them every time you walk onto set." I nod. Being in Pak's presence has the uniquely soothing effect I've encountered twice before—with the enlightened monk in South Korea, and with the queer artist Quentin Crisp. It's an existential kind of compassion: a kindness that makes you reflect on your problems with love, instead of anger. I've been diabolical to love, I reflect calmly. The intense creativity of filmmaking draws on the same part of the heart. Some think that a pram in the corridor is the death of the artist, and my life has been a constant struggle to prove this wrong.

"You're having a hard time, aren't you," Pak observes. And without him having to say any more, I know that my ex's young woman is not the cause of our breakup, but the symptom. I've always loved my daughter and my films—but I've only rarely been able to give her father the same attention and care. Pak gently pats my shoulder, and I feel infused with lightness. I will forgive my ex, I realise. I will acknowledge my own role in his pain, and move on. And one day, when we've healed enough to become friends, I will give him some David Beckham cologne—as payback.

The sun sinks to the tree line, a bloody, molten ball. "Here," says Pak, springing into action as Nic walks over to line up a shot. "If you do this, it looks more realistic." He pulls down a sprig from an overhanging bush, holding the leaves dead still in front of Nic's lens until the sun disappears.

PLAYING THE ENEMY

My fantasy of defecting to North Korea to make movies is dead. There's too much you can't do. The censorship began this morning: the Yangakkdo cleaning ladies drew a thick black cross through the note I left them, explaining the brown streaks on my washcloth were nothing more unpleasant than makeup. And now, Sun Hi won't let us shoot anything not explicitly on the itinerary. This includes the big cinema screen outside Pyongyang train station, the portrait painters in front of the Grand People's Study House, the black-market stall selling Chinese sweets and dried fish on Moran Hill, and a Coke can mysteriously left in a bin on Sungri Street. Sun Hi will neither acknowledge this proof that foreigners are not the only ones drinking Coke in Pyongyang, nor explain where it came from. And it's all thanks to Q.

When we began the day at the Leaders' statues at Mangyongdae, Team Gas was happy. Sun Hi was her cheeky self, parroting everything Nic and I said and wearing her koala cap at a jaunty angle. As thousands of soldiers and schoolchildren streamed up the steps to lay flowers at the Kims' huge bronze feet, Sun Hi chewed bubblegum and spoke off the cuff, working the camera like a pro: "Here we stand at the statues of the Great Leaders Kim Il Sung and Generalissimo Kim Jong Il. Our People are always longing for them. This is the day of the DPRK's foundation, a national holiday. People are coming from all parts of the country to greet them. We call Great Comrade Kim Jong Il 'Our Father,' because thanks to his policies, we defended our system of socialism. When he passed away, it was the bitterest agony for our People, and everyone felt heartbreak."

I stared at the rows of bowing people, their eyes fixed on Kim Jong Il's bronze head with the same intensity as the mourners who fell before his hearse, and asked Sun Hi the question that had plagued the blogosphere for months: "Were the tears your people cried the day he died genuine?"

Sun Hi's eyes widened in genuine surprise: "Of course! True grief comes from the heart! You can't make sadness!"

"Why did you love him so much?" I prompted, and Sun Hi, with the insolence of a teenager explaining wi-fi to a baby boomer, said: "It's hard for you guys to understand, because only in our country is there such love for the Leaders. But from when we are born, we get such care from our Party. We have a women's hospital where they don't pay for child. After birth, they are given modern medicines, like tonics and honey for their health. As I grew up, I learnt piano. Then I went to school and studied journalism at uni, all for free. In other countries, this can't happen. For example, I'm just an ordinary girl, who has bad teeth. When I go to the dentist, the government pays for it, and when I have bronchitis, I don't pay for the X-rays. Everything is in the People's interest. There are many countries which suffer wars, and the children suffer malnutritions, and the state doesn't care. But we have a good life here, and that's all thanks to the good policy of our General. That's why everyone loves our Great Leader."

I could feel Q hovering beside me, making sure we were filming Kim's statue in the correct wide. Q has performed his gaffer duties assiduously—but appears even more dedicated to monitoring everything we say. If he really is fluent in English, I figured, my next question would catch him out: "What happens, Sun Hi, when your people don't have enough to eat?"

Sun Hi only blinked once before resuming her sunny monologue:

"Yes. Many socialist countries are corrupted now, and we are the only socialist country in the world where everyone is united—and while we did have some hard days, we People think that not being with money is the only happiness. We have respect, we are all equal, and we have a peaceful life. That's why we could succeed in the Arduous March. If money was top of everything for us, we couldn't have done this." She shot me a *take that* pout, and I waited for her to blow a pink bubble and pop it for emphasis. But then Q said something softly in Korean, and Sun Hi turned white. She spat her gum into her hand, pulled off her koala cap and stalked off. She's refused to address our camera ever since.

Q gestured calmly for us to carry on, and Nic panned off Sun Hi onto the rows of red flowers displayed in brass jars at Kim Jong Il's feet. According to the silk sashes on the jars, countries as far away as Sweden, Indonesia, and Kenya were still sending in condolences, almost a year after Kim died. The fact that every country sent exactly the same jar, right down to the font on the sashes, was being accepted, apparently without question, by the people bowing reverentially before them. "Lady Gaga," I whispered to Nic, and she changed to a long lens to get close-ups. In private, we call our long, medium, and wide lenses Fatty One, Fatty Two and Fatty Three—after the way ordinary Chinese refer to the three Kims. But in front of our North Korean minders, our lenses are Lady Gaga, Taylor Swift, and Kim Kardashian. Sun Hi and Q don't know who these mega-celebrities are and—unless they check our viewfinder—what angle we're filming at.

At our next stop, the Juche Tower, Sun Hi watched our viewfinder like a hawk. We set up a majestic wide pointing back at the Dear Leaders' portrait in Kim Il Sung Square, and she made us stop: not because Kim Jong Il's face was cropped, but because it was out of focus. At the People's opera house, she criticised our close-up of the building's *Sea of Blood* mural—a six-metre mosaic of the pistol-toting heroine—for being off centre. We dutifully switched to Kim Kardashian for a symmetrical wide and rolled for ten dull minutes until Sun Hi was satisfied we weren't picking off close-ups of people in the background. It was only when we rewound that we realised we'd caught a moment of documentary gold: a pair of lovers, in khaki uniforms, weaving through the crowd. Their hands grip each other's waists, and as they walk away from camera, his fingers stray to her bottom and caress it—before working their way inside her pants. She biffs him with her briefcase, but lets him continue his anatomical explorations.

Unacknowledged fact #332: North Koreans like to have sex.

"You must not film that image," Sun Hi snaps, still cross with us three hours later when we attach Lady Gaga to get a portrait of Kim Jong Un across the water from our hotel. Censorship has continued to rule the morning, with our minders rigorously controlling where we shoot and eliminating many stunning landscapes from my film along the way. From the balcony of Moranbong Temple, they only let us point east, because the TV tower to the west was a "sensitive military installation." Outside the People's ice-skating stadium, Q let us shoot the promenading *hanboked* ladies, and the ruddy-cheeked boys practising backflips in the grass, but slammed his hand over the lens when a cavalcade of army trucks thundered past.

"No soldiers," Sun Hi said bluntly, and we watched sixty rusting jeeps, packed to the gunnels with skinny, bewildered boys in threadbare khaki uniforms, rolling through the intersection as jolly marching songs crackled from the rooftop speakers. I had the distinct impression that our minders didn't want the West to see just how unthreatening and folksy North Korea's notorious million-man army actually looks when viewed up close.

Even our trip to a local cinema was censored. I'd asked to film inside an ordinary suburban theatre, preferably one screening this year's latest hit. Instead, Q and Sun Hi took us to a magnificent stone palace in the middle of the city, with usherettes in diaphanous green *hanboks*. We found ourselves filming a rent-a-crowd of Party officers and workers, who had clearly been briefed not to blink when we shone our lights on their faces. I should have known it was a set-up: they were watching Mr. Ri's thinly veiled lesbian romance, *Do People Know You*, which was two years old. Somewhere out in the suburbs, ordinary North Koreans may have been going to the cinema to catch the latest matinee—but it sure wasn't here.

"This magnificent modern theatre was built by our Dear Leader for the cultural enjoyment of the People," said the theatre manager, a plump grandmother in a blue serge suit. "Before every movie, we always show something to expand the workers' general knowledge. That's why our cinema is so popular." I watched the rent-a-crowd gazing in rapture at a tedious documentary about how computers have revolutionised the Pyongyang workplace and begged the manager to let us film the projection room. To Western viewers, I explained, films shot on celluloid are nostalgic, revered for their beauty. It would be fascinating to see a place where it is used every day. Q and Sun Hi greeted my request with the same consternation they'd shown at the Pyongyang Film Studio when I asked to film the Steenbeck editing suites, telecine rooms, and processing labs. North Korea's reliance on old technology is not something they're keen to emphasise.

"Does she want me to get in trouble?" the manager whispered angrily to Q—and Sun Hi turned to us with an officious glare: "She cannot let us into the projection room because we don't have permission. There is no hierarchy in our country: everyone is equal. But still the manager comrade must check with her other comrades that the right forms have been signed." I had to satisfy myself with a solo portrait of the manager, smiling broadly in the unlit hall of the cinema. Sun Hi refused to be in the shot. "Oh come on, honeybun, you're a natural—you have the X factor!" I pleaded—and the comment, which only yesterday would have had Sun Hi begging me to repeat it so she could learn it by heart, sent her into a foot-stamping rage: "My job is to interpret, not answer questions. Stop making me do more!"

Q watched her stalk off. "Yes," he said, pleasantly. And I realized what had got Sun Hi into trouble back at the Leaders' statues: bubblegum. The fact she was chewing it while speaking of Kim Jong Il was already disrespectful. But the fact she was chewing it while wearing a Western baseball cap, and chatting spontaneously instead of reciting the usual polished spiel, made her performance downright blasphemous. Blasphemy can be punished with death around here. Sun Hi is distancing herself from Team Gas for one reason: she's scared.

That afternoon, when we finally decamp to the Taedong River to shoot the set of Mr. Ri's latest action pic, Sun Hi is as relieved as we are. We stand next to a chugging fifties generator truck, looking up at the gleaming hull of a real-life American spy ship. Captured in 1968, the USS *Pueblo* is now a floating museum, treasured proof of North Korea's military supremacy. It's an incongruous sight, with its bristling gun turrets pointed impotently at the Taedong Bridge as wooden fishing boats and canoes drift idly by.

We climb on board. The *Pueblo's* foredeck is crawling with an assortment of Chinese tourists, North Korean actors in World War II sailor suits, and a chain-smoking crew of riggers and special-effects people, three of whom fan the flames of a smoke machine. In the middle of the chaos, Mr. Ri, in combat gear and gold aviators, is trying to direct. No one shuts up when he rolls: he's not recording sound. "This ship invaded our territorial waters more than seventeen times," a prim soldier-guide tells the tourists. "Our navy captured the captain and all the sailors. They killed two and the rest were imprisoned alive. The US government sent a letter of apology asking for their ship back. We sent back the prisoners, but not this ship, as it is our trophy."

"Action!" shouts Ri over the guide, every inch the Commander of the Creative Group. A handsome North Korean marine grips a wheel on the main bridge, gazing over the curious tourists at an invisible flotilla of American frigates: "Seagull One to Seagull Two: we're surrounded by enemy vessels!" he says into a two-way—and Ri throws down his cap in disgust. "What is wrong with you?" he barks. "You're driving a battleship, not going for a walk on the beach! Calmness won't cut it. You have to do it like this." Ri lowers his glasses and delivers the lines with quiet machismo. "Again!" he yells, and the nervous actor redoes his take—as the smoke machine billows grey clouds all over the flash-bulbing Chinese. A camera assistant stands tip-toed on an apple box, coaxing smoke towards the actor's face with a small blue hankie. It's the sort of thing a Western gaffer might do if the high-tech gadgetry wasn't delivering. We may operate sixty years in the future, but sometimes an old-fashioned hankie does the trick.

"In our movie, we show the confrontation between our marines and the bastard Americans. We won this confrontation. That's the story," Ri declares as his crew move gear around for the next setup. A dignified man in a white captain's jacket waits beside me and Nic as gaffers rig up his lights. From the way the makeup ladies are fussing over him, he appears to be a movie star. We pick up our tripod to get out of the way, but Ri stops us, speaking fast. It sounds important—but Sun Hi is still too annoyed with us to translate. "Nicola, *bwaaaaah gung*," Ri declares urgently, making a panning motion with his hands. "Anna, 'Okay! Yeah!'" Ri says to me, giving a thumbs-up. "Action!" he yells at his crew—and before we can work out what's happened, we're on camera. The captain speaks enthusiastically to Nic, and Ri's lens points straight at my face. Nic pans, and I give the captain a hesitant, "Okay, yeah!"

"Cut!" Ri yells, and makes us do it again. His cinematographer, wearing a makeshift steadicam rig, is riveted by our digital Sony camera. He glides closer to Nic with each take, and by the fifth one, his softly whirring German Arri is making love to the Sony, the lenses so close to each other, the focus puller grazes Nic's ear.

"Comrade Ri's film is about the *Pueblo*, but it's also about how people come from all over the world to see it," says Sun Hi when we regroup under the gun turrets. She seems to have suddenly forgiven us for the gruelling events of the morning. She's wearing her Team Gas cap again and is flushed with pride. Nic and I, after all, have just successfully starred in a movie by the great Ri Kwan Am. Apparently, the captain was telling us how the North Koreans captured the ship, and my "Okay, yeah!" was Ri's idea of how an average Western media hack would react, when told such a heroic story.

Ri's so pleased he's granted us an interview. I meet him at the starboard gun ship, daunted. "Rule four says: *Acting depends on the director*," I begin, flipping open Kim Jong Il's manifesto.

Ri cuts me off. "Yes, yes. Acting is in the hands of the director, I agree. In your film, there is an evil miner. The actor you're using doesn't look like a baddie. So don't make him act evil. No one is that simple. Who would knowingly do a bad thing? He must genuinely think what he is doing is right." I nod, struck by how completely this contradicts Kim Jong Il's dictum that to play a bad guy, you must hate him with your very soul.

"Who are the foreign actors you're using?" I ask Ri, pointing at three blond men on the mess deck. They stick out like sore thumbs, these strapping, blue-eyed boys sitting uneasily in their ill-fitting sailor suits as the makeup ladies powder their skin. They are doing everything possible to avoid my gaze.

"They are the Dresnok boys. They're playing the Americans who pursued the vessel," Ri says dismissively—and I realise with a shock that we've stumbled on the progeny of the famous Joe Dresnok, North Korea's number-one movie villain. Dresnok snuck over the DMZ in the 1960s, along with Charles Robert Jenkins and two other American GIs, each soldier hoping to avoid punishment for misdemeanours they'd committed while stationed in the South. Dresnok's naive plan was to escape through North Korea into the Soviet Union, where he hoped to start a new life. Instead, he and his comrades were snapped up by Kim Jong Il, installed in mud huts with North Korean concubines, and put to work: playing the evil enemy in almost every military movie he shot.

According to a book Jenkins wrote about their ordeal, the uneducated Dresnok was a bully who beat up the other GIs to gain favour with their captors. Perhaps because of this, he is the most celebrated foreign actor in North Korea and is recognised all over Pyongyang, where he still lives. With Dresnok now retired, Jenkins safely on Sado Island, and the other two GIs deceased, Dresnok's sons are filling the ongoing demand for Yankee bad guys. They were born and raised

North Korean, but their fair skin indicates their mother is Caucasian. I wonder if she was one of Kim's kidnapped language teachers, or perhaps a dancer in his Joy Division—gifted to Dresnok in reward for his loyalty. I doubt that his sons are going to tell me—the murderous looks they're sneaking our way, as if Nic and I are personally responsible for the two million civilians killed in the war, suggests they've had to be more North Korean than the North Koreans to survive.

"Currently we are telling the hundred-year history of American invasion. We're telling the whole human race what happens in the end to invaders. We want to show who the real protector of happiness and justice is," Ri says grandly to my camera, as the tourists gather round to watch. "In rule two, *One must aim high in creation!*, our Leader stresses you must start small, and end big, bam, with something magnificent," Ri goes on. "Believe me, the audience will appreciate it. Also, it says here . . ." he riffles through the manifesto, looking for the page—but a loud Californian twang interjects: "I'm here to present $100,000 to get our ship back."

Ri, the tourists, and the crew look round in surprise. A grey-haired man in crumpled chinos is lurching unsteadily towards us. "And every day you don't give our ship back, we'll have to lower our offer by $10,000," he continues, giving our camera an imbecilic grin.

"Mr. Ri Kwan Am is a highly respected filmmaker and the director of this movie," I admonish the heckler, feeling responsible for the anger and embarrassment of the North Koreans around me.

"Oh great, nice to meet you!" the man says to Ri, with a mock salute. He seems slightly drunk, or mentally unhinged. Or both. Ri doesn't shake his hand, and the man doesn't offer.

"As I was saying," Ri says coldly, turning his back on the man and giving me an imperious stare, "in rule two —"

"And another thing!" the man calls out, photobombing Ri's interview again. "We're a believer in Jesus, and I hope you don't mind me saying, the principle of forgiveness—that when we confess our sins and own up to what we've done, we're forgiven—is a great way to live.

Have a nice day!" He waves and stumbles off. Nic and I watch him go, gobsmacked. We thought North Korea was an American-free zone, until we boarded the *Pueblo*. In the last five minutes, we've seen four. I turn back to Ri, but he's already walking away. "I need to shoot. We'll chat later," he says with quiet dignity, making a rolling motion with his fingers. His crew file behind him, stealing furtive glances at the flickering lights of the Sony.

I watch him go, cursing the dedication of Christian missionaries—who, even with the threat of imprisonment, persist in coming here. Thanks to the photobomber's desire to spread the Word, I've just lost a perfectly good interview.

Nic climbs through a narrow porthole into the engine room, and I hand her the Sony, trying to stay out of Ri's lights. Inside the cramped cabin, the oldest Dresnok, dressed as the captain of the USS *Pueblo*, is attempting to act. "Sir, trust me. With a little coaxing, we can snatch it out of their hands," he says, with all the animation of a satnav guide.

"Cut!" yells Ri. "Are you only going to do a good job if I swear at you? Do it with malice." Ri makes Dresnok stand and sits in his chair, doing a brilliantly sinister line read. Demonstrating is taboo in the West—directors are meant to help actors find the truth inside themselves, not force them to mimic. But when you're Commander of the Creative Group, clearly anything goes. Dresnok nods like a nervous puppy, and returns to his position. His second take is as stilted as the first. Ri waits for the cinematographer to rewind his mini DV. It's a crappy one-chip, guaranteed to look horrible on the big screen. I suspect Ri's using it for our benefit: lame proof that North Korea's gone digital. "Sir, trust me," Dresnok's words wind back, and Ri studies the monitor. Then he looks up: "You look good, but you can't act." Dresnok slumps with shame, and the crew burst out laughing. Ri grins at me, enjoying himself.

Later, as Ri's crew wrap their lights, I approach Dresnok with the friendliest smile I can muster. "Hello, is it true that you live here?" I say, and he surveys me with cold hatred: "Yes, I am living here." It's the same clipped accent I've heard in every North Korean doco I've watched—from the Air Koryo safety video to the saccharine biopics on Kim Jong Il. Perhaps Dresnok is the voice's original source—North Korea's go-to narration guy. It's bizarre, hearing a six-foot, blue-eyed blond speak like this. It's like talking to an android—or Arnold Schwarzenegger.

"Can I ask you a few questions?" I persist, and Dresnok's jaw clenches. "I am busy. Talk to the boss," he snaps. And stalks off.

None of which fills me with optimism, when Sun Hi runs up with the happy news that Ri has just cast me as Dresnok's wife. Western women are a rare commodity in Pyongyang—and after my dubious efforts on the *Pueblo*, Ri has written me a cameo. My scene is to be shot in two days' time. That's exactly forty-eight hours to work up a convincing level of adoration for the dead-eyed Dresnok.

"What's rule three again?" Nic asks innocently, ribbing me. "Isn't it *Emotions must be well defined?*" Sun Hi is already flipping open the manifesto. "You must study very hard," she says, overwhelmed by the task ahead of us. "All night, if necessary. To work with Senior Comrade Ri is a great honour." Nic stifles a giggle. I shoot her daggers. And start reading.

THE BODY AND EMOTION

TEAM GAS AND I ARE SITTING on the steps of Kim Jong Il's fake Swiss chalet. Goats graze in the meadow as the North Korean cast of *The Gardener* gathers around my laptop. On screen, Brian Monk, his sunny features unnaturally strained, studies the Origin Energy gas wells bordering his farm in Chinchilla: "When they first moved in, we thought it was just a test well. But then we saw five more go in, and realised this was a full-scale industrial drill. The methane has leaked out from the soil and is bubbling up in the Condamine River. They say the drills are no bigger than a tennis court—but you get the tape measure out—that's no bloody tennis court!" Brian looks at the huge compound of flaming pipes beyond the razor wire. Then he pulls out his wallet: "They'll spin you the spin because of this. Money. That's all it is. There's something wrong when multinationals can come here and take what they want, and my grandkids can get sick."

The North Korean actors nod in sympathy as the footage cuts to Brian's seven blond grandchildren playing in a desolate, scrubby paddock. "We first noticed something was wrong with the bore when the kids took a bath," Brian says. "The youngest started screaming, and when they got out, the kids' legs were covered in raw red burns. They also get skin rashes and headaches, and asthma-type symptoms." Brian's daughter-in-law cradles a toddler on her hip. He has red weals around his mouth. "We can't keep giving them Panadol," she says, exhausted with worry, "but every time we go to the doctor, he says we've all got the flu."

Brian takes us to a makeshift camp of caravans ringed in the dirt: "We come here when the wind blowing off the gas wells gets too strong. Little Jason has developed epilepsy, and they say fracking causes it, but we just don't know! We can't sell: no one wants a farm surrounded by gas fields. We're stuck. This is really our lift-off point," he says, gazing hopelessly at the caravans. He starts to cry. "It's hard, having to leave your own life."

The clip ends with Brian's son Dave standing over the bore—simmering with rage. "They sent in an inspection officer, but he wouldn't let us light the bore in front of him. He said it was against 'industry regulations.' The acceptable level of methane in water is 2 percent. You decide for yourself." Dave pulls out a boxy instrument as Brian touches a match to the bore. The water explodes in flames. Dave's instrument beeps like crazy, and the dial shoots into the red.

I shut the laptop and look at my North Korean actors. They look back in disbelief. "So the drills pollute the water, and then they cannot grow any food," Ms. Yun says quietly. The men stare at the meadow, trying to digest what they've seen. They seem bewildered that any government could let this happen.

"What advice would you give my actors?" I ask.

The two youngsters speak first. The athletic Miss N wants Kathryn Beck to play the gardener's daughter "with a strong sense of inner justice and love for her home town," and neat-as-a-pin Mr. Lee, as Sally's boyfriend Mitch, advises Matt Zeremes to "avoid chasing fame and fortune, and instead act as a true patriot for his country." I thank Mr. Lee, wondering what Matt, a hard-working father of two, would make of Lee's assumption that he only acts for fame. Mr. Lee looks reverently at his elder, the famous movie villain Ri Yon Chol.

With his broad, hard face, Ri Yon Chol makes a very convincing evil miner—the perfect foil for delicate Ms. Yun as my North Korean gardener. "If you play a villain, you need experience," Ri Yon Chol growls. "That's all I have to say. We've all read the script. Let's do it."

"We need to wait for Mr. Pak," I answer carefully. "He will direct you, to show me how it's done." Ri Yon Chol darkens, but the other actors look pleased. The venerable Pak clearly has their respect, despite the fact he's already fifty minutes late. I pull out my *Inner West Argus*, and Ri Yon Chol grabs it hungrily, poring over the photos of the Newtown flea markets, the high-rises going up in Erskineville, and a local mum who's made it big on *MasterChef*.

"Your train stations are not tidy," Ri Yon Chol notes disapprovingly, pointing out a picture of the rubbish-strewn platform at St Peters, with hipsters and goths slouching on graffiti-smeared benches. I have to agree that compared with the Yonggwang metro station, commuting standards in my 'hood are distinctly Third World. "What's going on?" asks a teasing voice, and there's Pak, forging his way through the bushes towards us, briefcase in hand. His cheeks are pink with alcohol. I bow, and he bows even lower, and we stand there giggling and out-bowing each other, the same way we clinked glasses the first time we met.

"Thank you for coming, sensei," I say, and he waves me away, chuffed.

"Come here," he says to the actors, and they assemble at his feet. Pak pulls out a well-thumbed copy of my script, speaking gently to Ms. Yun: "Karen is a gardener. She loves nature. She wants to preserve it for her daughter. You must have this love deep inside your heart." Ms. Yun nods. She's been studying the role for weeks now. She gave me her take on it earlier today, in Kim Jong Il's feudal Korean film set. Beijing tourists dressed in Yi Dynasty robes were posing for photos, and a Pyongyang bride in a meringue wedding gown stood under a parasol with her groom for a formal portrait. When it started to rain, we moved Ms. Yun into an antechamber next to the temple to continue her interview.

The chamber contained an incongruously springy red couch and bamboo wallpaper. Ms. Yun didn't seem fazed. "Karen has a mother's softness, but is as strong as a lion when fighting the evil deeds of big business," she began—and a trapdoor concealed in the wallpaper slid open. Two heavily made-up women, in leopard-print blouses and tight metallic skirts, peered out. They stared at the famous Ms. Yun, too starstruck to be embarrassed. They were obviously working girls, and the couch Ms. Yun was perched on was—as far as I could tell—where they plied their trade. Ms. Yun continued the interview as if the sex workers weren't there, and I followed suit, wondering if they serviced the studio's filmmakers—maybe even Pak himself. Perhaps the women were not embarrassed at all, but simply surprised by our intrusion. If the Koreans are anything like the Japanese, paid sex is a completely pragmatic activity, with none of the guilt-laden hang-ups still clinging to it in the West. Like so many other things I've encountered here, the only thing I was sure about was that I couldn't discuss it out loud.

Back on the Swiss chalet steps, Pak is busy humiliating Ri Yon Chol. "Comrade, you're playing the evil miner, but you look like a really bad guy already—so don't overdo it," he instructs, making the other actors laugh. Ri Yon Chol glowers with displeasure and lights a fag. "Hey, Anna, your casting ability is pretty poor, if you chose this actor based on his looks," Pak continues—and I want to leap to Ri Yon Chol's defence. I've seen him beating up communist workers as a gold-encrusted gangster in Seoul and sneaking into the Yankees' barracks on the DMZ to betray his comrades. Ri Yon Chol is brilliant. It's not his fault that he looks like a thug—underneath, he's probably as sensitive as the other actors, and just as keen for approval.

"I have to say, sensei, that I like Ri Yon Chol very much" is all I can manage, with my substandard Japanese. But I let Pak know that I mean it.

"Well then, Ri Yon Chol will prove you wrong in a minute," Pak says cheerfully and springs to his feet. "First, the lovers!" He herds Miss N and Mr. Lee to a stone path beside the chalet. Ms. Yun settles in the soft grass to watch, and Ri Yon Chol slinks into the shadows to study the *Inner West Argus*. Pak lights a new cigarette, watching Miss N practising tae kwon do in her high-heeled sandals. Each time she kicks, her khaki skirt billows above her thighs. "Hey, Anna," Pak calls. "If you're going to film something like this, do it low angle, so the audience won't be disappointed!" He mimes putting the camera underneath Miss N's skirt. She blushes and keeps on kicking. I'm too stunned to respond. Pak quickly waves his hand in the air, brushing the joke away. "Comrade Lee," he says, serious now, "you are Mitch, the awakened hero. Just like the playboy in our masterpiece *Myself in the Distant Future*, Mitch learns through the love of a devoted worker's daughter the error of his ways—and becomes a hero for the village." Mr. Lee nods and nervously stands in position.

"Action!" Pak snaps, and Mr. Lee saunters up to Miss N with exaggerated cool.

"Where are you from?" she asks him, continuing to practise her tae kwon do.

"I came from the North. You won't understand because you're not a comrade engineer," Lee replies, reaching out to touch her face. Then he stops, awkward with nerves. Miss N giggles.

"How do I—" Lee starts to ask—but Pak has already leapt in to demonstrate. "Don't approach her like a heinous criminal," he upbraids the embarrassed Lee. "Even in Europe, they don't do that. Do it as if you're yawning." Pak stretches his arms over his head, expertly letting one hand come to rest on Miss N's neck. "Doing it like this is art. Not the sleazy way you did it. Again!"

Lee repeats the scene, stretching clumsily and bumping Miss N on the nose. They burst out laughing, and Pak darkens with anger. "Stop!" he yells. "Do you think this is funny? How can you do a good job, with such an attitude? Comrade N: run around the building. Run to the hills and come back. Go! Now! Run!"

Miss N gathers up her skirt and runs off, as fast as her high heels will carry her. The others look on calmly. Pak turns to me, petulant: "She's only saying the lines. She's not acting from her body. An actor should *act*, for God's sakes." Pak smokes and sulks, until Miss N sprints back, red with sweat. "Go! Go into the scene!" yells Pak—and this time, they nail it. Mr. Lee brushes Miss N's hair off her face with seductive ease, and she grabs his wrist, punches him in the stomach, and sends him flying to the ground. "Good," says Pak, and saunters off. The young actors bow deeply, expressing their heartfelt thanks to his retreating back.

If Pak and Ri are anything to go by, being Commander of the Creative Group means being a bit of a dickhead, I decide. Nic raises her eyebrows at me—she's thinking the same thing. But Pak surprises us. He ushers Ms. Yun and Ri Yon Chol over to the grassy hill for their scene, and his entire demeanour changes. He plucks some wildflowers and places them delicately in Ms. Yun's hands, as if she's made of porcelain. "Pretend these are the sign you've made against coal seam gas," he whispers. "Action."

Ms. Yun turns to Ri Yon Chol, full of pain: "You work for us, but you take our money overseas. When our land is empty, you will run away —"

"STOP!" interjects Pak, and Ms. Yun blushes. "Anna, Comrade Yun is a kind person. She's only ever played nice ladies," he explains, "so it's hard for her to be angry."

I look at Ms. Yun: "Do you have children?" She nods, and I suggest she imagines the gas mine is making them sick.

"Yes, be really angry," Pak agrees. "Western emotions are different from ours: they are more overblown." It's an unusual observation, given the melodrama and sentimentality of North Korean movies. Then again, what's overblown to the North Koreans could be understated to us, and vice versa.

Pak stands beside Ms. Yun, their backs to the camera. "Imagine someone has died," he whispers, touching her arm. And suddenly, he starts to bounce up and down in the grass. "Squat and stand repeatedly twenty times," he orders. Ms. Yun does what she's told. We watch the two of them, bouncing up and down with the energy of teenagers. "This is connecting the body and the emotion!" pants Pak, waiting for Ms. Yun to finish. "Action!"

Ms. Yun spins around to Ri Yon Chol, her eyes flashing with rage: "We have to live with the destroyed land in sadness and in pain!"

Ri Yon Chol's mouth twists into a sly smile: "The gas we're extracting is not harmful."

Ms. Yun quivers, her beautiful eyes dissolving in tears: "Thousands of our townspeople will rise up against you!" Ri Yon Chol gazes calmly at the meadow, the softly bleating goats. "Where are they?"

It's mesmerising, like watching a real North Korean movie. Ms. Yun has the magnetic intensity of the ill-fated heroine in *A Broad Bellflower*. I feel strangely inspired seeing Ms. Yun and Ri Yon Chol battling out the coal seam gas issue on this remote Pyongyang hill, light-years away from the capitalist system that spawned it. "Cut!" Pak says, content. "That's how you do it," he says, nodding at me. I can't say the same for the dictator who trained him, but my mentor is a genius.

The artistry of our North Korean colleagues continues to dazzle us for the rest of the afternoon. Composer Mr. Pei, who has been rehearsing his rewritten version of the gardener's song for days, greets us outside the Pyongyang opera centre, which has an armed guard stationed somewhat pointlessly in front of its wide open doors. We follow him inside, expecting to be led to a small studio, where a few violinists, maybe even a quartet, will bring his composition to life. Instead, Pei ushers us into a five-hundred-seat auditorium.

A full 150-piece orchestra, in concert tuxedos, are tuning their instruments on stage. A woman in a black silk dress strums a gold harp, and an equally elegant woman waits at a grand piano. Pei takes a seat in the dress circle, fiddling with his glasses. "We put a lot of heart into this, because it's the first time an Australian director has come to work with us," he says, apprehensive. "We put more effort into it than we normally do."

Pak nods at the conductor. The lights dim, and a majestic singer in an apricot *hanbok* glides out from the wings. The conductor wafts his baton in the air, and delicately, the orchestra begins. It's the first time I wish our soundman had not exploded in Beijing. There is no mixing desk to plug into, and our boom and lapel mics are incapable of capturing the grandeur of Pei's score now filling the hall. Sam would have solved the problem in an instant. I place every recording device we've got in a circle around the conductor's brogues and hope for the best.

"When my native place is bright with the glow of spring, I sow affection-permeated seeds with mother's love . . ." the woman sings, in an ethereal soprano. The strings surge in a melancholy crescendo, and the woman gracefully sweeps the air with her sleeve: *"I earth the buds in autumn. I fertilise them with manure in the winter."* I look at Pei, surprised by the use of "manure" in such a romantic song—but he's lost in the woman's beautiful voice. I shelve it as another lost-in-translation moment and allow Pei's music to transport me.

After another extraordinary verse, the woman closes the song with a single, ethereal note: *"My native home, it's the best place to beeeeeeeeeeeeeeeeeeeeee."* She raises her arms, gazing over our heads at her own private vision of Sydney Park. The conductor puts down his baton. The musicians lower their instruments. Everyone looks at Pei. He turns to me. "Bravo! Bravo!" I shout, clapping madly, not caring if this is not how North Koreans behave in such a formal setting. Not only were Pei's lyrics more interesting than mine; his music was exquisite.

"Our Dear Leader said to make good music, the composer and director must be close friends, and drink together on a regular basis," says Pei, following us out. "For this reason, I must hug you." I oblige, surprised by this spontaneous show of affection. If the Japanese, as the cliché goes, are the "British of Asia," the Koreans—both North and South—are the Italians: quick to anger, quick to please, and unashamedly passionate. Pei hugs me tight for a very long time. He smells of peppermint and whisky. "So warm. So genuine. I want a souvenir," says Pei, and Nic takes our photo.

"I hope our actress can do your beautiful music justice," I whisper in Pei's ear—and he's so delighted he insists on travelling with us to our next shoot.

All the way to the Tae kwon do Palace, Pei conducts a post-mortem on his song, agonising about whether I really liked it, or if I was just being polite. I tell him repeatedly that he's written a masterpiece. So do Sun Hi, Nicola, Wang, and Q. It's not enough. "Yes, but did she really *like* it?" he asks the driver, for the umpteenth time. The driver's the only person still listening: the rest of Team Gas have given up. "I mean, she could just have meant she likes it in a professional sense, you know?" Pei frets. "Not a genuine, soulful one . . ."

The driver does what any self-respecting Australian would do when faced with such artistic wankery: he snaps. "She liked it, for fuck's sake. Now, for the love of God, shut up!" We laugh, and Pei grins happily. It's just what he needed to hear. Nic and I know exactly what the driver's said, without the translation. Filmmaking's like that. You can be working in an alien culture, but when the creative ego's involved, we're all as fragile as each other: identical needy lunatics.

We carry our gear into the cavernous stadium of the Tae kwon do Palace to discover forty-two black-belts in starched white uniforms lined up on a sprung stage. They do complex axe-kick patterns in perfect unison and chop wooden planks with knife-blade palms. They climb into a human pyramid, four people high—and a man does a string of backflips, somersaulting through the air towards a plank held by a woman balanced at the pyramid's top, snapping it in half with his foot. As the athletes defy gravity with these spectacular feats, Kim Jong Il looks down from the gods, above a red slogan: *Let us Practise Every Day and Become Iron-Fisted Masters, in Service of Our Beloved Generalissimo Kim Jong Il!* These fighters are the best in North Korea, and would rake in medals by the truckload if they were allowed to compete overseas. But the International Olympic Committee only recognises the South Korean version of tae kwon do, and North Korean black-belts are banned from the games. Foreign camera crews like us are the closest these athletes get to displaying their skills to the West.

Mr. Chen, a ripped fifty-year-old who has been appointed to choreograph the stunts in my film, has a problem with a line in the script: "She grabs him by the arm, throws him onto her back and dumps him on the mat." This has caused great consternation among his team—there is no tae kwon do throw to match the description. I explain, a little guiltily, that the sentence was written to fit into one line on the page rather than describe an actual move.

"No matter, here are three moves we prepared earlier," Chen says and claps his hands. A man and woman line up on the stage to bow—then execute three fights of death-defying intensity. At the end of each one, the woman sends the man flying with a gutcrunching punch, literally walking sideways up his body at one point to wrap her leg round his neck and snap him to the ground.

"Matt and Pete need to make the fight in your movie look real," Chen says solemnly, and claps his hands again. A broad-shouldered young man in camouflage pants, easily six foot five, bows at the nuggety Chen. They do a violent hand-to-hand combat sequence, which ends with Chen throwing his attacker through the air. The man slams on his back, then flips himself upright with a dazzling smile. It's as brutal as anything I've seen in Hollywood—with none of the clever cutting that is used to make the violence look real. I can't wait to show my actors what "doing your own stunts" means in North Korea.

We wrap the day on the twilit slopes of Moran Hill, a Pyongyang park famous for its group dancing. Most weekends, people come here to laze under landscaped trees over sizzling Korean barbeques. On national holidays, they dance. Q unwraps a picnic lunch of tempura and fried prawns on sticks, and Team Gas lie back in the grass, devouring the well-earned meal. I'm sure the group dancing on Moran Hill is a state-enforced activity: I've seen enough footage of Pyongyang's supposedly happy punters, waltzing in perfectly choreographed circles, to know that the collective joy is manufactured.

From behind a hedge, we hear the tinny sound of "Hwiparam": a folk song about a traditional wooden whistle, beloved by children on both sides of the DMZ. The driver is snoozing in the van with our Sony locked inside, and we don't want to incur the wrath he showed Mr. Pei by disturbing him, so Nic picks up her mini 5D and we climb through the hedge to investigate.

On a leaf-strewn path, people of all ages are dancing as a grandmother rides the volume on an old boom-box. Mothers swirl their scarves around each other flirtatiously, singing out loud. Two soldiers, their khaki shirts unbuttoned to their waists, weave arm in arm, followed by a line of ecstatic children doing their best to imitate them. *"La la la la la la, Hwiparam!"* The group sings as one, smiling broadly when they see our camera. I feel like we've stepped inside a jolly village song from one of Kim Jong Il's movies. If Pyongyang is a giant open-air musical, this is its most joyful scene. These people are undeniably happy, and their dancing is spontaneous. There's no way Q could have arranged for them to be there ahead of time: we chose to picnic on the other side of the hedge under six minutes ago.

I watch the dancing North Koreans, and the words of Chun, the TV entertainer from Seoul, come back to me: *Any song without politics becomes an instant hit in North Korea.*

"Hwiparam" is a song about a whistle. It doesn't mention the Kims once. Strangely, it has yet to be banned.

THE PROBLEM
OF GAY PEOPLE

LURKING IN THE BOWELS OF EVERY documentary is an ethical demon. The situations that awaken it vary—but they all boil down to the same impossible choice: honour the trust of your subjects, or betray it to entertain the audience. Michael Moore interviewed the CEO of General Motors twice for *Roger & Me*, but left the footage out of the film. Joaquin Phoenix pretended to be insane in *I'm Still Here*, then admitted it was all a stunt on Letterman. Sacha Baron Cohen duped his American subjects in *Borat* so often, their lawsuits ate up a large part of his box office. I'm not immune: in *Forbidden Lie$*, I was honest with Norma until I realised the only way I could catch her lying would be to lie to her myself; in *Helen's War*, I promised my aunt, anti-nuclear activist Dr Helen Caldicott, that I'd delete a scene where she dropped the F-bomb, then kept it in (with her eventual consent), because it was the most entertaining part of the film. And now, here I am with Q and Sun Hi in the Hana Music Information Centre, calmly aware that I'm about to deceive them.

Things go smoothly at first: the dewy-eyed guide with the flawless skin repeats her grief-stricken rendition of Kim Jong Il's final visit with impeccable precision—even crying on cue, just as she did the last time, when Kim's tattered glove appears on the LCD screen. Then Q shuts us down: "You must not use any images of the Dear Leader, or of Great Comrade Kim Jong Un." This is news to me. We've already filmed hundreds of portraits of the Leaders—and as long as they are not out of focus or cropped, Q has given us his blessing. Now, without explanation, the Hana Music Centre's blurry slides of Kim Jong Il with the DVD player, Kim Jong Il with the Hana workers, and Kim Jong Il with Kim Jong Un watching the Vienna Philharmonic play "The Blue Danube," are off limits.

I remember Nick Bonner's warning in Beijing: that if our minders ask us to do anything that seems nonsensical, we must obey. But when Q tells me I must delete the guide's speech, and the Kim Jong Il slides along with it, I rankle. Rushes are as sacred to the filmmaker as sources are to journalists: you protect them like a baby. I don't understand why the free world should be denied the chance to see Kim's holy glove because of some red tape at Hana Music. There's nothing offensive about the images: Kim's not wearing a kooky moustache; no one's photoshopped his hair. He's not wielding an Uzi like he does in *Kim Jong Il vs Hulk Hogan* or clomping around on puppet strings à la *Team America*. The slides are obviously for public consumption—they're playing in full view of the music-loving citizens of Pyongyang, who are plugged into the Hana Music Centre headphones, apparently enjoying the regime's latest hits.

I nod politely at Q, and turn to Nic with a sigh: "I'm terrifically tired." It's the code phrase we dreamt up in Beijing. She immediately knows what to do: "These are the files," she says to Q, pointing out the little square icons on the Sony's operating panel. "And this is how you wipe them." She highlights the offending clips and drags them into trash. The camera emits a conclusive *bing* but I'm not worried: the low-res versions of the clips still exist on the nano flash drive, connected to the back of the camera.

"We're happy to give you our hard drives later, so you can confirm they've been deleted," I add, making a mental note to copy the nano to my laptop tonight. "Yes," says Q, without his usual smile. Sun Hi looks between us, concerned. Then, to my horror, Q cancels our next shoot on the Taedong River Bridge, and Team Gas all pile back into the van to drive to the Yangakkdo at high speed. Q wants to check our drives immediately.

Nic and I sit in the back in nerve-racked silence. My lie has trapped us in a bigger one: if I don't pull the clips off the nano straight away, Q will know I've deceived him. "Let's get the camera ready to download," I say to Nic, and she starts unplugging cables from the front of the Sony. I hold the back of the camera in my lap—using the messy spaghetti of wires to discreetly unhook the nano drive and tuck it into my sock. I do it instinctively, as I would on any other shoot. It wouldn't be helpful to remember that right now I am in North Korea without a passport.

We follow Q into the Yangakkdo, trying to look relaxed, and he takes charge. Nic must wait with the camera in the cafe, and Sun Hi is to accompany me to my room. Ostensibly, she's there to help carry down the orange drives on which we store our masters. But she follows me like a shadow—even into the bathroom, as I look for a card reader. Clearly, I'm not going to be able to copy the nano in private—I'll have to do it in plain sight. "Oh look, a bra!" I say, scooping some underwear off the floor. Sun Hi turns bright red and giggles. Her sense of what's naughty sits around where my daughter's did when she was five. Sun Hi turns away in embarrassment, and I seize the chance to adjust the nano in my sock. Thank God my jeans are slightly flared, I think: that little bulge wouldn't just derail the shoot; it would derail *us* too.

We reassemble in the cafe, and Nic does the straight work of plugging the drives into the Sony to copy the high-res footage. Meanwhile, I rummage under the table for the nano, slide it into the card reader, and connect it right there on the table to my laptop. "Here's some stuff we shot yesterday," I say, and pull up a full-screen clip of the tae kwon do fights as the nano chugs away underneath. Sleight of hand, the gambler's skill, the magician's assistant: all proven ways of getting the mark to look the other way. In this case, the acrobatic Chen and his black-belts are working wonders on Q and Sun Hi. By the time the slides of Kim Jong Il are sitting in "Self-Saucing Puddings," the nano is clean and ready to check. Mission accomplished. I doubt Kim Jong Il's glove will ever end up in my film—and I'm aware that if it does, our friends could take the rap. But I will not let North Korea censor my right to decide. From his murky tank, Simon Sheen gives me a supportive blink. I blink back and, in defence of free speech, order a Coke.

The icy bubbles taste like freedom in the back of my throat—but we're not in the clear yet. Ms. K strides through the hotel's revolving doors and slides into the booth beside me. Whatever Q has told her has compelled her to leave the film festival building and hurry through the slogan-filled hedges to join us. Never one to let a crisis get in the way of a drink, Ms. K orders a Taedonggang beer, fixes me with her half-smile, and presents a contract. It's printed on recycled paper, the filaments pressed into a pale brown weft beneath an old copperplate font.

Two clauses immediately stand out. First, our North Korean collaborators can view any footage we film, and "will deal with customs regulation for viewed footage." And second, they "will not be held responsible for an irresistible situation" occurring during our shoot. Fair enough, I think: Ms. K is using the threat of customs confiscating our rushes to justify Korfilm's right to check them whenever it likes. More curious what an "irresistible situation" in North Korea could possibly be, I check the fine print. It lists "natural calamity, disease, and measures taken by the state." That doesn't sound reassuring. "Measures taken by the state" could mean anything—from Kim Jong Un declaring war on the West, to Pak being arrested for discussing *The Godfather,* to Nic and me being detained for possessing images of Kim Jong Il.

"You must sign now so we can make sure everything goes okay at the airport," Ms. K says evenly. And I know I can't sign. It's not the customs threat that's bothering me, although that's undeniably ominous—it's clause 3.1: that I "shall guarantee the film's accuracy and objectivity, and not use any narration or voice-over in the finished film." I assume this has been inserted to prevent me from making another *Red Chapel*, after Mads Brügger betrayed his North Korean subjects so comprehensively a year ago. But given my documentary fuses North Korean propaganda with coal seam gas, I'm going to need narration to help audiences make sense of it all. Protecting your footage is one thing; signing a contract you can't honour is where I draw my ethical line.

"Please delete clause 3.1," I say to Ms. K. "And I cannot sign for Unicorn Films without Lizzette seeing it." Ms. K puts down her beer, displeased. "I will check the clause," she says. "However, if you don't sign soon, we cannot help you in leaving." She beckons over a slender man in a suit, sipping tea at the bar. "This is Comrade Guk." I recognise him: Guk is the gatekeeper who stopped me breaking into Floor Five on my last trip. "Comrade Guk will inspect your rushes, so customs do not have to," Ms. K says with a pointed smile. "Please hand them over." I give Guk our three orange drives, and he looks at the cable sockets, puzzled. North Korean computer geeks, it appears, have yet to hear of FireWire. Blocking out the possibility that the inscrutable Guk will find a whole new list of clips we have to delete, I give him a FireWire cable, and head for the Tailor & Business Centre in the lobby.

The Yangakkdo's monolithic nineties computer sits on its lacy doily, the screen freshly dusted. According to *Lonely Planet*, the machine is set up for guests to send one email to the outside world, in the case of an emergency: but no one has actually done it to see if it works. I wait for the machine to groan to life, picturing Guk's comrades poised over their screens on Floor Five, waiting to see what I write. The business centre lady brings up whatever the North Korean version of Yahoo is, and I type Lizzette's address into the utilitarian header. The keys, when I tap them, pop like bubble wrap. They haven't been used for a very long time.

Hi Lizzette

Filming going well, Korfilm sending contract. Must sign asap, to assist rest of shoot ----- and departure. Trust ok, x Anna

I press *Send*, hoping Lizzette will realise the hyphens stand in for a whole lot of things I can't possibly say. The business centre lady shuts down the computer, and I make my way back through a mob of freshly de-bussed tourists. They lean excitedly over their cameras, sharing pictures of the Kim statues at Mangyongdae. As Nic and I follow Team Gas out to our van, they watch us with envy. These people have been cooped up in a bus for three days and shunted from photo-op to photo-op, with no contact with North Koreans other than their guides. "Where are they taking you today?" asks a Canadian academic, his cabin fever making him look slightly insane. Last night in the non-revolving restaurant, he confessed to me that Pyongyang is fifth on his bucket list, but the rest of North Korea is first. "To the countryside," I say, trying not to gloat, and skip outside.

When Pyongyang visitors want to see something farm-related, they are normally taken to marvel at lovingly tended rows of "Kimjongilia" flowers in the botanical gardens north of the city. But Ms. K has a remarkable ability to get us into places not on the tourist radar. When we were planning the shoot, I'd emailed asking if we could see a cooperative farm like in *Urban Girl Gets Married*, and Ms. K exceeded even her own high standards: "Let us go to the People's Magnificent Taedong Apple and Turtle Farm!" she'd replied.

From what I can work out, the Apple and Turtle Farm is in Taedong County in South Pyongan province, two hours from Pyongyang. The province is split into one *up* (village), one *rodongjagu* (worker district), and twenty-one *ri* (towns). My map indicates we are currently on Sochon Street, heading west. We could be on the road to nowhere, for all I care—I'm just glad to be escaping Korfilm. Team Gas seems to share my relief: as we speed along the highway, suffused with the joyful optimism that kicks off all road trips, the driver puts "Hwiparam" on

the stereo, and my North Korean comrades, in their koala caps, start
to sing.

"*La la la la Hwiparam,*" warble Mr. Wang and Sun Hi, as the driver
imperiously waves our travel permit at the third checkpoint we've
passed in ten minutes. The soldier peers at Nic and me curiously and
waves us on. *"HWIPARAM!"* sings Team Gas triumphantly—then Sun
Hi stops and leans over with sudden concern. "What can we do about
the problem of gay people?" she whispers. I look at Nic. Sun Hi's ignorance of the West is almost total: she doesn't know of George Clooney,
Madonna, Bowie, or The Beatles. Her ideas of how Westerners live are
cobbled together from *The Sound of Music*, *Mary Poppins*, *Bend It like
Beckham*, *The Pelican Brief*, Tchaikovsky's *Swan Lake,* and the snatches
of slang we taught her before Q shut her down. We've been itching to
enlighten Sun Hi for days. Now we're in the countryside, with Ms. K
safely back on an island in Pyongyang, and no Man in Black taking
notes. The camera isn't rolling, and Q is taking a break from his surveillance duties to enjoy the scenery. This is our chance.

"Well, Sun Hi," I begin gently, "where we live, gay people are not
a problem. In fact, we believe they have a right to live normal lives,
like everyone else. Our government is even considering allowing them
to marry. And every year, in Sydney, gay people put on sparkly underwear, and dance in the streets. There are men dressed as women and
women dressed as men, and big strong girls on motorbikes with top-
less girlfriends. There are gay people from the army, the police, and the
government. They all march and do group dancing and throw sequins
at the crowd. They carry banners criticizing our politicians, and afterwards, they go to a stadium and dance until dawn, sometimes on illegal
drugs. The parade is called Mardi Gras, and it is broadcast on national
TV. It is celebrated by six hundred thousand non-gay people and their
families—which is roughly the population of Tasmania—who all turn
up in the streets to clap."

Sun Hi looks queasy: "Ah, that's a joke, right? You're making fun!"

I shake my head. "It's true. In New Zealand and some parts of

America, gay people can get married, by law. Some of my best friends are gay, with children. You know, two mums with a little boy, or two dads with a little girl. It's all completely fine."

Sun Hi gasps in horror. I can almost hear the synapses exploding in her brain. "I'm sorry, too much," she says, and turns very quiet. I leave Sun Hi contemplating her lap in a state of mute shock and turn my attention to the road. We've been driving through what seems to be one huge barley field for an hour now—the neat furrows interspersed with people pulling ox-drawn carts and carrying hessian sacks. A fine mist blurs the valley into soft greens and greys. It is as serenely pretty as the Thai countryside of my childhood—without the Coke ads.

I scour the landscape for signs of the other North Korea, the one even Nick Bonner says exists outside the cosy bubble of Pyongyang. The rumours are horrific: the coastal town of Wonsan, romanticised in North Korean tourist brochures as a laid-back seaside resort, purportedly contains a barbed-wire gulag, to which old people are lured with promises of retirement, then put to work. Defectors from the North speak of farmers being shot for raiding communal orchards to feed their families. Footage smuggled from the east shows gangs of orphans as young as five begging for food in the streets and huddling together in burnt-out basements to sleep. Even the United Nations, with its staunch reliance on fact over rumour, maintains that malnutrition is rife, with a third of the people outside Pyongyang lacking basic food and sanitation at any one time.

The road we're on, however, either runs through an unusually prosperous part of the country, or the starvation is much further away. The people working in the fields, so far, seem purposeful, well fed, and fit. As we approach a new military checkpoint on the border of South Pyongan province, the benign normality starts to shift. A little boy, no more than four, stands alone on a muddy path in a dirty blue sailor suit, looking stunned. The people walking past ignore him, and further on, a group of farm workers see our van and immediately scurry into the field, as if in fear of being accosted. As the guard unlocks the wire gate to let us through, ten people waiting on the other side quickly bicycle past us, their eyes lowered under sodden hoods. In the pannier of the closest cyclist, I see two shaggy puppies, strung together by their necks. Their tongues loll with thirst, but they don't squirm—their legs appear to be broken. These are the first dogs I've seen in my entire time in North Korea. They don't look like pets.

"In front of you is an endless paradise you can't see anywhere else in the world," intones the Taedong Apple and Turtle Farm video as we enter the foyer. "Yearly, it processes thirty thousand tonnes of fruit and fifty thousand tonnes of fruit products. We owe it to the grand ideas of our Great General. He provided us with a sea of apple blossoms!" The boiler-suited ladies feeding apples onto a space-age conveyor belt morph from virtual to real, as the guide leads us onto a glass platform, looking down on a processing machine the size of a nuclear reactor. The ladies from the video wear plastic booties and caps and move over the white floor with scientific precision. They are feeding perfect pink apples into a twisted chrome pipe that could double as a Marc Newson sculpture. At the other end of the pipe, shiny bottles stamped with the Taedong logo glide along a conveyor belt, pumped full of the Great General's life-prolonging nectar.

"It is true this factory produces the highest quality juices, soaps, and shampoos," the guide says, ushering us into a sky-lit vestibule that features Kim Jong Il in a field of apple blossoms, stroking his double chin. "This is the very lift the Great General used, when he came to give us his benevolent guidance." The guide and Sun Hi step back from the elevator door, so we can admire the gold sign above it: *Our Dear Leader Kim Jong Il used this lift on July 21, 2011*. We are then led along a second glass walkway, suspended over more processing labs. Some contain tank-sized vats of shampoo, others massive cylinders of yellow and pink soap. All are suspiciously empty. "Where are the workers?" I ask.

"They are having a break," Sun Hi replies, not very convincingly.

The long white corridor to the visitors' centre is also worker-free. In a brightly lit shop, an aggressively rouged lady in a duck-egg blue uniform welcomes us to peruse aisles of jams, pickles, and cosmetics, all made on the farm. High on the wall, a TV is mounted on an altar, wreathed with flowers. It is playing *We Met Again on Mount Myohyang*, a film celebrating Kim Jong Il's love of nature. "Our Fathers found a great gold mine in Habiro Valley," a noble park worker is telling his lover. "But our Great Leader had the mine abandoned, saying: 'Mount Myohyang is more precious than gold.' So we carved his song of love on the rocks." The video cuts to a huge red slogan etched on a granite cliff. Then it segues into a karaoke-style clip of ruddy-cheeked factory girls singing as they polish apples on a factory floor. There are more workers in this one shot than we've seen in the entire Taedong Apple and Turtle Farm for the last forty minutes.

The guide takes us out into the drizzling rain to admire six huge greenhouses, each one perfectly smooth, grey, and empty. "Our Great Leader removed all the coal mines in this area, so our produce would not be damaged," says the guide, and I'm seriously beginning to wonder if he removed all the workers too. Maybe Sun Hi's right, and they're just resting somewhere. Or maybe the regime is too energy-poor to keep this factory running all the time, and uses it as a fruit-themed side-show for inquisitive visitors. Kim Jong Il's love of nature could also be fake—but the propaganda devoted to it indicates the regime considers environmentalism important. The Dear Leader's green cred has been mythologised in movies, plays, and books. In *Kim Jong Il: A Life*, the young Kim decides to find out why low-flying swallows forecast rain:

> Kim Jong Il closely observed the flight of swallows for months. At last he learned the reason and said to his great-grandfather: "When it is about to rain, insects, not swallows, fly low first, because their wings become moist and heavy. The swallows fly low to catch the insects." Struck by his cleverness, Kim Po Hyon embraced the boy lovingly and exclaimed, "What a wonder child I have in my family!" The vil-lage elders admired the boy, calling him a child prodigy. And he was loved by the People too, for his outstanding intelligence and wisdom.

"Where does the energy for this farm come from?" I ask the guide, aware that while North Korea has made noises about using renewable since 2011, the bulk of its electricity is still derived from hydroelectric dams and fossil fuels.

"We are building many solar farms and wind turbines," says the guide, without hesitation. Then he lowers his voice to Sun Hi, his lapel mic picking up every word: "Should I tell her we use coal-fired power?"

"No, don't bother," Sun Hi answers. "Her country is being destroyed by gas mines. Just say something about that." The guide nods, and turns to us with a sympathetic smile. "Anyway, I just want you to know that coal seam gas is very bad. I feel very sorry for your farmers."

Sun Hi continues to massage her translations when we walk next door into an amphitheatre of concrete tanks. Long-necked turtles crawl on the mossy cement as a handful of workers in gumboots sluice them with hoses. The worker closest to us is wearing a floppy white seventies sunhat and flower-print blouse, rocking that retro-feminine look I now recognise as North Korean worker chic. "These turtles are very good for enhancing the brain function," says the guide, lifting out an animal to show us its slimy, sharp brown teeth. "We grind up their blood and bones and feed it to the children before their exams."

"*Ewww!*" Nic, Sun Hi, and I say, sharing a moment of girly horror. The guide laughs: "Turtle brain has a real kick, when you mix it in alcoholic drinks."

Sun Hi titters nervously

"What did he say?" I ask. Her translation is pure poetry: "It is also beneficial for the adults' health."

We drive up a steep hill facing the apple orchards. The trees stretch all the way to a low shelf of mountains bordering the valley. The rain has started to fall in soft grey sheets, and Q holds a plastic protector over Nic and the camera, so she can line up her shots. It's quiet and still in our plastic cocoon, and the cottages nestled below look as pretty as a Normandy postcard. The village, at least, appears to be inhabited: in three minutes, I count eight bicyclists and four walkers, and two schoolboys carrying posies of red flowers. They noodle along in their sailor suits, chatting contentedly. Then they look up and see us and immediately split apart—disappearing into the alleys as fast as they can without breaking into a run. Nic attaches Kim Kardashian to the Sony to get an extreme wide. The orchard's main road dissects her shot in a straight line, right up to the foot of the mountains. "When you frame it symmetrically like this, it looks like something from one of your movies, doesn't it?" I say to Q. It's the first time I've directly addressed him.

He looks at me with his intelligent, heavy-lidded eyes. "Yes," he says, smiling.

With our landscapes in the can, Nic and I stretch out in the van, glad to be out of the rain. We pass wide wet fields and copses of birch and people hunched over bicycles in black tarpaulins, flapping along the highway like bats. Behind high stone walls, we glimpse the odd thatched roof, the occasional mural of Kim Jong Il. We plunge into a long tunnel, and on the other side of it, through the trees, I spot what looks like a town. "Please can we stop, Tongji Q? It's the only town we've seen," I beg. Q looks at me carefully in the rearview mirror—making a point of waiting for Sun Hi to translate. Then he tells the driver to stop. As long as we don't leave the road, we may pick off a few shots. Q doesn't get out to check the viewfinder: we're either too far away from Pyongyang for it to matter, or he's unfamiliar with the power of the photoscopic lens. Nic attaches Lady Gaga to the Sony, and the town sits magnified before us.

The clay buildings are narrow and up to six storeys high, the roads between them unpaved. People walk to and fro under umbrellas, gathering around the tents of a ramshackle market tacked to the edge of a muddy square. No one is skeletal—but the knife-sharp cheekbones on several faces suggest that three meals a day could be a luxury. A man in a faded army jacket squats under an awning, cobbling shoes, and a girl in a skirt balances side-saddle on the back of her boyfriend's bicycle. Through a ground-floor window, we see a string of plastic flowers looped along a wall, and people sitting beneath it, eating from steel bowls. Further back there's a large but decrepit building, flanked by a low wooden stage and framed by the red-and-white slogans we've seen in Pyongyang. In the foreground, three twelve-year-old girls skip along a path, pushing hula hoops. The low-slung cottages they're skipping past, while distinctly impoverished, are clean. . . .

"You must stop now," Sun Hi says firmly, and we climb into the van, treasuring our thirty-two seconds of uncensored access. I give Q a grateful smile. He reaches over to hold the camera so Nic can buckle her seatbelt, and his cuff rides above his wrist. On the smooth skin of his inner arm, faded with age, are five tattooed numbers. They look functional, not decorative: like the ID tattoos worn by the survivors of Auschwitz. Before I can study them, Q's cuff slides back down, and he turns to the front. We drive into the twilight, lapsing into the companionable chatter of a road trip successfully shared. Sun Hi grills Nic about what "rents" and "mortgages" are, and Mr. Wang and the driver idly dissect some Pyongyang soccer game.

But Q is silent. I gaze out at the misty fields, stunned. So what if I can't put Kim Jong Il's glove in my movie, or if Dresnok hates me and our scene tomorrow is a disaster? Who cares if we don't get our rushes out of the country, or I end up making a movie that no one understands? What does it matter that I've lost my marriage, when my daughter is thriving, and I know that she's safe at night? Q, a father of four, appears to have gone through more than I ever will.

Nic packs up the Sony to discover we've lost our lens cap—probably back on the highway, in front of the town. I tell her not to worry. Compared with whatever hell Q has survived, the idea of filling out lengthy insurance forms now feels like a luxury.

SPINSTER TIME

"YOU BOWL, THEN TURN WITH GREAT joy to your husband, and say: 'Strike!'" says Ri excitedly. I nod, and he barks at the makeup lady: "Brush her hair, for God's sakes, or she'll look like a spinster!" Sun Hi giggles, but doesn't translate. In my wildest dreams, I never thought I'd end up in a white jumpsuit with Joan Collins hair, playing an "evil American bowling secretary" in Pyongyang. The bowling alley has a nineties monitor, three pink lanes, and a Lady Di poster on the wall. It's part of a secret labyrinth of snooker bars, karaoke discos, and ping-pong rooms tucked away in the mysteriously named "Underfloor" of the Yangakkdo Hotel.

Ri strides to the camera and looks at me expectantly. All I know is that my character likes purple mascara and is married to the oldest Dresnok. The middle Dresnok is playing a Yankee spy with whom I am apparently required to flirt, but Sun Hi considers this too risqué to translate. I squint through the lights at Ri's twenty-man crew. "What's my motivation?" I ask, feebly.

"Just tell her it's real," Ri snaps—and turns to Dresnok. "It's a shame your chest doesn't bulge out," he grumbles, butting out his fag. "Action!"

I hurl the bowling ball at the pins, narrowly missing a squatting man waiting to catch it. "Strike!" I say stiffly and look straight down the barrel. Ri darkens. Film stock is expensive: most North Korean actors only get two takes. "I'm sorry, I fucked up," I mumble, and everyone looks at me in shock.

Ri mutters something, and even the Dresnoks laugh. "He said: 'She thinks it's digital,'" Sun Hi translates, enjoying the putdown. It takes me four more takes to finally nail the over-the-top Californian gaucheness Ri is looking for. He scutinises my face, then yells at the makeup lady: "Younger! Prettier! Younger!"

The makeup lady whips out some frosty pink gloss, which she promises will knock a decade off sun-damaged Australian skin. Ri surveys me with pity: "You've been directing a long time, haven't you? It makes you look tired." I apologise, pointlessly, for my wrinkles, and he chuckles and walks off.

"Where do you get your products?" I ask the makeup lady, who is rocking an eighties sun-visor over fifties hair. "Some are made here, some from China," she replies, and I show her my lipstick: "Do you use Chanel?" She glances at the tube with bored disdain, a look most North Koreans cultivate when confronted with Western products. "No. This one makes you prettier," she says and smears her pink gloss on my lips.

Powdered and pouffed, I join the sullen Dresnoks under the lights, feeling like Norma Desmond from *Sunset Boulevard*. She had five hours to transform herself into an object of desire for younger men; I've had five minutes. In this scene, I must wipe Husband Dresnok's brow with a cloth, while Spy Dresnok makes eyes at me. All right, Mr. Ri, I'm ready for my close-up, I feel like saying, reminding myself there's nothing tragic about being fortysomething, as long as you're not trying to be twenty-five.

"Positions!" calls Ri, and Mr. Wang drops the boom to answer his phone. He wanders off, and Ri scowls but doesn't resist as I attach a radio mic to his lapel. He knows he has to let me shoot my film, so I will act in his. "Action!" he yells finally, and I sashay over to Husband Dresnok as sexily as I can, hips gyrating and eyelashes fluttering, reaching up to seductively dab his huge, sweaty forehead. He freezes in horror, and the entire crew titters.

Sun Hi turns bright red: "Comrade Ri said *offer* him the cloth, not *touch* him with it!" she says, trembling with embarrassment.

The frustrated Ri slumps in a deck chair under Lady Di and stares at his script for a very long time. "We'll just have Dresnok pick up the cloth alone," he declares finally—and sacks me. I slink off under the Dresnoks' gloating gaze, back through the shadowy Underfloor. Team Gas follow in supportive silence. I feel like I've let down my country.

In the foyer, Ms. K has good news. Lizzette's email got through: the contract is good to sign. But Guk, the rushes checker, looks worried. I ask him what's wrong, already preparing myself to kiss our footage goodbye. "I am sorry, but I cannot view your drives," Guk says, and I realise what the problem is. Our high-res Sony files are recorded at the latest codec, viewable only with sophisticated software. North Korea doesn't have it. I copy the software onto one of the drives and hand it to the ecstatic Guk. He hurries back to his comrades on Floor Five in a state of geeky euphoria. If Kim Jong Un's next rocket launch is a success, I sure as hell hope it isn't because I just gave North Korea QuickTime X.

"Let us dine with the workers of the Pyongyang Film Studio!" Ms. K beams, and I remember, a little sadly, that in forty-eight hours we'll be gone. Team Gas is with us right to the end: Q's surveillance services are still required on tomorrow's trip to the DMZ. But the North Korean filmmakers are wrapped. We join them in the meadow of Kim Jong Il's European film set, where a picnic table has been spread with platters of shredded cabbage, kimchi, and beef. The braziers are already smoking, and the artists are all there in floral barbeque aprons: Mr. Pei the composer, Mr. O the cinematographer, Mr. Kang the designer, Ms. Jang the rom-com writer, the April 25 Military Film Studio director, actors Ms. Yun and Ri Yon Chol, and Mr. Ri and his crew—but thankfully, no Dresnoks. Pak, the respected leader, stands and welcomes us with glasses of *soju*. We tie on our aprons and sit down.

"Anna, I will come out of my tomb to help you make your movie," says Pak with a charming smile, and everyone toasts our project.

"I hope *The Gardener* will advance Australian and DPRK friendship," Ms. Jang adds warmly. "There are lots of movies depicting motherly love. But your film says the best way to show it is to pass to the next generation a clean environment. That's a novel idea to me, and why I like your film. When it's made, people will learn not just about green issues, but how we can show our love for our children." The filmmakers nod solemnly, and we all toast each other again. Then, with the speechifying out of the way, everyone slaps beef on the braziers and gets down to gorging. Nic and I film and graze, enjoying the camaraderie of our North Korean friends. They chat in the soft afternoon light, the aprons shielding their pristine shirts from the sticky barbeque.

"Do you ever fall in love with your leading men?" I ask Ms. Yun, who is unusually relaxed, having eschewed her normal tea for *soju*. She giggles. "Goodness, I've acted a married woman so often, I can't fall in love with my partner every time. He's normally a soldier or a worker, and I go into character to act the feeling. But I never fall in love to the point of destroying my family."

Pak raises his glass to her fondly: "Well said, Comrade Yun. You might find this unfamiliar, Anna, but here we consider the whole country one big family, and look out for one another. When we make a film, it's a microcosm of society. As the director, I take on the father's role. I care for everyone. Every morning, I look at everyone's faces—and if someone looks troubled, I'll inquire. If someone suffers a misfortune, or falls ill, we help that person. We aren't just creating art, but bringing everyone together into a family with a father, mother, brothers, sisters, and grandchildren. If something goes wrong, the director's leadership is to blame."

"What happens to the director, if something goes wrong?" I press Pak, taking advantage of his candid mood. Perhaps he's decided to let it all hang out, now we're at our last supper. The Man in Black is out

of earshot at the other end of the table. "Directors who fail find it difficult to make a film again," Pak says quietly. "But if you're good, you're
given more movies to make, and it can be quite tough. In my case, I'd
like some rest, but I keep being told to make new movies. I find it a bit
tiring, but directing is the only thing I can do. So I bear with it and keep
on going." I wonder if Pak has the option to retire. He seems strained
behind his courtly smile. Does he keep working because he wants to
contribute, or because the regime gives him no choice?

If Pak is trapped, then his love for his comrades, and theirs for
him, are what sustains him. His wisdom and humour have made him
their undisputed leader—the living embodiment of everything Kim
Jong Il was meant to be, but wasn't. *Great Man and Cinema* recounts
unbelievable tales of Kim flying his crews through snow storms in heli-
copters, carrying their gear up mountains, and even hunting animals
for medicine when a scriptwriter's wife got sick:

> The officials said the weather was very inclement and advised him to
> go when it abated. Comrade Kim Jong Il said they should not post-
> pone, even for a while, to save the patient from death. He put on his
> fur cap and went hunting that minute. That night many wild animals
> were caught. Comrade Kim Jong Il was bright with joy as he came
> back to Pyongyang in a car loaded with them. He told the officials to
> carry the animals to the scriptwriter promptly. Just as devotion makes
> the flower bloom even on a stone, so his great love turned into a mys-
> terious elixir of life and enabled the patient to recover from her incur-
> able disease miraculously.

Even if he was having an affair with her, it's hard to imagine Kim Jong
Il shooting lynx in the freezing snow for a lowly scriptwriter's wife. But
I can see Pak doing it. The only person who doesn't appear to share the
general adoration of the man is the bad-guy actor, Ri Yon Chol.

"Hey, Pak, if you're going to play father, show Anna how to cook
her beef!" Ri Yon Chol yells at Pak over the spitting coals—and Pak

reaches out with his chopsticks, too late, to pull a charred scrap of meat off my brazier.

"You telling me how to do my job, you bastard?" Pak grins—but there's anger in his eyes. It's the same animosity I noticed when they rehearsed on the hill: whatever history these two share, it's not pleasant.

"What movies have you made with Comrade Pak?" I ask Ri Yon Chol, hoping he'll reveal the cause of their conflict. He bursts into derisive laughter: a sure sign I won't get an answer.

Sun Hi tugs on my sleeve. "Anna, Comrade Designer made something for you," she says, and Mr. Kang holds out an intricate watercolour of actress Susan Prior in a North Korean smock and floral headscarf.

"I am not familiar with Australian national customs," says Mr. Kang, his glasses fogged up by the barbeque smoke, "but it is important you dress her practically, with a tool bag of gardening shears, and a scarf to shelter her when she toils. If ladies in your country wear sunhats, that could be okay too." I thank Kang for his beautiful picture, transported back to the days of hand-drawn animation and costumes sewn from scratch. Our budget stretches to one pair of thrift-shop overalls, and if we're lucky, an embroidered logo. I decide that Susan must wear a headscarf. The look may have been out since Helen Reddy sang "I Am Woman" in the tie-dyed 1970s, but in honour of Kang, we'll resurrect it.

"She has no idea about the affairs of our country, none at all," I hear Mr. O saying to Pak in Japanese. Everyone is tipsy now, and the conversation is boisterous.

"That's true. Our newspapers mainly speak about your prisons," I intrude, hoping my childish Japanese will soften the fact I've just raised the taboo of the gulags.

Pak shoots me a look and slips back to Korean: "God, if only she knew how much harder it is now," he says to O. "We filmmakers used to be at the top, didn't we . . . ?" Pak raises his glass in ironic celebration, and O, with a sympathetic nod, clinks and drinks.

"Hey, you mustn't say things like that," Mr. Pei interjects. "Her investors have spent a lot of money sending her here. They'll be embarrassed!" I suspect Pei is more worried about the Man in Black than our investors.

But Pak ignores his warning. "Anna, there is a seismic shift coming in our country," he says, deadly serious. "That's something the DPRK can show the world. Everything is going to change. Let's sing!"

Q and Ms. Yun immediately stand and remove their aprons, smoothing their hair. *"Where have the seeds of love blossomed?"* Ms. Yun begins sweetly, sweeping her arm to invite the whole group to share her joy.

"Have they sprouted near the window where learning echoes?" chimes in Q, making Nic and me look up in astonishment. The man who has said nothing but yes for the last thirteen days has a surprisingly beautiful baritone.

"My endless love has blossomed in the bosom of my comrades," Pak joins in, the love in his eyes for the people around him both sorrowful and warm. *"My love when I am happy, my happiness when I am sad,"* sings the whole table, swaying to the beat. *"My endless love has blossomed in the bosom of my comrades!"* Everyone cheers and Mr. Pei blushes with pride. The song is his, from the war drama *My Happiness*. I turn to Pak, determined to find out what he meant by a "seismic shift," but he grabs my wrist: "Shut up. Now you must share a beloved song, from your country."

Twenty faces turn to me expectantly. Bloody hell. The only anthems Australians sing with the same kind of patriotic fervor are AC/DC's "Highway to Hell," Cold Chisel's "Cheap Wine," and, at a pinch, the Peter Allen–penned Qantas jingle "I Still Call Australia Home." My own favourite, Nick Cave's moody ballad "From Her to Eternity," would bomb with this crowd. They're after something saccharine—which is not a quality the hardbitten cynics of my motherland are known for. Quietly cursing Pak, I take a swig of *soju* and choose the most asinine thing I can think of. "It's a beloved children's song,"

I announce. "It's about a bird." The table clap with delight, and in my pathetic soprano, I let rip: *"Kookaburra sits in the old gum tree; merry, merry king of the bush is he; laugh, Kookaburra, laugh, Kookaburra, gay your life must be."* The filmmakers nod, trying to clap to the beat. Before they can join in the chorus, I've finished, and everyone laughs with relief. Everyone, that is, except the Man in Black—who continues to clap to a 4/4 beat, lost inside the strange mechanical universe of his mind.

"Thank you for recollecting the Australian people's pure and innocent childhood," Pak says kindly, patting my hand. But Sun Hi looks appalled. "What is 'gay'?" she whispers, clearly picturing a country so decadent even the birds are homosexual.

"It's just an old word meaning 'jolly,'" I say, putting her out of her misery.

Pak grabs my hand, impatient. "Anna, let us make a film together," he says and pulls a newspaper from his satchel. "Comrade Translator, pull yourself together," he says, nudging Sun Hi.

She dutifully scans the article he's circled. "This is about a mentally handicapped man in Pyongyang, who through the devotion of his family and comrades had a happy and productive life," she explains.

"It is a really moving story," Pak adds enthusiastically. "Let's make a film about him. Take it!"

I slide the paper into my bag, stunned by Pak's choice of subject. North Korea is notorious for its treatment of the disabled: according to the 2014 UN report on the country's human-rights abuses, handicapped babies are seen as "impure" and are relocated to remote areas, along with their families. Some are sent away forever to secret "treatment" facilities; others are killed at birth. With North Korea's disabled population sitting at a lowly 3.4 percent, against the 10 percent world average, it is doubtful the majority survive to adulthood. I'm sure Pak isn't intending to make a critique of the regime's abuses; but even a straight Kim Jong Il–style propaganda movie in which a disabled hero devotes himself to the nation and no ill-treatment is revealed would be a subversive act. It would fly in the face of Kim's rule that the hero must be physically beautiful and promote the idea that all people, including the disabled, are worthy of respect.

"Read it when you get home," Pak says casually, as if there's nothing unusual in what he's proposed. I'm still thinking about it two hours later, when we climb in the van to drive to the Yangakkdo. Night has fallen, and the driver makes me sit in the front to distract the soldiers. "Hi there!" I wave sunnily at the first checkpoint, and the guards wave us on, too astonished to query our lack of a curfew permit. Pak, Ms. Yun, and Ri Yon Chol chat with Team Gas in the back—and Nic and I share a smile, delighted our comrades have decided to keep drinking with us at the hotel. But then, the driver stops beside an ovoid skyscraper towering over the lightless river. Ms. Yun gets out, shakes my hand through the window, and hurries off into the topiary hedges.

We drive on, down a bumpy side street I haven't seen before. A soldier steps out of the darkness to stop us, and this time, my friendly "Hello" doesn't deter him. "Where is your permit?" he barks at the driver—and I can feel our North Korean friends become tense. Then a voice growls from the back of the van: "What the fuck do you think you're doing, comrade?" The soldier, furious, marches to the window—to find Ri Yon Chol leaning out, wearing his most evil scowl. The soldier's eyes widen in recognition.

"Yes, it's me, you bastard," Ri Yon Chol sneers, with jaded indifference. "Now let us through." The soldier steps back, starstruck. "Nice to know my ugly mug is good for something," Ri Yon Chol says pointedly to Pak, and the old man gives him a grateful nod. We round a bend and head down a bumpy hill to a cul-de-sac of low-rise tenements. These buildings don't have the fresh paint and flower boxes of Yonggwang Street: they are buckled and dirty, the window panes either cracked or gone. Ri Yon Chol mumbles his goodbyes and disappears into the shadows.

"Are you going to join us at the hotel, sensei?" I ask Pak, desperately hoping he's not going to disappear too. I want to talk about his film idea over some sake. I'm certain there's more he wants to share.

He smiles, but says nothing. We turn onto a highway, and I realize it's not the one leading back to our hotel. The North Koreans lapse into an apprehensive silence. This area, after curfew, is dangerous. I try again: "Do you think we can talk some more, Tongji Pak?" He ignores me and says something softly to the driver. The driver slows to a stop beside a desolate stretch of dirt and barbed wire. A line of pale, decrepit buildings is visible through the gloom, miles in the distance. Pak swings open the van door and climbs out. The North Koreans whisper goodbye.

I jump out, bewildered. Pak turns in surprise and holds out his hand: "Goodnight, Anna. You must go back now." I hold his hand, unable to work out what's going on: "Thank you, sensei, thank you for everything," I say, and he breaks into his usual smile: "Don't be silly. The pleasure's mine. Now off you go." He gestures at the van with his head but doesn't let go of my hand. We stand there, staring at each other, and his smile disappears. His hands start to tremble, and his eyes fill with tears. "When will I ever see you again?" he asks.

I clasp Pak's hands tight. I wish I could disappear with him into the darkness and meet his family. I wish I could take him back to Sydney to meet mine. I wish I could give him a hug and tell him how much he's taught me. I wish we could make a film together. Instead, I climb quietly into the van, and Pak bends down to pick up his satchel. The driver does a rapid U-turn, and I peer back through the night to see my mentor hobbling over the dirt in his neatly pressed chinos, picking his way over the rubble to whatever place he calls home.

OUR DIVIDED NATION

Ms. K's BOSS IS DRUNK AGAIN. We're in the meeting room on Floor Five, facing his muu-muued sidekick and two Party officials. The self-entitled smiles on their smooth young faces indicate that these boys are not here on merit, but because they have fathers higher up in the ranks. The problem of Pyongyang's privileged twentysome-things, who grow up sheltered from hardship, is tackled in the 1997 drama *Myself in the Distant Future*. The playboy anti-hero ignores the pleas of his hard-working father and spends his time playing Pac-Man and cruising Pyongyang in a Japanese convertible. Then he falls in love with the humble labourer who has built his high-rise condo. After many ideological discussions on the banks of the Taedong, she finally converts him to the Juche ideal of self-sacrifice—and he devotes him-self to serving the nation.

"Ms. K tells me today you will visit the DMZ," says the boss, and I shift on my chair, trying to cushion my bruised coccyx. North Korean funfairs may contradict the horror stories we hear in the West—but North Korean massages do not. Last night, Nic and I vis-ited the Spa & Fitness Centre on the Underfloor for a much-needed shiatsu. I went in second and found Nic spread-eagled on a bench, glaze-eyed with shock. The masseuse pulled the curtains shut before I could find out what was wrong. "Off!" she ordered, adjusting the sweatband on her white seventies tennis ensemble. I stripped and lay on my back, and she tucked a rice sack between my shoulder blades. Then she placed her muscled hands on my shoulders and slammed them down hard. Crack! went my back, and she laughed. "You feel pain?" she asked.

"Yes. Pain!" I grunted—and she proceeded to crack every bone in my body, with intensifying force. By the time she'd flipped me on my stomach, I was ready to surrender, but my tormentor had something else in mind. She jabbed one thumb on top of my skull, and shoved the other up my arse—avoiding digital sodomy by a millimetre. Then she rammed her thumbs towards each other and pinioned me to the bench—like a pig on a spit. "Pain," she observed, with professional pride. I was too traumatised to speak.

I am now fully prepared for whatever surprises the most militarised border on earth has in store after my night of pain. "I'm looking forward to seeing the DMZ," I tell Ms. K's boss. "But I am worried about what will happen to our footage at the airport."

Ms. K's boss nods sympathetically. "Comrade Guk is doing you a favour by checking your rushes," he says. "Hopefully, you will have a smooth exit. Isn't that right, Comrade K?" Ms. K emits an unhelpful giggle, the only response she ever gives her boss. He frowns. "I want to apologise on behalf of Korfilm for Comrade Wang," he says. "Apparently, his sound recording was not up to scratch."

"No, no, he was wonderful," I enthuse. "And so were your filmmakers. They have taught me so much. In fact, I should apologise for my bad acting. I only shoot video, so it was wonderful to learn about the complex demands of celluloid." The Party officials nod, pleased by my deference to North Korea's artistic superiority.

"You all taught each other," Ms. K's boss says with finality, and nods impatiently at his sidekick. She pulls two contracts from a red velour folder and slides them towards me.

Korfilm's demands are set out in bold copperplate, in English and Korean. The no-narration clause is still there. "Bugger," I say. "I thought we were deleting 3.1?" Ms. K looks at me, surprised, then giggles apologetically at her boss. He glances at the offending clause, and bursts out laughing: "Yes, yes, that is just a stupid mistake by our translators. The Korean version is the right one. Just sign that." They all stare at me, and Ms. K gives me a pen. There's a pleading look in her eyes.

I have no idea what the Korean contract says. I certainly don't trust Ms. K's boss. Then I think of Nic on the forty-seventh floor, recovering from her massage and packing the little Korean dolls she's bought for her mother. Nic needs to get out of here as much as I do. She's put my film before her safety, and I'm the reason she's here. I sign the contract blind, and give Ms. K's boss an envelope with €30,000 in cash.

"Wonderful!" says Ms. K's boss, lurching to his feet. "The contract and the money are not important. What is important is our bond, and your important film." He picks up the duty-free bag of scotch, which, after my last disastrous attempt, I've prudently left by the door. "Why so heavy?" he asks, letting out a comic groan. "It's important alcohol," I say coolly, not bothering to hide my annoyance with this hypocritical drunk. The Party officials do a double take, but Ms. K's boss cackles. "Wonderful," he says again—and squeezing unsteadily around the table, he staggers out of the room.

Ms. K and I look at each other, two working mums in our forties, and share a moment of deliciously sexist disdain. We've both had to go the extra mile, so men above us can take the credit. There are exceptions of course, but in general, I've found women bosses to be more collaborative. I doubt Ms. K has had the luxury of finding this out.

"How can you work for someone like that?" I ask her, when we're safely back in the corridor. "It's 9 a.m. and he was pissed! You've done the work, and he can't even get a bloody translation right! You should be the boss of Korfilm."

Ms. K gives me her rueful smile: "Maybe I will be, if you make a good enough film." I look at the carpet, riddled with guilt. A "good" film in North Korean terms, the one guaranteed to get Ms. K promoted, would be a Kim Jong Il puff piece. I already know my film cannot be an apology for the Kims' brutal regime. But where it will end up sitting, in that grey void between the West's "beyond evil" story and the propaganda of Pyongyang, remains a mystery.

"Let us go on a road trip," says Ms. K happily and ushers me to the stairs. Her friendly smile makes me want to ignore the brutality altogether and make a film that simply humanises the generous North Koreans I've met. As we step into the stairwell, a door behind us swings open and a young woman with a tense expression hurries out. There's just enough time before she closes the door to glimpse a bank of monitors, displaying what appears to be security-camera footage. Two, maybe three, men in headphones sit in a row, gazing intently at the screens. The pictures they are watching look a lot like the hotel rooms on my floor. I could be wrong: I've had less than three seconds to look. But what I've seen is enough to turn the rumour that Floor Five is used to spy on foreign guests from a paranoid fancy to a real possibility.

"It's a shame the enemy aren't around today," a soldier muses to our driver. We're driving under concrete tank traps, poised to drop onto the narrow road that leads to the DMZ. The famous border cuts Korea in half across the thirty-eighth parallel: a latitude chosen somewhat arbitrarily by the Americans and the Soviets at the end of World War Two to delineate their spheres of political influence. Contested by both Kim Il Sung and his American-backed adversaries in the South following the creation of the socialist Democratic Peoples' Republic of Korea and the capitalist Republic of Korea in 1948, the continually shifting border was finally fixed permanently in 1953—when the DPRK, China, and the UN command forces signed the armistice agreement to end the Korean war.

The demilitarized zone is 250 kilometres long, four kilometres wide, and, despite its name, the most heavily armed border on earth. Because the Korean War ended in a ceasefire rather than a peace treaty, America and North Korea are still technically at war. Their armies stand ready to strike at the merest provocation, and the DMZ is booby-trapped with a million landmines. In the Joint Security Area in Panmunjom, the two Koreas face each other across a painted white line. Soldiers on both sides will shoot dead anyone who tries to cross it.

"What's her movie about?" the soldier asks our driver.

"Something to do with gas mines destroying her land," he mumbles, "but we won't get to see it."

The soldier digests this as we pull up outside the Joint Security Area gate. "Why can't we see it? What's wrong with it?" he wants to know.

"If I tell you, we'd get into trouble," says the driver, and orders us out of the van. He's not allowed to drive any further: we must walk the rest of the way.

"You can't take that with you," the soldier says, frowning at our Sony. Apparently, the camera is too big. Nic picks up her mini DV instead, and we follow our minders into the guard post. As busloads of Chinese tourists walk freely through the gate, Ms. K negotiates with an obstinate guard, increasingly flustered. Even without our professional camera, Nic and I are still Western media. Whatever permit we have, it's not enough. "They need an access fee," Ms. K says, looking unusually rattled. I fish out what's left of our petty cash, and she hands it over. The guard barks something at Ms. K, and she stays in the guard post as Q, Sun Hi, Nic, and I walk through.

"Do *not* walk anywhere except where I tell you!" a twenty-something soldier with matinee-idol looks instructs the tourists in fluent Mandarin. We fall into single file. It's not a difficult order to follow: since 1953, skirmishes over this small patch of land have killed five hundred South Koreans, fifty Americans, an unknown number of North Koreans, a few defectors, and one tourist—who wandered into the bushes to do yoga one day and was promptly shot. Despite this, the path we're filing along is pretty and serene. Birds sing in thickets above our heads, and wildflowers line the paving stones. Every fifteen metres, as if to remind us we're not in a nature reserve, a soldier stands to attention with his rifle against his chest, gazing sternly into space.

"This is a monument to the glorious Korean People's Army fight for freedom," our soldier-guide says, pointing at a megalith on a viewing platform above the Joint Security Area. "Its total length is 9.4 metres, which signifies the year it was built by our Great Leader. The height is 4.15 metres, which signifies the date of birth of our Great Leader. At the bottom you can see our national flower, *Magnolia sieboldii*." The tourists lean forward to snap the flower—but Nic and I film the South Korean viewing platform facing us across the valley. It has coin-operated binoculars and fronts a modern glass building. Two decades ago, I stood there with my father, trying to spot North Koreans. Now I'm surrounded by them—and the South Koreans are weirdly absent. Perhaps they have better things to do out there in the free world. Seoul is only sixty-two kilometres away, but all I can see of it from here is a line of gently undulating hills.

If it weren't for the observation towers, the DMZ would look a lot like a national park. Unofficially, it is. The place has been deadly to humans, but a godsend for animals. For six decades, they've roamed freely between the fortified fences—creating what ecologists now recognize as one of the most significant temperate habitats in the world. There are 2,900 plant species, 320 kinds of birds, and seventy different mammals thriving in the mountains, prairies, and marshlands of this accidental wildlife sanctuary—including the near-extinct Korean tiger, Amur leopard, Asiatic bear, and the icon of North Asian art, the red-crowned crane. Just as Chernobyl proved in the 1980s, the removal of humans from the food chain can do wonderful things for nature. In 2005, the DMZ's beauty so captivated CNN media mogul Ted Turner, he offered to finance any plan to turn it into a peace park and UN-protected World Heritage Site.

That's not happening anytime soon, judging from the firepower on display in the Joint Security Area. We follow our soldier-guide

down to a row of deceptively humble blue cement huts on a neat concrete square. The place is oppressively quiet and crackling with tension. South Korean soldiers, in high-tech camouflage uniforms, glare
at their distinctly poorer cousins across the white demarcation line.
Their grim, robotic postures make them look like actors in a particularly pretentious interpretive dance. If it weren't for their guns, I'd
be giggling. As it is, I join the tourists in the main hut in respectful
silence. The table the American and North Korean generals sat around
when armistice negotiations began in 1951 has been perfectly preserved—right down to the miniature flagpoles and microphones posi-
tioned on each side of the line. Horrifically, both powers continued to
kill Korean civilians while conducting these talks, one of the sadder
facts about the Forgotten War. I pose for Nic in the chair where US
Lieutenant General William K. Harrison, Junior sat, making sure the
North Korean soldier behind me is in frame. A South Korean soldier
faces him through the window, stiff and blank. Neither flinches when
Nic's camera flashes. They are brilliant at pretending we're not there.

We move on to Armistice House, a gabled Korean manor surrounded by lush gardens. "On 25 June 1950, America invaded North
Korea," states our soldier-guide solemnly. "After sustaining significant
damage, America suggested talks. Right here is where the agreement
was signed." There is a long table covered in green baize, framed by the
flags of America and its allies. The walls are hung with photographs
of Kim Il Sung talking with the enemy brass and detailed charts of
American war crimes. I walk into the sun, overwhelmed by the insanity
of war. There are no benches to sit on, but a small stone plinth offers
a comfortable ledge. I perch on it and take out my *Inner West Argus*. A
snap of Australian CSG protests in the middle of the DMZ, I figure,
will make for an interesting contrast. "How dare she sit there?" someone yells in Korean—and a dog barks in the distance. I look up from
the paper to see Q hurrying towards me, gesturing frantically for me
to stand.

Apparently, I've committed a major crime: the writing on the plinth is as sacred as Kim Jong Il. Sun Hi, shaky with fear, translates: "The American imperialists, instigators of a provocation raid on Korea, knelt down before the heroic People of Korea and signed the armistice agreement here on 27 July 1953." My incursion has had one advantage: it's compelled our handsome guide to leave the tourists to investigate. "Exactly what movie are you making here?" he asks, alert behind his smile.

"It's about evil capitalists destroying her farms," Sun Hi says quickly, before I can answer.

The soldier stops smiling. "She must delete the image with the foreign newspaper on our monument," he says.

"The article is only about Australian gas drilling," I reason. "It's not about your country. In fact, I'm making a film in your style, to stop the mines."

He raises his beautiful brows in surprise. "You like our films?" His curiosity betrays his innocence. He can't be more than twenty-two.

"What do you think of my country?" he asks. I tell him that I think his people, and their films, are wonderful. "What do you think of Australia?" I fire back.

The soldier breathes in sharply, and rocks on his heels. "I'm going to get in trouble for this, aren't I?" he mumbles to Q. I'm not sure why he's deferring to Q: in his casual shirt and grey slacks, Q is not a Party official, or even a designated guide. He is just our gaffer—an Average Joe from Pyongyang. But from the nervous way the soldier awaits Q's response, it seems that Q has real power.

Q blinks slowly and nods: "It's okay. You can tell her." The soldier squares his shoulders, and faces our camera. We have to tilt up to catch his eyes: he's at least six foot four. "Ma'am, a lot of countries, including Australia, made the mistake of fighting us in the war," he begins, in a respectful tone. "They should not have done it. They were just the lackeys of America."

I nod politely, assuring him I do not condone any of the wars my country has followed America into. In my peripheral vision, I can see Q following every word. "What do you know of Australia?" I press. "Bondi Beach? Mel Gibson? *Mad Max*?"

The soldier's eyes light up at *Mad Max*, but Sun Hi's not going there. "Do Australian visitors who come here have no moral code?" she says, brutally changing the subject, and the soldier laughs: "Of course not. The Australians are fine," he says kindly, and holds out his hand. I shake it.

"I'm relieved to hear that," I say, smiling. "Now tell me what Mel Gibson movies you've seen." The soldier giggles and shoots a look at Q, as if he can't believe my audacity. "Ma'am, just as you and I can stand here smiling at each other, I hope we can forge a new peace between our countries," he says. "I hope you can portray in your movie the tragedy of our divided nation." He's grinning broadly, but there's a yearning in his eyes. He still hasn't let go of my hand. He holds on to it all the way back to the van, as if it's an umbilical cord to the world outside.

The tragedy of my young friend's divided nation stays with me on the highway back to Pyongyang. What would it feel like, I wonder, if a hostile, foreign force suddenly shut Queensland off from the rest of Australia? Bad example: the banana benders are so crazy, the rest of the country would be relieved. The west coast of America from the east, then: the border slicing straight down, from North Dakota to Texas. Families severed for sixty years. No trade. No news. No hope. How would that be? The Koreans I've met on both sides of the DMZ long for reunification. The real tragedy is both China and the US have a strategic interest in stopping it. And now, a new generation of South Koreans are too prosperous to care. To the future-focused twenty-somethings driving the Korean Wave in Seoul, the North Koreans are a deluded, redundant nuisance.

I wonder how the soldiers in Pyongyang would react to this news. There are a thousand of them watching us right now as we follow Q along the Taedong's banks to get pick-up shots of the USS *Pueblo*. The soldiers are lined all the way up the hill in symmetrical rows. It's something I would love to film: these fresh-faced boys, with their identical uniforms and stern expressions, look just like the military portraits the regime stages in Kim Il Sung Square to convince the West of its power. But instead of Kim Junior 2.0 standing solemnly in the foreground, Nic and I are there in our sloppy jeans, filming the *Pueblo's* hull. We can feel the soldiers' unwavering gaze drilling holes into our backs. We're flesh-and-blood targets, after all: the very enemy they've been trained to kill. Then I remember my soldier friend at the DMZ. I turn around and fix the closest row of soldiers with a sunny grin. "Gidday! How's it going?" I say. The soldiers blush and giggle—their boyish warmth rippling back through the crowd, like a Mexican wave. By the time Nic's finished filming her close-ups, a thousand faces behind us are smiling. If Q wasn't there, I suspect they'd applaud us for a job well done.

"WE HAVE CONCERNS WITH YOUR FOOTAGE," says Guk, as I copy the *Pueblo* files onto my laptop back at the Yangakkdo. Ms. K has scheduled our meeting over lunch, and our cables are coiled around plates of noodles and *omurice*—a popular Japanese egg snack stuffed with rice.

"What are your concerns?" I ask, wondering how many of our eighty hours Guk has actually watched. Even without sleeping for two days, he'd only be able to get through half the rushes—unless he fast-forwarded—or had assistants. Guk is alert and well rested: Korfilm has obviously given him a team.

"There are three major problems," Guk says coolly, sipping his tea. "First, we do not appreciate the way Senior Comrade Pak speaks positively about Western films. Second, there are too many soldiers in every exterior shot. And third, most serious of all . . ." Guk looks gravely at Ms. K and Q, and my mouth goes dry. He's going to make me delete the flirting lovers in khaki, or wipe everything we filmed with Pak. "The third problem I must show you direct," Guk continues—and expertly navigates QuickTime X to pull up our interview with Ms. Yun in the brothel.

Everyone cranes over the laptop. Ms. Yun is reciting a slogan that all North Korean actors learn, as part of their ideological training: *"Oh Glorious Fatherland, let Us Devote our Hearts to Your Greatness!"* she chants, then bursts into a fit of embarrassed giggles. It is clear she thinks the slogan sounds ridiculous. Q and Ms. K frown at Guk, and I look at Nic. Ms. Yun's laughter is one of the only times our North Korean subjects have shown anything close to subversion in the face of the Party line. I already know it must be in the film.

"That's no good at all." Ms. K frowns, and I reluctantly reach for the laptop, to delete the clip. But Guk waves my hand away, pausing the image. "I want you to understand why this is a serious offence," he says, pointing at Ms. Yun's left breast. "See your microphone wire? It is obscuring the image of Great Comrade Kim Jong Il." Nic and I peer at the offending wire, and sure enough, two millimeters of it sits over Kim's right eye on the badge pinned to Ms. Yun's collar.

"Oh," I say, concealing my relief. "I am sorry. We can matt out the wire in the edit." Ms. K, Q and Guk confer urgently in Korean, and I busy myself with my noodles. Guk and Ms. K are uncomfortable with what Q is saying, but finally, Ms. K nods.

"If you remove the wire and the line of Comrade Pak saying that he likes *The Godfather*, we have no more problems," she says. "I personally think you should delete all your landscapes with soldiers in them, but Comrade Q says this is unfair, as everywhere you go in Pyongyang there are soldiers, and you obeyed his instructions as faithfully as you could." I look at Q, astonished by this show of solidarity. "Yes," he says. And smiles.

Q's loyalty to Team Gas continues when we drive to the Arirang Mass Games, the final stop of our shoot. We're cruising north along the river, and as the sun dips behind the buildings, Q makes the driver stop, so we can capture an unscheduled, golden hour shot of Pyongyang's workers bicycling on a leafy path. The sun blazes pink in the river, and the workers glide along in contented silence, headed for home. All seems well in their world; somewhere just out of frame, you can imagine their grandmothers, gently lifting kimchi out of terracotta pots, in preparation for dinner.

Boom! Boom! Boom! Sixty thousand feet stamp in unison as Arirang, North Korea's annual propaganda extravaganza, starts. The feet belong to thirty thousand schoolchildren—the same kids Lizzette and I saw practising under the overpass on our first trip. They are sitting in a huge rake across the arena, holding their placards above their heads. Every few seconds, the children flip the placards, making the images on the rake shift and change, like a giant LCD screen. A rose-framed pistol dissolves to a red-crowned crane, to Kim Jong Il's birthplace on Mount Paektu, to stallions prancing beside a waterfall. It is an astonishing display of ingenuity and precision. It makes Cirque du Soleil look like amateur hour at the country pub. According to the Guinness World Records, Arirang is the largest event of its kind in the world. And it is defiantly analogue: instead of using computerised lighting displays and digitally generated graphics, North Korea has successfully transformed thirty thousand cheering children into human pixels.

That's just the backdrop. In the arena itself, which is the size of a small Pacific atoll, a thousand more children join soldiers, gymnasts, comedians, dancers, acrobats, and opera singers in exquisite unison, creating spectacular patterns with their bodies. *"My love has blossomed in the bosom of my comrades,"* they sing, as human hyacinths bloom and wither across the shifting sands of the stadium and shimmering waves of blue-clad girls break against a pixelated sunset. The show moves from high kitsch to pathos as the performers recreate the cherished Korean folk story of two young lovers separated by an imperialist oppressor. As the lovers call to each other across a red silk sea, aerialists dressed as nuclear rockets fly through the air, shot from a cannon suspended in the roof.

Arirang is an extravagant metaphor for the divided Korea, a dazzling two-hour dream in which a Juche-inspired revolution makes the two Koreas one. The show ends with Kim Jong Il appearing on the rake in a halo, as the lovers reunite and two thousand marching girls in patent leather boots wave their swords in triumph.

Team Gas, Nic, and I spill into the night, surrounded by exuberant crowds. There are no food stalls or coffee vans outside the stadium—just a few flimsy tables selling hand-painted posters of the show. As we move through the chattering throng towards the van, the child performers surge from the stadium, their faces flushed with pride. Ms. K was not lying: they really do love it. Hundreds more of the cast pour out in a tsunami of sequins, plunging us inside a fantastic parade. It's camp and macabre, a G-rated Mardi Gras: mums in chicken suits and dads dressed as rabbits mingle with unicycling clowns, while bloodied soldiers walk along with girls in gossamer gowns, their vampy makeup doing nothing to hide their innocence. Even the defiant marching girls seem fragile and shy close up. Do they know what they're missing out on? Are they just pretending to be happy because they're scared? I turn off my Western thought track. I already know the answer. These people, tonight at least, are genuinely happy. It's a bliss born of togetherness—and ignorance.

Someone bumps my shoulder, and I turn to see a young man, his khaki shirt hanging loose, his eyes masked by black wraparounds. He does not belong in this picture. He has the arrogance of a punk, the edge of a rebel, the swagger of youth. He wears a cynical, *fuck you* expression, as if he already owns the future. He's the first North Korean I've seen who looks like he knows—beyond any shadow of doubt—that his country is a confection of lies. The man melts into the crowd, and I climb into the van. I think of Jiro Ishimaru, the brave Japanese journalist who for years has worked with a defector to smuggle in USB sticks of South Korean TV shows and Western films to show North Koreans what life is really like on the other side of their propaganda wall. If the man who just bumped into me is anything to go by, it's working.

Team Gas chat contentedly in the back, and I watch the euphoric faces glide past in a blur. I hope that these resilient, painfully isolated people will never have to be bombed. I hope that when their bubble is shattered, as it surely will be, it will be shattered by knowledge and not by war. I hope, most of all, that in freedom's name, or in Juche's name, or in any other name, their blood will never have to be shed.

SYDNEY

The present, 8 p.m.

On September 14, 2012, Nicola and I left Pyongyang without a fuss. Ms. K returned our passports without explanation, and the customs guards stopped us photographing soldiers in the airport but left our footage alone.

Q, Ms. K, and Sun Hi stood on the other side of the barrier, waving us through. We'd slipped Sun Hi the Kate and Wills wedding stamp inside a box of Clinique and given Q a USB stick taped to a bottle of scotch. The stick contained pictures of Nic and me with our North Korean friends throughout the shoot. It also had my contact details in Sydney. Q promised to share it with the filmmakers—especially Mr. Pak. Ms. K graciously accepted a pink Japanese credit card holder, and the driver gleefully sequestered my Kim Kardashian perfume along with some Mild Seven cigarettes. All woefully inadequate compared with what Team Gas had given us, but it had to do.

I buckled myself into my Air Koryo seat, and the hostess welcomed me back. As the Ilyushin's wheels kissed Kim Jong Il's socialist paradise goodbye, I held my camera to the window, ready to catch the farmers who had tossed flowers at us the first time we flew in. The women were still there in the rice paddy, their skirts bunched around their waists. But this time, strangely—or not strangely at all, depend-ing on how you view it—they didn't look up. They just kept pulling reeds from the mud, their heads resolutely bowed.

On the plane from Beijing, I watched an exquisitely violent South Korean movie, the kind Hollywood directors now study for new ideas. It told the story of identical twin brothers who work in a circus: one good, one bad. Abandoned by their mother at birth, the evil brother murders young girls to dull his pain; the good brother, loyal but guilt-ridden, covers his twin's bloody tracks. The film ends in an empty circus tent with the brothers beating each other to the death. After the saccharine fantasy of Arirang, it was easy to see this film as the South Koreans' more cynical response to the tragedy of their divided world.

My documentary, *Aim High in Creation!*, premiered at the Melbourne International Film Festival in late 2013, causing delight and conster-nation. I wasn't surprised—the combination of Kim Jong Il and coal seam gas was always going to be a stretch. Audiences in Paris, Seoul, Amsterdam, Romania, Myanmar, St Petersburg, Doha, and New York enjoyed the humour and camaraderie of our North Korean friends—but Sydney CSG activists were troubled by its linking of their cause to a totalitarian regime; the ABC felt its depiction of North Korea was "naive" and buried it in a late-night time slot; and Ms. K, I later dis-covered through Nick Bonner, was unhappy about the way my actors had carried a banner of Kim Jong Il on Bondi Beach.

A-list film festivals like Sundance, which had embraced Mads Brüggers' anti–North Korean diatribe *Red Chapel*, unanimously rejected *Aim High*. Perhaps, as a middle-aged mother, my appearance in it as a gonzo-style frontman was too bizarre—or perhaps my sym-pathetic view of the North Korean filmmakers contradicted the main-stream horror story too radically. Conservative pundits who hadn't bothered to watch the film slammed me for using "taxpayer dollars" to be an apologist for the regime, and journalists who had seen it vari-ously labeled it intriguing, hilarious, excellent, surreal, and dotty.

The Australian government refused to give Mr. Pak a visa to

attend the Melbourne premiere; instead, Nick had to take a copy into Pyongyang. The North Korean filmmakers were allowed to watch my short drama *The Gardener*, but not the documentary it sat inside. I'm relieved to report that after staring at Nick's laptop in silence for some time, Pak and his colleagues gave my little film the thumbs-up. If you'd like to make up your own mind, *Aim High in Creation!* can be viewed on Netflix and DVD. If you've really drunk the Kool-Aid, you may want to make a North Korean propaganda film of your own—in which case, aimhighincreation.com is a great place to start.

I've written this book to share all the things I discovered about North Korea and its filmmakers that, for reasons either artistic or political, I had to leave out of my film. The hermit kingdom has changed since we shot there: contrary to initial hopes that the country would become more permissive under Kim Jong Un, North Korea has continued to test its missiles, execute its dissenters, and threaten the West at every opportunity.

And on both sides of the fence, the propaganda war continues to rage. North Korea releases videos of New York being nuked by Taepodong-2 rockets and calls Obama "a monkey in a tropical forest," while the West runs satirical spoofs about Kim Jong Un being voted "the sexiest man alive" and archaeologists finding a "unicorn lair" in Pyongyang. Sony attracts audiences to its Kim Jong Un assassination comedy *The Interview* by accusing North Korea of hacking, and agencies as august as *The Telegraph* and the *Huffington Post* continue to push the North Korean horror story from every conceivable angle—giving equal weight to the UN's exhaustively fact-checked reports on the country's human-rights abuses and completely unsubstantiated rumours.

On May 17, 2014, Chosun Ilbo's widely reprinted article about Kim Jong Un executing his ex-girlfriend and members of her Unhasu orchestra for "making porn" was kiboshed, when Hyon Song Wol, the woman in question, appeared alive and well on North Korean television to salute Kim Jong Un for his "heavenly trust and warm care." In January 2015, Shin Dong Hyuk, the survivor of Camp 14, recanted parts of his story, admitting he hadn't spent his entire North Korean life in the gulag and had not been tortured at age thirteen. In May 2014, former New Mexico governor Bill Richardson, who has been to North Korea several times, warned that the North Korean rumour mill was "out of control." This was a problem, he said, "because we know so little about Kim Jong Un and his true intentions and governing style."

I agree with Richardson. In fact, I'd love to swap travel stories with him sometime and hear his theory about the dancing people on Moran Hill. Fuelling the North Korean rumour mill does not just damage our chances of finding a more productive and diplomatic way of dealing with the country; it also harms the people who, through no fault of their own, happen to live there. Mr. Pak and the filmmakers I met deserve the courtesy of being understood before they are damned as guilty by association. They may be "ignorant" by the hyper-connected standards of the free world, but they are also intelligent, generous, principled human beings, who, as Nick Bonner observed in Pyongyang, "love their kids, and just want to get through the day."

I am no apologist for the Kims and am deeply grateful that I live in the West. But I hope the next time you see a report on Fox News or YouTube accusing North Korea of executing two hundred Christians by flame-thrower, or feeding a disgraced general to starving dogs, you'll remember Mr. Pak and his friends. I hope you'll acknowledge, as I have, that the truths of their country are more complex than what we're normally told—and that while the gulags and malnutrition rates are both horrifically real, North Korea is also home to at least sixteen million people who, despite the propaganda they're fed and the restrictions they have to endure, are trying to lead normal lives. Lives full of dreams and desires and love, about which we never, ever hear. I hope you'll endorse Mark Twain's view that travel is fatal to prejudice, bigotry, and narrow-mindedness—and keep an open mind.

I'm lying on my couch as I write this, watching the evening settle in behind the bowling club trees. The gas mine in Sydney Park is history, thanks to the courageous campaigning of Stop CSG Sydney. My daughter is spending the night with her father, with whom I now have a distant, but civilised, friendship. My time in Pyongyang, a place so removed from everything I know of the world, feels more like a dream than a memory. If it weren't for the media visa stamped in my passport, I'd wonder if I'd actually been.

But then I see Mr. Pak, my silver-haired mentor, holding my hand on the edge of that dirty highway. And I know that his tears, and the compassion he showed me, will stay with me forever.

ACKNOWLEDGMENTS

MASSIVE GRATITUDE TO MY WONDERFUL AGENTS, Fiona Inglis and Dan Lazar, inspirational publishers Cate Blake and Ben Ball at Penguin and Cal Barksdale at Arcade, and my impeccable editor Nikki Lusk. Thank you all for your patience, wisdom and belief.

I'm also hugely grateful to my fearless *Aim High in Creation!* collaborators: Dean O'Flaherty and Kate Breen at Unicorn Films, Mark Woods and Claire Dobbin at the Melbourne International Film Festival, the Solrun Hoaas Documentary Foundation, Alan Erson and the ABC, Ross Woods and Sam Griffin at Screen Australia, Dan Fill at Chocolate Liberation Front, Ruth Hessey, Pat Fiske and OzDox, Piers Nightingale at HighPoint, Johannes Schonherr, Nate Bolotin at XYZ, Jill McNab at Vendetta, and our generous crew and subjects in Seoul. For their talent, chutzpah, and heart, I thank actors Susan Prior, Peter O'Brien, Elliott Weston, Kathryn Beck, and Matt Zeremes, DOPs Geoffrey Simpson and Justine Kerrigan, composer Dale Cornelius, sound wizards Craig Carter and Andrew Neil, photographer Wendy McDougall, editors Melanie Sanford, Cyndi Clarkson, and Karryn de Cinque, and the entire Aussie cast and crew.

Nothing would have been written without Mary Ann Jolley, who gave me *that* present, and the brilliant Nick Bonner (best flea-market companion ever!) and his dynamic team at Koryo Tours—who made our shoot in the Democratic Peoples' Republic of Korea possible. In Pyongyang, I am indebted to the kind assistance and support of the Korean Film Export & Import Corporation, the hard-working staff at Korfilm and the Yangakkdo Hotel, our delightful DPRK film crew, and the extraordinary filmmakers and guides who embraced our anti–Coal Seam Gas mission with generosity, humour and grace. Thank you, Mr. Pak, Mr. Ri, Ms. Yun, Mr. Pei, Mr. O, and all your colleagues, for sharing your world, and showing us that filmmakers, wherever they are, are family.

For her compassion, perspicacity, and a trip I'll never forget, deepest thanks to producer Lizzette Atkins. For her comradeship, beautiful shots, and surviving the Underfloor with a smile, I thank cinematographer Nicola Daley. For defeating the Sydney Park gas mine and fighting CSG across Australia, my loyalty and respect goes to Stop CSG Sydney, Lock the Gate, Brian Monk and his family, activist Tony Pickard, and courageous farmers and environmentalists everywhere.

Last and not least, loving thanks to my multifaceted family: Aline and Flav, Sonya, Brett, Hex and the boys, Snake and Max, Grish and Nina, Miranda and Scotty, Roy, Shirley, and Duncan, Henny and Mary, Mary Alice and Susie, and my parents, Richard and Alison. Arlene—you're glorious. Grace—couldn't have done it withoutcha. Darling Ava—you are my sun.

ABOUT THE AUTHOR

ANNA BROINOWSKI FELL INTO FILMMAKING BY accident—when she unearthed Japan's queer, Yakuza, and Otaku subcultures in the cult hit *Hell Bento!!* She's directed ever since. Anna's latest documentary *Aim High in Creation!* sold to Netflix USA and inspired her DIY North Korean propaganda film workshop, which she travels around the world. Other films include *Forbidden Lie$,* about hoax author Norma Khouri; *Helen's War,* about anti-nuclear campaigner Dr Helen Caldicott; and *Sexing the Label.* They've won some shiny things, including three AFIs, a Silverdocs Award, the Rome Film Festival Cult Prize, a Walkley, the Al Jazeera Golden Award, a Russian Film Critics' prize, Best Director at *Films Des Femmes,* and Best Nonfiction Screenplay from the Writers Guild of America. Before filmmaking, Anna was an actor and rock violinist. She dropped out of Law, toured her bilingual play *The Gap* to Japan, and has written for *The Guardian*, *BBC Magazine*, *Tokyo Journal*, *The Sydney Morning Herald*, *Black + White*, and others. This year, Anna received a PhD from Macquarie University for her thesis on documentary and deception. Born in Tokyo and raised in the Philippines, Burma, Canberra, Japan, and Iran, Anna currently lives in Sydney with her daughter, a wise Glaswegian, and a three-legged cat called Tripod.